The Impact, Legitimacy and Effectiveness of EU Counter-Terrorism

Counter-terrorism law and policy has been prominent and widespread in the years following 9/11, touching on many areas of everyday life from policing and border control to financial transactions and internet governance. The European Union (EU) is a major actor in contemporary counter-terrorism, including through its development of counter-terrorism laws for application within the Union. This book undertakes a multi-disciplinary and empirically informed analysis of the impact, legitimacy and effectiveness of EU counter-terrorism.

Taking into account legal, societal, operational and democratic perspectives, this collection connects theoretical and practical perspectives to produce an interdisciplinary and multi-stakeholder study of how we might measure and understand the impact, legitimacy and effectiveness of EU counter-terrorism. Bringing together a select group of experts in the field, particular emphasis is placed on understanding the practical experience of implementing and assessing these measures gathered from and with end users, including law-makers, policy-makers, security services, industry partners and civil society.

This edited collection will be of great relevance to scholars and policy-makers with an interest in counter-terrorism law, EU law and security studies.

Fiona de Londras joined Durham Law School as Professor of Law and Co-Director of Durham Human Rights Centre in 2012. Her research and teaching are in the fields of human rights and comparative constitutional law.

Josephine Doody joined Durham Law School as Research Fellow in September 2013. Her research interests lie at the intersection between criminology, sociology and human rights law.

Routledge Research in Terrorism and the Law

Available titles in this series include:

The United States, International Law and the Struggle against Terrorism
Thomas McDonnell

Counter-Terrorism and Beyond
The Culture of Law and Justice After 9/11
Nicola McGarrity, Andrew Lynch and George Williams

Counter-terrorism and the Detention of Suspected Terrorists
Preventative Confinement and International Human Rights Law
Claire Macken

Gender, National Security and Counter-terrorism
Human Rights Perspectives
Margaret L. Satterthwaite and Jayne Huckerby

Surveillance, Counter-Terrorism and Comparative Constitutionalism
Fergal Davis, Nicola McGarrity and George Williams

Homeland Security, its Law and its State
A Design of Power for the 21st Century
Christos Boukalas

Anti-Terrorism Law and Normalising Northern Ireland
Jessie Blackbourn

The Impact, Legitimacy and Effectiveness of EU Counter-Terrorism
Fiona de Londras and Josephine Doody

The Impact, Legitimacy and Effectiveness of EU Counter-Terrorism

Edited by
Fiona de Londras and Josephine Doody

Routledge
Taylor & Francis Group
LONDON AND NEW YORK

First published 2015 by Routledge

2 Park Square, Milton Park, Abingdon, Oxon OX14 4RN
711 Third Avenue, New York, NY 10017, USA

Routledge is an imprint of the Taylor & Francis Group, an informa business

First issued in paperback 2017

British Library Cataloguing in Publication Data
A catalogue record for this book is available from the British Library

Library of Congress Cataloging-in-Publication Data
The impact, legitimacy and effectiveness of EU counter-terrorism / edited by Fiona De Londras and Josephine Doody.
pages cm. — (Routledge research in terrorism and the law)
Includes bibliographical references and index.
1. Terrorism—European Union countries—Prevention. 2. Judicial assistance—European Union countries—International cooperation. 3. Terrorism—European Union countries—International cooperation. I. De Londras, Fiona, editor. II. Doody, Josephine, editor.
KJE8780.I47 2015
363.325'16094—dc23
2014043129

ISBN: 978-1-138-85413-0 (hbk)
ISBN: 978-1-138-09795-7 (pbk)

Typeset in Garamond
by Apex CoVantage, LLC

Contents

Notes on contributors

J. Peter Burgess is a philosopher, political scientist and cultural historian. He is currently Research Professor at the Peace Research Institute Oslo (PRIO) and Senior Researcher at the Institute for European Studies at the Vrije Universiteit Brussel. He is Editor of *Security Dialogue*, an international scholarly journal dedicated to innovation in security research and Series Editor of the Routledge/PRIO 'New Security Studies' collection.

Yulia Chistyakova is a Research Associate in the School of Applied Social Sciences, Durham University. She has held research posts at the universities of Stirling and Leicester and has taught criminology and political science at the Open University. Before moving to the UK, she worked as a sociologist at the Siberian Branch of the Russian Academy of Sciences, and undertook independent research for the MacArthur Foundation.

Fiona de Londras joined Durham Law School as Professor of Law and Co-Director of Durham Human Rights Centre in 2012. She also holds adjunct/visiting professorships at the University of New South Wales and University College Dublin. Her research and teaching are in the fields of human rights and comparative constitutional law.

Josephine Doody joined Durham Law School as Research Fellow in September 2013. Her research interests lie at the intersection between criminology, sociology and human rights law.

Ben Hayes is a fellow at the Transnational Institute who has worked for the civil liberties organization, Statewatch, since 1996, specializing in international and national security and policing policies. Ben also works as an independent researcher and consultant for organizations including the European Centre for Constitutional and Human Rights, Cordaid, the Heinrich Boll Foundation, the European Parliament and the European Commission.

Lucy Hoyte is a Research Assistant at The Dickson Poon School of Law, King's College London.

Chris Jones is a researcher for Statewatch, where he has worked since 2010. His work examines policing, migration, military and security issues in the UK and EU.

Médéric Martin-Mazé is a Research Associate at the Department of War Studies, Kings College London.

Cian C. Murphy is the Academic Co-Director of the Center for Transnational Legal Studies (CTLS) – a Georgetown University led partnership of law schools in which King's plays a key role. At CTLS, he teaches The Rule of Law under Globalization, European Human Rights Advocacy (experiential learning course with Nuala Mole of The AIRE Centre) and the core course, An Introduction to Transnational Law and Governance.

Bruno Oliveira Martins is an Assistant Professor at Aarhus University. He was a political adviser at the Delegation of the European Commission in Israel, Visiting Fellow at Egmont Institute and at the EUI, and EuroMeSCo Exchange Fellow at Ben-Gurion University of the Negev, Israel. He completed his PhD at the University of Minho, in Portugal. Current research interests include EU security, counter-terrorism, European constitutionalism and international security.

Rosemarijn van der Hilst is a Senior Researcher and defended her PhD thesis at the Norwegian Centre for Human Rights, Putting Privacy to the Test: How Counter-Terrorism Technology is Challenging Article 8 of the European Convention on Human Rights.

Mathias Vermeulen is a Research Fellow at the European University Institute (EUI) in Florence, Italy, and a PhD candidate at the Research Group on Law, Science, Technology & Society at the Vrije Universiteit Brussel.

Aldo Zammit Borda was Research Associate on the EU FP7-funded project Securing Europe through Counter-Terrorism: Impact, Legitimacy and Effectiveness (SECILE) at King's College London and is now a Senior Lecturer in Law at Anglia University. He holds a Bachelor of Arts (2000) and Doctor of Laws (2003) degree from the University of Malta.

1 Introduction

The impact, legitimacy and effectiveness of EU counter-terrorism

Fiona de Londras and Josephine Doody

More than a decade after the attacks of 11 September 2001, we have entered a security age that is post 'war on terror' but nonetheless heavily concerned with the national and transnational threats posed by terrorism and terroristic violence. In this world, counter-terrorism laws and policies are prominent and widespread, touching on many areas of everyday life from policing to border control, to financial transactions and internet governance.[1] The European Union (EU) plays a significant role in contemporary counter-terrorism through its development of counter-terrorism laws for application within the Union, as well as in its capacity as an international security actor. While there are some studies on select EU counter-terrorism laws and policies,[2] a comprehensive, multi-disciplinary and empirically informed analysis of the impact, legitimacy and effectiveness of EU counter-terrorism within the Union itself is absent from the literature This collection fills that gap.

This book presents some findings from, but also goes beyond, a major FP7-funded study entitled SECILE (Securing Europe through Counter-Terrorism: Impact, Legitimacy and Effectiveness).[3] This research was undertaken by a consortium of Durham University, King's College London, the Supreme Court of Latvia, the Centre for Irish and European Studies, Statewatch, the National Maritime College of Ireland and the Peace Research Institute Oslo in 2013–14. Fundamentally, this study was concerned with understanding how we can ask – and how we can properly answer – three difficult questions about counter-terrorism in the EU context: 1.What are,

1 See for example E. Guild and F. Geyer (Eds.), *Security versus justice? Police and judicial cooperation in the European Union* (Ashgate, 2008); A. Baldaccini and E. Guild, *Terrorism and the foreigner: a decade of tension around the rule of law in Europe* (Brill Nijhoff, 2007); C. Eckes, *EU Counter-terrorist policies and due process: the case of individual sanctions* (Oxford University Press, 2009); F. Davis, N. McGarrity and G. Williams (Eds.), *Surveillance, counter-terrorism and comparative constitutionalism* (Routledge, 2014).

2 See for example C. Murphy, *EU counter-terrorism law: pre-emption and the rule of law* (Hart, 2012); R. Deibert, J. Palfrey, R. Rohozinski and J. Zittrain (Eds.), *Access controlled: the shaping of power, rights and rule in cyberspace* (MIT, 2010).

3 Full details are available online at www.secile.eu

and how can we assess, the impacts of EU counter-terrorism? 2. How can we assess whether or not counter-terrorist measures introduced by the European Union are legitimate? 3. How can we assess whether or not EU counter-terrorist measures are effective? In exploring the answers to these questions, the study also considered what the concepts of impact, legitimacy and effectiveness might be said to mean in the context of EU counter-terrorism.

Taking into account legal, societal, operational and democratic perspectives, this collection connects theoretical and practical approaches to produce an interdisciplinary and multi-stakeholder understanding of how we might understand and measure the impact, legitimacy and effectiveness of EU counter-terrorism. This is done through the use of both inter-disciplinary desk research and the presentation of results from concentrated engagement with practitioners, policy-makers and civil society undertaken as part of SECILE. Through this combination of theoretical and empirically informed work, we aim to bridge gaps in understanding between theoretical perspectives on the one hand, and operational and practical views on the other.

Although counter-terrorism law and policy is an active field of research across disciplines and jurisdictions,[4] there is a need to advance the state of knowledge in order to create a deeper, broader and more practicable body of work. This book contributes to that process. The state of knowledge as it currently stands is often defined by discipline, jurisdiction or measure. Thus, while there is a large amount of work on the concepts of legitimacy, impact and effectiveness in law, sociology and democratic theory, there is a dearth of work on these concepts as understood in a multi- and inter-disciplinary manner, where the insights from diverse disciplines are synthesized rather than merely presented alongside one another. Bearing in mind the existing literature, it is appropriate that a comprehensive, multi-level and multi-disciplinary understanding of the legitimacy, impact and effectiveness of EU counter-terrorism should be developed. The aim of this book is to develop such an understanding, taking into account multiple operative, theoretical, doctrinal and practical perspectives and empirical evidence as to the impact, legitimacy and effectiveness of EU counter-terrorism measures to date. Furthermore, while there is advanced inter-disciplinary research on particular counter-terrorist measures,[5] there is less research on counter-terrorist law and policy seen as a general and comprehensive phenomenon, particularly within the European Union. In addition, much of the research

4 Counter-terrorism is examined across a range of disciplines including, for example, criminology, mathematics and politics: M. Deflem, *Terrorism and counter-terrorism: criminological perspectives* (JAI Press Inc., 2004); V.S. Subrahmanian, *Handbook of computational approaches to counterterrorism* (Springerlink, 2013); L.K. Donohue, *The cost of counterterrorism: power, politics and liberty* (Cambridge University Press, 2008).

5 N. Keijzer and E. Van Sliedregt, *The European Arrest Warrant in Practice* (TMC Asser Press, 2009).

produced is academically driven and focuses entirely or substantively on advancing the theoretical and normative understandings of legitimacy, effectiveness and impact to the detriment of a practical and operable outlook. This book transcends these fragmentations by producing insights that are both normatively innovative and of practical utility. Ultimately, it is intended to present not only sophisticated and rigorous understandings of these concepts, but also workable and functioning tools through which these normative advances can be translated into practice by law- and policy-makers at the European level. By identifying best practice in the incorporation of human rights concerns in designing and implementing European security measures, the insights presented in this collection can help to ensure that future measures are not in contravention of human rights standards.

The focus of this book is EU, rather than national, counter-terrorism. This reflects both the particular nature of EU counter-terrorism and the relative lack of critical analysis of how EU counter-terrorism law and policy are made, applied, and reviewed. As a supranational body, the EU inevitably works in a somewhat different way to national law- and policy-making systems, not least as it may be unable to move quite as quickly as national systems can to introduce legally binding counter-terrorist measures in the wake of a particular attack. One can hardly imagine, for example, the passage of a new Directive in less than a week, whereas notorious and repressive national measures have been introduced in just such a timescale after terrorist attacks.[6] Thus, counter-terrorism by a supranational institution such as the EU, with its own particular constitutional and institutional arrangements, raises particular questions that require attention from scholars and civil society. The decision to focus on the EU alone is also motivated by the extraordinary growth of counter-terrorism law and policy in the Union since 2001. From a Union with essentially no counter-terrorism law in August 2001, the EU has developed a vast infrastructure of institutions, laws and policies concerned with countering terrorism.[7] Thus, given its relatively new nature as well as its rapid growth, the EU's system of counter-terrorism requires scholarly attention, not least as we enter into new phases of EU involvement in international security, including countering the threat posed from ISIS (the 'Islamic State of Iraq and the Levant') and developing Union-wide responses to the phenomenon of 'foreign terrorist fighters'.

Although the contributions to this collection focus on the EU, the insights presented have relevance beyond Europe for a number of reasons. These include the globalized nature of terrorist threats and security solutions and the development of legislative imperatives at UN level (recently reemphasized

6 For example, the UK's Prevention of Terrorism Act 1974 was introduced in less than a week after the Birmingham bombings.

7 B. Hayes and C. Jones, *Catalogue of EU counter-terrorism measures adopted since 11 September 2001* (SECILE Consortium, 2013).

by the passage of Security Council Resolution 2178 on foreign terrorist fighters), and the global application of new security technologies. Thus, this book presents Europe as a security innovator in theoretical and operational terms. This is of particular significance as responses to terroristic threats are increasingly undertaken on a regionalized basis such as, for example, regional responses to Boko Haram in Sub-Saharan Africa.[8]

The book is organized into three parts, which attempt to identify ways to ask key questions and to understand the relationship between the three concepts that can be applied in the real world when policy-makers are making and reviewing counter-terrorist measures. Part I establishes the doctrinal and theoretical framework by cataloguing existing measures and reviewing the institutional framework in place within Europe. Part II advances various disciplinary understandings of the key concepts by drawing on legal, societal and democratic approaches. Part III complements this with a fresh perspective from operational end-users and civil society across three case studies. Broadly speaking, impact relates to the effect or consequence a counter-terrorist measure has. It can be positive or negative, or it can be both simultaneously when considered across multiple referents. It is subject to change over time, depending on the context (periods of *de jure* emergency or normalcy, for example). Effectiveness relates broadly to the extent to which a measure achieves its intended outcomes. Measuring or assessing effectiveness from societal, legal and democratic perspectives poses particular challenges because of information deficits and/or monopolization, a failure to take second order effects into account, the conflation of compliance with effectiveness within official monitoring mechanisms, and institutional limitations. The third concept, legitimacy, is a nebulous term that can be said to comprise numerous different strands, including input legitimacy, process legitimacy, output legitimacy, outcome legitimacy, effective legitimacy, descriptive legitimacy and normative legitimacy. It is closely linked with effectiveness within the counter-terrorism context as measures that are deemed to be effective seem to enjoy enhanced legitimacy.

Part I EU counter-terrorism: its scope and institutions

In Chapter 2, Hayes and Jones base their findings on the first concerted attempt to catalogue all relevant EU counter-terrorism measures (CTMs) adopted since 11 September 2001 (neither EU institutions nor external evaluators have produced a comprehensive repository). The stock-take identified a surprisingly large body of counter-terrorism legislation: 238 specific EU measures, of which 88 – or 36 per cent – are legally binding (or 'hard

8 European Parliament, *Resolution on Nigeria – recent attacks by Boko Haram*, 2014/2729 (RSP). The EU imposed sanctions on Boko Haram including an arms embargo, asset freeze and travel ban in June 2014.

law') in the Member States, meaning that they have direct effect or require transposition by the Member States in the form of new national laws or practices. Further research identified three noteworthy trends that challenge conventional wisdom about the impact on EU Treaty obligations and the values and principles therein. First, transposition to domestic law without delay took place in only 2 per cent of cases. Not only were Member States frequently slow to implement EU CTMs, but in many cases they did not implement them at all until faced with legal action by the European Commission.[9] Second, the failings on the part of the Member States with regard to implementation of EU CTMs were compounded by a frequent failure on the part of the EU institutions to include provisions for review in the legislation itself.[10] These problems were exacerbated by systematic failures to conduct the reviews that were mandated, and by subsequent failures to make the findings of those reviews that did take place available and accessible to the public.[11] Third, despite the relatively wide range of consultative, legislative and review procedures at their disposal, the EU institutions have, at best, underutilized these resources and, at worst, applied them in a manner that ignores crucial issues of civil liberties and human rights, necessity and proportionality, and accountability and democratic control. All of this makes it extremely difficult for citizens, and even for specialist researchers, to understand what EU counter-terrorism policies exist, where they came from, how they relate to one another, what they seek to achieve, whether they have been properly and uniformly implemented, whether they are effective in achieving their aims, or whether there are other, unintended consequences. In this context, the prospects for addressing the democratic

9 Parliament and Council Directive 2001/97/EC amending Council Directive 91/308/EEC on prevention of the use of the financial system for the purpose of money laundering – Commission [second anti-money laundering Directive]; Parliament and Council Directive 2002/58/EC concerning the protection of personal data and the protection of privacy in the electronic communications sector [the 'e-Privacy Directive']; Council Directive 2004/80/EC relating to compensation to crime victims; Council Directive 2004/82/EC on the obligation of carrier to communicate passenger data [the 'API Directive']; Parliament and Council Directive 2005/60/EC on the prevention of the use of the financial system for the purpose of money laundering and terrorist financing [Third anti-money laundering Directive]; Parliament and Council Directive 2005/65/EC on enhancing port security; Parliament and Council Directive 2006/24/EC on the retention of data generated or processed in connection with the provision of publicly available electronic communications services or of public communications networks and amending Directive 2002/58/EC; Parliament and Council Directive 2007/64/EC on payment services in the internal market amending Directives 97/7/EC, 2002/65/EC, 2005/60/EC and 2006/48/EC and repealing Directive 97/5/EC; Commission Directive 2008/43/EC setting up, pursuant to Council Directive 93/15/EC, a system for the identification and traceability of explosives for civil uses; Council Directive 2008/114/EC on the identification and designation of European critical infrastructures and the assessment of the need to improve their protection; Directive 2009/16/EC on port State control (Recast).

10 B. Hayes and C. Jones, *Report on how the EU assesses the impact, legitimacy and effectiveness of its counter-terrorism laws* (SECILE Consortium, 2013).

11 Ibid.

deficit long associated with EU decision-making – which is widely viewed as particularly acute in the area of security and counter-terrorism – appear remarkably constrained. The authors call for fundamental reforms to existing agenda-setting, decision-making and review processes.

Building on the legal framework outlined by Hayes and Jones, Doody presents a comprehensive account of the current EU counter-terrorism institutional framework in Chapter 3. She identifies the key actors and their roles in the process of securing Europe. Other works address the issue but, in the main, presuppose a pre-existing knowledge of the institutional labyrinth that is the EU.[12] This chapter adopts a descriptive approach. It asks a number of questions: 1. Who proposes EU counter-terrorism measures? 2. Who adopts them? 3. Who makes the decisions regarding legislation? 4. What groups contribute to this decision-making process? 5. Who oversees the implementation of the legislation? In this way it attempts to penetrate the institutional complexity that is the EU security architecture and provide an accessible overview of the existing actors and their roles. Third, it reflects upon the complexity identified by other authors and asks whether this situation has improved over time. Part I gives the reader a firm introduction to the current counter-terrorism measures in use in the EU institutions involved in their development, thereby enabling the reader to move on to Part II and to begin considering differing disciplinary perspectives on EU counter-terrorism.

Part II Disciplinary perspectives on EU counter-terrorism

In Part II, Vermeulen analyses the ways in which law – and especially public law, with an emphasis on human rights law – understands the concepts of impact, legitimacy and effectiveness in the context of counter-terrorism. Based on a wide-ranging comparative analysis, he argues that from a legal perspective 'impact' can be understood as the *negative* effect a counter-terrorism measure has on the protection of human rights. In this respect, an impact might be direct or indirect. A direct negative impact of a

12 D. Keohane, 'Special report 1: The EU and international terrorism', (European Policy Analyst, September 2005, The Economist Intelligence Unit Ltd. 2005); L. Lugna, 'Institutional framework of the European Union counter-terrorism policy setting' (2006) *Baltic Security and Defence Review* Vol. 8; D. Casale, 'EU institutional and legal counter-terrorism Framework' (2008) *Defence Against Terrorism Review* Vol. 1, No. 1; C. Kaunert and S. Léonard, 'Supranational governance and European Union security after the Lisbon Treaty – Exogenous shocks, policy entrepreneurs and 11 September 2001' (2012) *Cooperation and Conflict* Vol. 47, No. 4; J. Monar, *The external dimension of the EU's area of freedom, security and justice: progress, potential and limitations after the Treaty of Lisbon* (Swedish Institute for European Policy Studies, 2012); T. Renard, 'EU counterterrorism policies and institutions after the Lisbon Treaty' (2012) *Center on Global Counterterrorism Cooperation Policy Brief*; J. Argomaniz, 'Post 9/11 institutionalisation of European Union counter-terrorism: emergence, acceleration and inertia' (2009) *European Security* Vol. 18, No. 2; D. Bigo, P. Bondotti, L. Bonelli & C. Olsen 'Mapping the field of EU internal security agencies', Paper produced for the Changing Landscape of European Liberty and Security (CHALLENGE) Project of the Centre for European Studies (CEPS).

counter-terrorism measure results in decreased (often procedural) safeguards for terrorist suspects, while an indirect negative effect manifests itself over time so that safeguards are reduced in a general sense (not only for suspected terrorists) and there may therefore be a slow erosion of the rights-based protections that these safeguards provide for the population as a whole. Whereas impact can be understood as the negative human rights implication(s) of counter-terrorism measures, Vermeulen argues that a counter-terrorist measure is considered effective if it is successful in producing an intended, positive result (in the context of counter-terrorism, this is likely to be the improved prevention or prosecution of terrorism-related activities). Finally, counter-terrorism measures might be considered legitimate if their effectiveness and impact are assessed within a predetermined period of time by a public justificatory deliberation mechanism that has the capacity to change or discontinue the measure. These conclusions are based on a substantive comparative study of how law deals with counter-terrorism. Looking at the European Court of Human Rights, in particular, Vermeulen finds that it rarely comments on the indirect impact of counter-terrorism measures, but instead focuses on the direct impact of a specific counter-terrorism measure on the (procedural) dimension of a specific human right. Similarly, the European Court of Human Rights rarely discusses the effectiveness of a given counter-terrorism measure; nor does it take effectiveness explicitly into account when determining the legality, necessity or proportionality of a counter-terrorism measure. This reflects the fact that the Court is reluctant to second-guess governments' assessments of what might be the most prudent or expedient policy to combat terrorism, even if it is presented with statistical evidence that at least suggests that a measure is not particularly effective.[13] Instead of analysing the effectiveness of a particular counter-terrorism measure per se, Vermeulen argues that the Court tends to assess the effectiveness of the safeguards that accompany extraordinary counter-terrorism powers.

Approaching these questions from a societal security perspective, Martin-Mazé and Burgess point out that the impact of security measures on society must be contextualized by an understanding of society as the product of a long-term process of historical differentiation. It is thus crucial to recognize that measures taken in the name of security will play out differently across different social contexts, where economic well-being, political systems, and cultural traditions are unequally distributed in the first place. While security measures may have value added in one specific societal sector, they may also have a detrimental impact in others. This chapter aims to clarify the character and dynamic of the societal impact of security measures, the dependency upon the actual security 'added value' they produce, and the political and social legitimacy required to sustain them. In this respect, Burgess and Martin-Mazé argue that assessing the effectiveness of counter-terrorism

13 See for example, the use of stop and search powers under Section 44 of the UK Terrorism Act 2000.

measures requires attention to both the positive and negative benefits of such legislation, and to the fact that specific measures have consequences for both primary and secondary audiences.

Chistyakova considers the impact of counter-terrorism on EU democracy in Chapter 6. She begins by outlining different theoretical and disciplinary perspectives on democracy and security, with particular emphasis on the legitimacy and accountability of security policies. Then, she focuses on counter-terrorism policies in the EU, and considers the extent to which these decisions can be said to be democratically legitimate: can EU citizens see themselves as authors of counter-terrorist policies and can they hold decision-makers to account? Chistyakova establishes that, from cosmopolitan and liberal perspectives, EU institutions can provide the necessary mechanisms of accountability, thus making the line of authority and power more transparent and accessible to citizens. From a communitarian perspective, EU institutions suffer from a 'democratic deficit' and only nation-states can guarantee the true legitimacy and accountability of security policies. The chapter argues that neither of these two perspectives is sufficient in order to understand the legitimacy and impact of counter-terrorism on democracy in Europe. It is important to examine critically the discourses, institutions and practices of counter-terrorism at both national and supranational levels. Chistyakova asks whether less protection of fundamental rights, and lower standards of legitimacy and accountability, should be tolerated by European democracy in order to provide security to its citizens, or whether such exceptionalism undermines the legitimacy of democratic institutions. She concludes that more rational and informed debate is needed in order to challenge the normative foundations and assumptions that underpin the practices and institutions of counter-terrorism in Europe, and to be able to question the extent to which they are consistent with democracy.

In the final chapter of Part II, Oliveira Martins examines how the emergence of EU counter-terrorism policy in the aftermath of the terrorist attacks of 9/11 challenged some of the foundations of the Union. By expanding its security portfolio in the direction of counter-terrorism, the EU inevitably brought about debates on the relationship between security and justice, questions of privacy and data protection, and on the broader respect for fundamental rights more generally. In this process, the legitimacy and the social appropriateness of some of these counter-terrorism measures have been questioned, both at the societal level and in front of, or by, European institutions such as the European Parliament or the Court of Justice of the EU. This chapter argues that the constitutional foundations of the EU play a decisive role in granting legitimacy to EU counter-terrorism law and policy and to ensure its recognition as socially acceptable. Combining sociological institutionalist theory with insights from the New Haven school, namely its process-orientated conception for fostering legal order, it crosses legal and political science traditions to explore the ways that EU counter-terrorism law and policy acquire and maintain social appropriateness.

Part III Practical perspectives on EU counter-terrorism

The growing literature on EU counter-terrorism law and policy tends to focus on European-level institutions (Commission, Council and Parliament), offices (the Counter-Terrorism Coordinator), and agencies (Europol and Eurojust).[14] Thus, the implementation of EU counter-terrorism law and policy by law enforcement officials within the Member States has gone without significant scrutiny. Chapter 8 by Murphy, Zammit Borda and Hoyte seeks, in part, to address this gap in the literature. The chapter sets out the perspectives of governmental officials, prosecutors, police officers and other law enforcement agents drawn from three focus groups held under the auspices of the SECILE Research Consortium. Each focus group took one of three case studies as its subject: the European Arrest Warrant, counter-terrorist finance or border control databases. The perspectives gleaned from these focus groups addressed key themes in EU counter-terrorism and broader security narratives: the necessity of cooperation as a corollary of EU integration, the relationship between cooperation on the basis of mutual recognition and the establishment of trust among different agents, and the challenges of legitimacy in legal and social terms.

Doody and van der Hilst present a complementary analysis from the perspective of civil society. In December 2013, the University of Durham, together with the Peace Research Institute Oslo (PRIO), organized a focus group consisting of civil society representatives from various EU Member States to discuss the operation of EU databases and systems of information exchange in the context of counter-terrorism, EU measures aimed at disrupting the financing of terrorism and the European Arrest Warrant in the context of counter-terrorism. The University of Durham conducted a further ten interviews with key policy-makers across Europe. The objective of this focus group and the series of interviews that followed was to develop an empirically informed understanding of the perceived impact, legitimacy and effectiveness of EU counter-terrorism measures among these stakeholders. In this chapter, Doody and van der Hilst present the findings of their engagement with civil society. A number of questions guide the work. The chapter is divided into three sections: impact, legitimacy and effectiveness. First, it asks what these concepts mean: 1. How can they be measured? 2. What factors need to be considered? 3. Where do these definitions fit within the wider discourse of impact, legitimacy and effectiveness? It then applies these definitions to the three case studies.

Chapter 10 brings the book to a conclusion. The preceding chapters outline the practical and normative insufficiencies in the conceptualization, implementation and assessment of the EU's counter-terrorist measures, systems

---

14 O. Bures, *EU counterterrorism policy: a paper tiger?* (Ashgate, 2013); R. Bossong, *The evolution of EU counter-terrorism: EU security policy after 9/11* (Routledge Publishing, 2012); A.M. Salinas de Frias, K. Samuel and N. White (Eds.) *Counter-terrorism: international law and practice* (Oxford University Press, 2012).

and infrastructure. In this chapter, which draws on insights from those that precede it, de Londras makes a key recommendation for reform: i.e. to 'close the loop' by means of effective, participatory and evaluative review of the operation of EU counter-terrorism on a periodic basis. The chapter proposes a mechanism of institutional review, drawing on, but also adapting, national models, which embraces the core principles of participation and transparency suitably adapted to a security context.

Part I

EU counter-terrorism

Its scope and institutions

2 Taking stock

The evolution, adoption, implementation and evaluation of EU counter-terrorism policy

Ben Hayes and Chris Jones

1. Introduction

Before 9/11, only a handful of the (then) 15 European Union (EU) Member States had dedicated terrorism legislation,[1] while relevant international conventions dealt only with specific terrorism-related offences, the suppression of terrorist financing and the protection of potential nuclear and aviation targets.[2] After 9/11, counter-terrorism moved rapidly to the forefront of the

1 Those states were France, Greece, Italy, Portugal, Spain and the UK.

2 See the International Civil Aviation Organization (ICAO), *Convention on offences and certain acts committed on board aircraft*, 14 September 1963. Available online at http://www.refworld.org/docid/3ddca03d4.html (accessed 3 October 2014); International Civil Aviation Organization (ICAO) *Convention for the suppression of unlawful acts against the safety of civil aviation*, 23 September 1971, 974 UNTS 177. Available online at http://www.refworld.org/docid/3ae6b37a14.html (accessed 1 October 2014); International Civil Aviation Organization (ICAO), *Convention for the suppression of unlawful acts against the safety of civil aviation*, 23 September 1971, 974 UNTS 177. Available online at: http://www.refworld.org/docid/3ae6b37a14.html (accessed 3 October 2014); UN General Assembly, *Convention on the prevention and punishment of crimes against internationally protected persons, including diplomatic agents*, 14 December 1973, No. 15410. Available online at http://www.refworld.org/docid/3ae6b3afc.html (accessed 3 October 2014); UN General Assembly, *International convention against the taking of hostages*, 17 November 1979, No. 21931. Available online at http://www.refworld.org/docid/3ae6b3ad4.html (accessed 3 October 2014); UN General Assembly, *Convention on the physical protection of nuclear material*, 26 October 1979, No. 24631. Available online at http://www.refworld.org/docid/3dd8fbec4.html (accessed 3 October 2014); United Nations, *Protocol for the suppression of unlawful acts of violence at airports serving international civil aviation, supplementary to the Convention for the suppression of unlawful acts against the safety of civil aviation*, 24 February 1988, UN Treaty Series 1990. Available online at http://www.refworld.org/docid/3ddcac634.html (accessed 3 October 2014); UN General Assembly, *Convention for the suppression of unlawful acts against the safety of maritime navigation*, 10 March 1988, No. 29004. Available online at http://www.refworld.org/docid/3ae6b3664.html (accessed 3 October 2014); UN General Assembly, *Protocol for the suppression of unlawful acts against the safety of fixed platforms located on the continental shelf*, 10 March 1988, UNTS 1678, I-29004. Available online at http://www.refworld.org/docid/3dda0fff4.html (accessed 3 October 2014); UN General Assembly, *Convention on the marking of plastic explosives for the purpose of detection*, 1 March 1991. Available online at http://www.refworld.org/docid/3dd90f0c7.html (accessed 3 October 2014); UN General Assembly, *International Convention for the suppression of terrorist bombings*, 15 December 1997, No. 37517. Available online at http://www.refworld.org/docid/3dda06ddc.html (accessed 3 October 2014); and UN General Assembly, *International Convention for the suppression of the financing of terrorism*, 9 December 1999, No. 38349. Available online at http://www.refworld.org/docid/3dda0b867.html (accessed 3 October 2014).

EU's policy agenda, with the result that the current 28 members of the European Union are now obliged to implement a vast body of legislation and policy. This includes a common legal definition of terrorism and terrorist offences,[3] and a host of substantive criminal and procedural laws and mechanisms for cross-border police cooperation, as well as scores of supplementary security and preventative measures. In addition, numerous EU bodies and agencies have been given a mandate to implement or coordinate EU counter-terrorism policies.[4]

As part of the SECILE project, we developed a catalogue of the counter-terrorism measures (CTMs) adopted by the European Union since 9/11, explored the extent to which those measures have (or have not) been implemented in accordance with the requirements of the legislation and evaluated the application of mechanisms used to assess their impact, legitimacy and effectiveness by the EU institutions. This chapter provides a summary of our key findings. Section 2 begins by outlining the evolution of the EU counter-terrorism agenda and describing the voluminous body of legislation we identified. Section 3 examines the extent to which those CTMs requiring transposition by the Member States (i.e. new national laws or practices) were implemented in accordance with the binding legal requirements therein and to the satisfaction of the EU institutions, and outlines some of the factors affecting the transposition process. Section 4 analyses the application of the various mechanisms at the institutions' disposal for reviewing the potential impact and practical application of EU CTMs at the various stages of the legislative process (*ex ante*, deliberative and *ex post*). Section 4 also examines the substantive reviews of EU counter-terrorism policy conducted to date. Section 5 draws some brief conclusions.

2. Terrorism fatigue: cataloguing EU measures

As data collection exercises go, identifying and collating EU CTMs proved an arduous undertaking. Material was gathered from the websites of the EU institutions and the archives of the civil liberties organization, Statewatch, where both authors work. Individual legal acts and policy documents were included if they fulfilled two criteria: 1. they had, at some point in time, been part of the EU's counter-terrorism agenda; 2. they had been adopted or approved by an EU institution or body, or otherwise represent the official policy of the European Union.[5] We discovered that, if both legislative and

3 Framework Decision 2002/475/JHA on combating terrorism of 7 February 2013.

4 Among the EU agencies and bodies established or empowered to deal with terrorism-related issues are EUROPOL (the EU police office), EUROJUST (the EU judicial prosecutions unit), Frontex (the EU border management agency), the EU Police Chiefs Operational Task Force, the EU Counter-terrorism Coordinator, the European Maritime Safety Agency and the EU Agency for Network and Information Security (ENISA).

5 B. Hayes and C. Jones, *Catalogue of EU counter-terrorism measures adopted since 11 September 2001* (SECILE Consortium, 2013) pp. 17–18.

non-legislative instruments are taken into account, the EU has adopted at least 238 separate counter-terrorism measures between 9/11 and the summer of 2013, equivalent to almost twenty per year. Before providing an overview of our findings, we outline three key features of EU decision-making that help to explain why the EU counter-terrorism agenda appears to be so bloated.

The sense of urgency caused by the moral panic invoked by terrorism

The origins of the EU's counter-terrorism agenda can be traced to the Conclusions of the extraordinary EU Justice and Home Affairs (JHA) Council convened on 20 September 2001 in response to the 9/11 attacks. These conclusions called for concerted action in thirty-three specific areas, with a further eight measures relating to cooperation with the US.[6] A month later, the US Government wrote to the European Commission with a further forty specific requests regarding cooperation on anti-terrorism measures.[7] By now, the EU had adopted its first counter-terrorism roadmap, containing sixty-four detailed objectives, the majority of which were marked as urgent.[8] An update of the roadmap published in 2002 showed significant progress with regard to almost all sixty-four objectives.[9]

Among the expedited measures were proposals for Framework Decisions on Terrorism[10] and the European Arrest Warrant (EAW),[11] published on 25 September 2001 (i.e. just two weeks after 9/11), both of which the European Commission had already prepared in accordance with an EU Action Plan of 2000 to implement the principle of mutual recognition in civil and criminal matters.[12] (These two Framework Decisions were politically agreed by the Member States following just) six weeks of negotiations;[13] less time than it subsequently took to translate the text into all of the EU's official languages. The speed at which agreement was reached is notable

6 *Conclusions adopted by the Council (Justice and Home Affairs)* on 20 September 2001, 12156/01, 25 September 2011.

7 *Text of US letter from Bush with demands for EU cooperation*, Statewatch news online, October 2001. Available online at http://www.statewatch.org/news/2001/nov/06uslet.htm (accessed).

8 *Coordination of implementation of the plan of action to combat terrorism*, 12800/1/01, 17 October 2001.

9 *European Union action plan to combat terrorism – Update of the roadmap*, 13909/1/02, 14 November 2002.

10 *Proposal for a Council Framework Decision on combating terrorism*, COM(2001) 521 final, 19 September 2001.

11 *Proposal for a Council Framework Decision on the European arrest warrant and the surrender procedures between the Member States*, COM(2001) 522 final, 25 September 2001.

12 *Draft programme of measures for implementation of the principle of mutual recognition of decisions in civil and commercial matters* (OJ 2001 C 12/01). Available online at http://eur-lex.europa.eu/LexUriServ/LexUriServ.do?uri=OJ:C:2001:012:0001:0009:EN:PDF.

13 The two Commission proposals were published on 19 September 2001. Political agreement was reached by ministers at the EU Justice and Home Affairs Council meeting on 6–7 December 2001.

given that the 1996 EU Convention on Extradition that the EAW replaced had taken almost four years to agree to and had not yet been ratified by all Member States. There was even less debate over the EU legislation implementing the far-reaching UN Security Council Resolution 1373 on counter-terrorism, which also contained the EU's first terrorist blacklist;[14] the relevant texts were simply faxed around the EU's foreign ministries two days after Christmas and adopted by written procedure when none objected.[15]

The frantic pace of legislative activity has not, of course, been maintained throughout the intervening years since 9/11. However, the powerful sense of urgency returned after the terrorist attacks in Madrid in March 2004 and London in July 2007, each event producing substantial pressure to adopt legislation that Member States had hitherto been unable to agree on. The controversial Data Retention Directive,[16] which was declared unlawful by the Court of Justice of the European Union (CJEU) in 2014,[17] is a good example of this: the European Parliament had twice voted to reject such a proposal but reversed its position in the immediate aftermath of the 7/7 bombings. However, by 2009, even the EU Counter-Terrorism Coordinator (CTC) was talking of 'counter-terrorism fatigue' caused by 'a string of other global crises with more immediate impact on peoples' lives' (i.e. the financial crisis and economic depression).[18] At the time of writing, in September 2014, things have come full circle again and counter-terrorism has moved back to the centre of the EU policy-making agenda with the establishment of a Caliphate in parts of Iraq and Syria and concerns about radicalization and returning foreign fighters. Central to the 'new' proposals is a Directive obliging airlines to share more data about passengers (PNR: passenger name records) with security agencies – another measure that the European parliament has already rejected[19] and one whose potential effect might well contravene the CJEU ruling on the Data Retention Directive (DRD). As one study of the potential ramifications of the DRD judgment suggests, the

---

14 *Council Regulation (EC) No 2580/2001 of 27 December 2001 on specific restrictive measures directed against certain persons and entities with a view to combating terrorism*; *Council Common Position of 27 December 2001 on the application of specific measures to combat terrorism* (2001/931/CFSP).

15 This process is detailed in 'EU announces first lists of terrorists and all refugees to be vetted', *Statewatch news online*, January 2002. Available online at http://www.statewatch.org/news/2002/jan/02euterr.htm

16 B. Hayes and C. Jones, *The EU Data Retention Directive: a case study in the legitimacy and effectiveness of EU counter-terrorism policy* (SECILE Consortium, 2014).

17 European Court of Justice, Judgment of the Court (Grand Chamber) In Joined Cases C-293/12 and C-594/12, 8 April 2014. Available online at http://www.statewatch.org/news/2014/apr/eu-ecj-data-ret-judgment.pdf

18 EU Counter-Terrorism Coordinator, 'EU counter-terrorism strategy – discussion paper', 15359/1/09 REV 1, 26 November 2009. Available online at http://register.consilium.europa.eu/doc/srv?l=EN&f=ST%2015359%202009%20REV%201

19 European Parliament, 'Civil Liberties Committee rejects EU Passenger Name Record proposal' press release, 24 April 2013.

proposed PNR Directive 'is not compatible with the required precision and clarity the CJEU demanded' with regard to purpose and use, retention of data, the amount of data gathered, and access to and transfer of data.[20]

Mission creep and the diffusion (and normalization) of EU CTMs

The sense of urgency generated by acts of political violence has also enabled the broader counter-terrorism agenda to incorporate measures that have little or nothing to do with countering-terrorism *per se*, and to disburse them throughout the legislative and operational branches of the EU JHA and security architecture. Following the terrorist attacks in Madrid on 11 March 2004, the European Council adopted a fresh declaration on combating terrorism containing 57 specific measures, many of which were new.[21] As Statewatch observed at the time, '27 of the proposals have little or nothing to do with tackling terrorism – they deal with crime in general and surveillance'.[22] In June 2004, the roadmap was replaced by an EU Plan of Action on Combating Terrorism containing at least 129 specific measures divided across seven strategic objectives.[23]

In 2007, following the 7/7 bombings in London, the EU's counter-terrorism programme was renewed again with the adoption of a new EU Counter-Terrorism Strategy subtitled Prevent, Protect, Pursue, Respond,[24] seemingly inspired by the UK's CONTEST strategy (Prevent, Pursue, Protect, Prepare). Although the EU strategy was described as new, the updated action plan that accompanied it had changed little from the previous version. In any case, there were now so many CTMs in the plans that they had become unintelligible to all but seasoned observers of EU JHA policy-making. Moreover, the objectives and measures set out in the EU's action plans and counter-terrorism strategy had already spawned a series of sub-programmes on different aspects of counter-terrorism, each with its own dedicated action plans or implementing measures, including:

- Radicalization and recruitment
- European critical infrastructure protection
- Strategy on terrorist financing
- Customs initiatives
- Proliferation of weapons of mass destruction

---

20 Prof. Dr. F. Boehm and Prof. Dr. M.D. Cole, 'Data Retention after the judgement of the Court of Justice of the European Union', *Greens/European Free Alliance*, 30 June 2014, pp. 65–71. Available online at http://www.statewatch.org/news/2014/jul/ep-greens-dt-ret-study.pdf

21 *Declaration on Combating Terrorism*, 25 March 2004.

22 Statewatch, 'Statewatch "Scoreboard" on post-Madrid counter-terrorism plans', *Statewatch news online*, March 2004. Available online at http://www.statewatch.org/news/2004/mar/swscoreboard.pdf

23 *EU Plan of Action on Combating Terrorism*, 10586/04, 15 June 2004.

24 *The European Union Counter-Terrorism Strategy*, 14469/4/05 REV 4, 30 November 2005.

- Civil protection and crisis management
- Chemical, Biological, Radiological and Nuclear (CBRN) protection
- Integrated border management
- Information management strategy
- Security research.

By this stage, there were apparently so many components to the EU counter-terrorism agenda that no more consolidated action plans or road maps were produced. As the European Commission acknowledged in its 2010 review of EU counter-terrorism policy,[25] while the core strands of the counter-terrorism strategy (Prevent, Protect, Pursue, Respond) remained integral, much of the action plan had been taken up by the broader EU Internal Security Strategy[26] and the new multi-annual work programme and action plan for the area of justice, freedom and security (the Stockholm Programme).[27]

It is also important to stress that while our catalogue of 238 CTMs includes the *legislative* acts stemming from these sub-programmes, many of the measures contained therein are non-legislative, and for the most part require specific actions to be undertaken by EU agencies and national security forces; for example, the second iteration of the radicalization and recruitment action plan contained 79 specific measures.[28] These operational measures were excluded from our database, which would otherwise have been much bigger.[29]

Lack of democratic scrutiny and transparency

The public was not allowed to know what the seventy-nine measures in the counter-radicalization plan were. The Swedish Presidency, which oversaw the update of this plan, was 'of the firm opinion that the revised version of the Radicalisation and Recruitment Action Plan should be a public document',[30] but all the specific actions were redacted from the publicly available

25 *EU Counter-Terrorism Policy: main achievements and future challenges*, COM(2010) 386 final, 20 July 2010; *Taking stock of EU counter-terrorism measures*, SEC(2010) 911 final, 20 July 2010.

26 *Draft internal security strategy for the European Union: 'Towards a European Security Model'*, 7120/10, 8 March 2010.

27 *The Stockholm Programme – An open and secure Europe serving and protecting citizens*, OJ C 2010 115/01.

28 *Revised EU Radicalisation and Recruitment Action Plan*, 15244/08 EXT 1, 14 November 2008.

29 Also omitted are EU agreements with third countries that contain basic counter-terrorism commitments. This is because from 2005, standard counter-terrorism cooperation clauses began appearing in all new and updated EU association agreements (which set out the framework for cooperation with third countries) while having only negligible effect on 'domestic' EU counter-terrorism policy. External policies and treaties with third states covering specific counter-terrorism policy issues are included, but the numerous agreements between EU agencies such as EUROPOL and EUROJUST and their counterparts in third states, which include a counter-terrorism dimension, are not.

30 *Revised EU Radicalisation and Recruitment Action Plan*, 15374/09, 5 November 2009.

text. All the other key documents relating to the EU's radicalization and recruitment strategy received the same treatment. Needless to say, if the public and civil society is prevented from knowing what a particular EU strategy entails, it is impossible for them to try and ascertain its legitimacy or effectiveness, or otherwise play any part in the democratic process.

As will be discussed further below, the democratic deficit that has long been synonymous with EU decision-making has been particularly pronounced in the area of JHA and security policy, with long-standing concerns about national sovereignty leading to the European Parliament being excluded from key counter-terrorism decisions altogether. Indeed, many of the earliest documents relating to EU counter-terrorism were only in the public domain because Statewatch published them on its website. As one exasperated MEP asked the Civil Liberties Committee Secretariat in 2002, 'How can Statewatch get a copy of the EU-US mutual legal assistance agreement when we apparently cannot? I am very glad they do get it, but it is frankly humiliating that we as a Parliament have to depend on a leaked copy from an NGO'.[31] While the European Parliament (EP) now has a much greater role in the EU legislative process, and transparency is much improved,[32] the Member States acting within the EU Council still retain substantial control over the security and counter-terrorism agendas (and complete control over operational issues), despite extensions to the mandate and powers of the European Commission in these areas.

The problem of the democratic deficit with regard to the evolution of the EU counter-terrorism agenda – as opposed to specific CTMs – is now as closely related to the lack of scrutiny of the executive functions of the Council of the EU as to the earlier lack of transparency.[33] As we will see in the following section, more than a hundred sets of Council Conclusions covering every conceivable aspect of EU counter-terrorism policy were identified by our cataloguing exercise.[34] This body of soft law has shaped the entire legislative and operational counter-terrorism agenda and ensured that it has remained at the centre of the EU policy-making edifice, yet there is no national or European parliamentary scrutiny of the drafting or adoption of Council Conclusions and very little media or public interest in their content. Furthermore, while the powerful governments among the 28 Member States clearly exert significant influence, it is the General Secretariat of the Council, which – on behalf of the Presidency of the day – drafts these agenda-setting documents.

Finally, whereas the role played by the General Secretariat of the EU Council raises concerns about democratic control of the EU

31 Source: personal correspondence between members of the European Parliament's Civil Liberties Committee seen by the authors and cited in Ben Hayes's PhD.

32 Articles 1, 11 and 16, Treaty on European Union.

33 D. Curtin, *Executive Power in the European Union: law, practice, and constitutionalism* (Oxford: Oxford University Press, 2009).

34 B. Hayes and C. Jones, *supra* note 5.

counter-terrorism agenda, the increasing involvement of the security and defence industry in many of the security and counter-terrorism policies overseen by the European Commission[35] gives rise to concerns about democracy, accountability and undue corporate influence over critical issues affecting the fundamental rights of everyone in the European Union.[36]

Taking stock: the 238 EU counter-terrorism measures

Between September 2001 and the summer of 2013, the European Union adopted at least 238 separate counter-terrorism measures. Of these 238 adopted measures, eighty-eight, or 37 per cent, are legally binding in the Member States (hard law), meaning that they have direct effect or require transposition (new national laws or practices) by the Member States. The following table shows the breakdown of the different instruments and outlines their purpose and impact.

The sheer scope of the EU's counter-terrorism agenda gives rise to two major concerns. First, as the annual British Social Attitudes report found in 2007, 'The very mention of something being a counter-terrorism measure makes people more willing to contemplate the giving up of their freedoms'.[37] 'It is as though society is in the process of forgetting why past generations thought these freedoms to be so very important' cautioned the authors.[38] Second, the EU's counter-terrorism agenda has become so bloated as to make it extremely difficult for citizens and even specialist researchers to understand which specific policies fit in where and why, never mind what those policies do, where they came from, whether they have been properly implemented or whether they are effective. Put another way, our catalogue of well over 200 largely impenetrable measures – many of which simply cannot be understood in isolation – does little to inspire confidence or

---

35 This includes Commission initiatives on: support for the EU security and defence industries (see for example *Towards a more competitive and efficient defence and security sector*, COM(2013) 542 final, 24 July 2013); European critical infrastructure protection (e.g. *Commission staff working document on a new approach to the European Programme for critical infrastructure protection: making European critical infrastructures more secure*, SWD(2013) 318 final, 28 August 2014); security research (e.g., European Commission (2004) *Research for a secure Europe: report of the group of personalities in the field of Security Research*); and cybersecurity (now incorporated into Pillar III of the Digital Agenda for Europe 2020, see http://ec.europa.eu/digital-agenda/en).

36 These issues are explored in B. Hayes, *NeoConOpticon: the EU security-industrial complex* (Amsterdam: Transnational Institute/Statewatch, 2009). See also B. Hayes (2012) 'The surveillance-industrial complex' in K. Ball, K. Haggerty and D. Lyon (Eds), *Routledge handbook of surveillance studies* (New York: Routledge, 2014), pp. 167–175.

37 'New British social attitudes report published today', National Centre for Social Research press release, 24 January 2007.

38 M. Johnson and C. Gearty, 'Civil liberties and the challenge of terrorism' in A. Park, J. Curtice, K. Thomson, M. Phillips and M. Johnson (Eds), *British social attitudes: perspectives on a changing society, the 23rd report* (London: Sage, 2007), p.143 at 169.

Table 1 EU counter-terrorism measures by instrument

Instrument	*Quantity (+drafts)*	*Purpose, impact*
Action plans and strategy documents	**26**	Sets the EU counter-terrorism agenda through legislative and/or operational programmes that represent a political commitment on the part of EU Member States, institutions and agencies to develop and implement specific policies, legal measures or frameworks for cooperation.
Regulations	**25** (+13)	Legal acts that apply directly without requiring national laws to implement them (though states are free to transpose as long as effect is the same). All EU institutions, Member States and individuals must comply with Regulations.
Directives	**15** (+8)	Legal acts that are binding on the Member States in terms of the results to be achieved, but leave to the discretion of national authorities the methods by which these results may be achieved.
Framework Decisions	**11**	Legally binding acts used exclusively in the fields of police and judicial cooperation in criminal justice matters between 1999 and 2009. Similar in effect to Directives insofar as they require Member States to achieve particular results without dictating the means of achieving those results.
Decisions	**25** (+4)	Legally binding acts that may have general application, in which case all Member States must take steps to comply, or they may be directed at specific addressees, meaning that only those subject to the Decision must comply.
Joint Actions	**1**	Legally binding instruments under the Common Foreign and Security Policy that provide for the deployment of financial and/or human resources to achieve a specific objective. May also lay down basic rules on how such initiatives should be implemented.
Common Positions	**3**	Legally binding agreements between the Member States on the position to be taken with regard to international matters such as strategic relations with third countries, negotiating positions in international fora or the domestic (EU) interpretation of international laws and conventions.
Recommendations	**9**	Not legally binding but representative of a political commitment on the part of EU institutions/bodies or Member States toward specific conduct, or they outline the goals of a common policy.
Resolutions	**4**	Not legally binding but used to signify political agreement to act in a given area.
Conclusions	**111**	Not legally binding but used exclusively by the EU Council to set the policy agenda by signifying political agreement among the Member States as to the type, nature or content of specific measures.
International agreements	**8**	Legal effect varies according to the type and nature of the agreement. In the area of counter-terrorism, EU treaties have been used to ensure EU cooperation with the US as well as to provide a legal basis for the exchange or transfer of personal data with/to third states.
Total	**238** (+25)	

assuage widely held concerns about negative impacts on fundamental rights or the unchecked accrual of powers by police and security forces.

3. Too little, too late: the implementation of EU CTMs

As well as cataloguing the extent of EU counter-terrorism, we examined the implementation of EU counter-terrorism measures by the Member States. The research was constrained in two important ways. First, we limited our study to the eighty-eight legally binding EU counter-terrorism measures identified during our cataloguing exercise. Of these, only fifty required formal transposition, meaning that the Member States were obliged to introduce new laws or policies to implement them.[39] This is not to say that the CTMs we excluded do not have a significant legal or practical effect, but rather that their application is achieved through different mechanisms.[40] Second, it was not possible to assess qualitatively the implementation of fifty separate EU CTMs by the twenty-eight EU Member States as this would have necessitated some 1,400 investigations into domestic law-making processes.[41]

To understand the extent to which the Member States had implemented the fifty relevant CTMs, we examined implementation reports from the Member States and EU institutions (where available) and the use of infringement proceedings by the European Commission, i.e. legal action against Member States for failing to comply with EU law. This allowed us to make some basic determinations about the extent to which specific CTMs had been implemented at national level in accordance with the requirements therein, and to the satisfaction of the EU institutions. Although the absence of comparable qualitative data meant that it was not possible to ascertain the precise reasons for the inconsistent implementation of specific CTMs, we did identify some of the factors that may help explain delays, failures or otherwise inconsistent application of EU law. These include the type of legislative procedure (normal parliamentary processes, also known as primary legislation, versus delegated powers, statutory instruments and implementing regulations, etc.), a predilection for gold plating (i.e. the incorporation of additional provisions into national legislation implementing EU texts), the

39 Fifteen Directives, eleven Framework Decisions, three Common Positions, and three international agreements.

40 EU Regulations, for example, have direct legal effect, which means that they do not require transposition into national law, although significant practical steps may still be required to enforce or apply whatever rules it is that the Regulation seeks to achieve. Similarly, while all EU Decisions are legally binding, some are addressed to the EU institutions rather than the Member States, with the effect that the latter need not do anything in terms of implementation. In the same vein, only three of the eight EU agreements with third states on counter-terrorism measures require some form of transposition in the Member States (the others affect private data controllers and EU institutions). See further B. Hayes and C. Jones, *Report on the transposition of EU counter-terrorism measures* (SECILE Consortium, 2013).

41 See B. Hayes and C. Jones, *supra* note 16 for an example of such a study.

structure of the state in federal or decentralized countries, the obligation to consult different stakeholders, including civil society, the legal drafting techniques employed, the length of the transposition process and a lack of coordination between different administrative departments.[42] Looking more broadly at the evolution of EU counter-terrorism policy and the controversies that have accompanied it, concerns about the impact of specific measures on human rights, about the surrender of powers to other Member States or EU agencies, and about proportionality and accountability have also played a role in determining the acceptability, and hence the practical application or implementation, of EU CTMs in the Member States.

Our research produced two startling findings. First, only one of the fifty CTMs we examined was found to have been implemented within the requisite time period by all of the Member States and to the satisfaction of the EU institutions (by this we mean that no infringement proceedings were launched, and no censures or complaints against the Member States were recorded in the implementation reports). Somewhat ironically, rather than introducing new counter-terrorism powers or practices, the one seamlessly transposed EU measure concerned the introduction of a peer review mechanism by the Member States for evaluating one another's counter-terrorism systems and structures, a framework which required only the lightest touch in terms of implementation (see further section 4.4.1, below).[43] Second, we found that where the European Commission had the power to initiate legal proceedings against Member States for failing to implement EU law – as it can in the case of EU Directives – it did so in respect to eight out of the eleven relevant CTMs (see Table 2, page 24). Ultimately, the Commission can bring the matter before the CJEU and request the imposition of substantial fines. For example, the Commission sought a daily penalty payment of €315,036.54 from Germany for its failure to implement provisions transposing the Data Retention Directive, after its national implementing legislation was ruled unconstitutional.[44] As noted earlier, the Directive itself has now been ruled unlawful by the CJEU.[45]

In December 2014, new powers were introduced allowing the European Commission to pursue infringement proceedings in respect of other types of legislative instrument used in the former third pillar, including Framework

42 B. Hayes and C. Jones, *Report on the transposition of EU counter-terrorism measures* (SECILE Consortium, 2013), pp. 17–18.

43 *Council Decision of 28 November 2002 establishing a mechanism for evaluating the legal systems and their implementation at national level in the fight against terrorism (2002/996/JHA)*. Available online at http://eur-lex.europa.eu/LexUriServ/LexUriServ.do?uri=OJ:L:2002:349:0001:0003:EN:PDF

44 European Commission, 'Data retention: Commission takes Germany to Court requesting that fines be imposed', 31 May 2012. Available online at http://europa.eu/rapid/press-release_IP-12-530_en.htm

45 European Court of Justice, *Judgment of the Court (Grand Chamber) in joined cases C-293/12 and C-594/12*, 8 April 2014. Available online at http://www.statewatch.org/news/2014/apr/eu-ecj-data-ret-judgment.pdf

Table 2 Infringement proceedings for failure to implement EU CTMs

Directive	*Infringement proceedings*
Parliament and Council Directive 2001/97/EC amending Council Directive 91/308/EEC on prevention of the use of the financial system for the purpose of money laundering – Commission (second anti-money laundering Directive)	Italy
Parliament and Council Directive 2002/58/EC concerning the protection of personal data and the protection of privacy in the electronic communications sector (the e-Privacy Directive)	Greece Portugal
Council Directive 2004/80/EC relating to compensation to crime victims	Italy
Council Directive 2004/82/EC on the obligation of carrier to communicate passenger data (the API Directive)	Poland
Parliament and Council Directive 2005/60/EC on the prevention of the use of the financial system for the purpose of money laundering and terrorist financing (third anti-money laundering Directive)	Belgium Spain France Ireland Poland Sweden
Parliament and Council Directive 2005/65/EC on enhancing port security	Estonia UK
Parliament and Council Directive 2006/24/EC on the retention of data generated or processed in connection with the provision of publicly available electronic communications services or of public communications networks and amending Directive 2002/58/EC	Austria Germany Greece Ireland Netherlands Sweden (2010 and 2013)
Parliament and Council Directive 2007/64/EC on payment services in the internal market amending Directives 97/7/EC, 2002/65/EC, 2005/60/EC and 2006/48/EC and repealing Directive 97/5/EC	Poland
Commission Directive 2008/43/EC setting up, pursuant to Council Directive 93/15/EC, a system for the identification and traceability of explosives for civil uses	No
Council Directive 2008/114/EC on the identification and designation of European critical infrastructures and the assessment of the need to improve their protection	No
Directive 2009/16/EC on port State control (Recast)	No

Decisions. Thus, further legal action to ensure the application of EU counter-terrorism policy can be expected.

The democratic legitimacy of decision-making in the EU, and more specifically within the Council of the EU – particularly with regard to the former third pillar where Member States monopolized the decision-making process to the exclusion of the European Parliament – is ostensibly derived from Member States' democratic systems. However, the European Commission frequently takes those very same states to task for failing to implement properly the measures they have developed. Clearly, the consensus reached within the Council is something that many feel they can discard if the final decision is not to their liking. While the exact reasons for this fall beyond the scope of our analysis, it should be of some concern to the Commission and for all those who wish to see common and consistent application of law across the EU. This is particularly so given the stated goal of the EU to create a common 'area of freedom, security and justice'.[46]

4. Assessing the impact, legitimacy and effectiveness of EU CTMs

The magnitude of the task facing anyone hoping to understand how EU counter-terrorism law has been transposed is compounded by a failure to include, on a systematic basis, provisions for review in the legislation itself, failures on the part of the EU institutions to conduct those reviews and failures to make available reviews that have been conducted.

The EU has at its disposal a wide range of consultative, legislative and review procedures that can be employed to evaluate measures implemented by its institutions. These come in the form of pre-legislative or *ex ante* assessments, assessments made during the decision-making process, and post-legislative or *ex post* assessments. If applied in full to the EU law- and policy-making process, these procedures have the *potential* to provide for a competent – if not comprehensive – evaluation of the impact, legitimacy and effectiveness of all EU CTMs, from conception through to design, adoption and implementation. Our research looked at the way the various review processes have been applied in practice in order to ascertain the extent to which the EU has sought to assess and evaluate the quality of its counter-terrorism *acquis*. The findings should be considered in the light of repeated promises on the part of EU institutions to better involve the public in their policy-making procedures, commitments that are intimately linked to public disquiet about the EU itself. The violent protests against the EU in 2001 (in Genoa and Gothenburg) sparked the first inter-institutional debate about European governance and how to 'get citizens more actively involved in

46 Article 67, Treaty of Lisbon. Available online at http://register.consilium.europa.eu/doc/srv?l=EN&f=ST%206655%202008%20REV%207

achieving the Union's objectives and to offer them a structured channel for feedback, criticism and protest'.[47] There was further soul-searching following the rejection of the EU constitution by French and Dutch voters in 2005 and the launch of Plan D for Democracy, Dialogue and Debate.[48] Despite the democratic reforms brought about by the Treaty of Lisbon, perceptions about the democratic deficit and an EU that has grown too large and powerful were frequently invoked after the results of the 2014 European Parliament elections.

Ex ante assessments of EU CTMs

Public consultations

Our research findings provide food for thought about the extent to which the EU has fostered democracy, dialogue and debate in the counter-terrorism field. Despite the decade-old commitment on the part of the European Commission to consult the public more widely, our research was only able to identify three public consultations for the eighty-eight legally binding counter-terrorism measures we identified, equating to a rate of 3.4 per cent. Although the Commission is only committed to public consultation on major initiatives,[49] this is a poor return for an area that has proved so controversial, but one that is representative of the JHA policy framework as a whole: from January 2002 to December 2012, a total of 1,395 JHA policy and legal texts were adopted by EU institutions, yet information published by the Commission suggests that since June 2002, there have been just thirty-four public consultations on JHA policy issues (equating to a rate of 2.4 per cent).[50]

The three public consultations concerned the Directive on the retention of telecommunications traffic data for law enforcement purposes,[51] the Decision to establish the Visa Information System (VIS),[52] and the Directive on

---

47 *European Governance: A White Paper*, COM(2001) 428 final, 25 July 2001.

48 Communication from the Commission to the Council, the European Parliament, the European Economic and Social Committee and the Committee of the Regions, *The Commission's contribution to the period of reflection and beyond: Plan-d for democracy, dialogue and debate* (com (2005) 494, 13 October 2005). Available online at http://eur-lex.europa.eu/lexuriserv/lexuriserv.do?uri=com:2005:0494:fin:en:pdf

49 *Towards a reinforced culture of consultation and dialogue – general principles and minimum standards for consultation of interested parties by the Commission*, COM(2002) 704 final, 11 December 2002.

50 See further B. Hayes and C. Jones, *Report on how the EU assesses the impact, legitimacy and effectiveness of its counterterrorism laws* (SECILE Consortium, 2013). Available online at http://www.statewatch.org/news/2013/dec/secile-how-does-the-EU-assess-its-counter-terrorism-law.pdf

51 Directive 2006/24/EC of 15 March 2006. Available online at http://eur-lex.europa.eu/LexUriServ/LexUriServ.do?uri=OJ:L:2006:105:0054:0063:EN:PDF

52 Council Decision of 8 June 2004 establishing the visa information system (VIS), 2004/512/EC. Available online at http://eur-lex.europa.eu/legal-content/EN/TXT/PDF/?uri=CELEX:32004D0512&from=EN

critical infrastructure protection.[53] In each case, the adoption of the measure was treated as a foregone conclusion and only the VIS consultation demonstrated a clear understanding of impact from a fundamental rights perspective.[54] The critical infrastructure consultation paper made no mention of fundamental rights, while the data retention consultation failed to canvass opinion on the impact of the proposed Directive on privacy and data protection.

Impact assessments

As well as improved public consultation, the Commission's better law-making Communication of 2002 also promised a more 'systematic approach to assessing the impact of initiatives, especially legislative ones'.[55] This would entail the employment of a 'general-purpose impact analysis tool' to be implemented 'gradually from 2003' and 'applied to all initiatives undertaken under the Commission's programme of work'.[56] The Commission promised to provide legislators with 'more accurate and better structured information . . . having regard to economic, social and environmental aspects'.[57] In 2006, an Impact Assessment Board was established within the Commission 'to provide independent quality control and quality support for Commission impact assessments', examining 'all draft impact assessment (IA) reports against the quality standards set out in the IA guidelines, and [issuing] opinions with recommendations on how the impact assessments should be improved'.[58] As with public consultations, the eventual aim was also to carry out impact assessments 'for all major initiatives, i.e. those which are presented in the Annual Policy Strategy or later in the Work Programme of the Commission'.[59]

It is clear that the use of impact assessments for CTMs has become more systematic over the years, in particular with regard to Directives and Regulations. Nevertheless, only twenty-two of the eighty-eight legally binding

53 Council Directive 2008/114/EC of 8 December 2008. Available online at http://eur-lex.europa.eu/LexUriServ/LexUriServ.do?uri=OJ:L:2008:345:0075:0082:EN:PDF

54 Questions included 'what are the eventual impacts on illegal immigrants?'; 'what are the eventual impacts on asylum seekers?'; and 'which impacts will the implementation of the VIS have from the data protection point of view?' European Commission, 'Consultation of Visa Information System (VIS)'. Available online at http://ec.europa.eu/dgs/home-affairs/what-is-new/public-consultation/2004/consulting_0018_en.htm

55 European Commission, 'Communication from the Commission on Impact Assessment', COM(2002) 276 final, 5 June 2002. Available online at http://eur-lex.europa.eu/LexUriServ/LexUriServ.do?uri=COM:2002:0276:FIN:EN:PDF

56 Ibid.

57 Ibid.

58 European Commission, '*Impact Assessment Board Report for 2012*', p.3. Available online at http://ec.europa.eu/governance/impact/key_docs/docs/iab_report_2012_en_final.pdf

59 Ibid.

counter-terrorism measures (25 per cent) we have identified were subject to such evaluations. The twenty-five Decisions have had four assessments (16 per cent), the fifteen Directives have had eleven (73 per cent), the eleven Framework Decisions one (9 per cent), and the twenty-five Regulations six (24 per cent). It is worth noting that no legislative proposal that originated in the Council (rather than the Commission, which only gained the full 'right of initiative' in respect of JHA policy after 2005) has ever been subjected to an impact assessment. Eight of the twenty-five Decisions were proposed by national delegations within the Council,[60] as were six of the eleven Framework Decisions[61] and one of the twenty-five Regulations.[62]

The impact assessment process is supposed to result in a decision-making aid that provides legislators with 'more accurate and better structured information on the positive and negative impacts' of the proposals, 'but not taking the place of political judgment'.[63] Although we did not analyse the content of the impact assessments that we identified, it is important to stress that they are inevitably highly politicized due to the number of differing

60 Eurojust (2000) *Initiative of the Portuguese Republic, the French Republic, the Kingdom of Sweden and the Kingdom of Belgium with a view to the adoption of a Council Decision setting up EUROJUST with a view to reinforcing the fight against serious organised crime*. Available online at http://register.consilium.europa.eu/pdf/en/00/st10/st10357.en00.pdf; peer evaluation of Member States' counter-terrorism provisions (Spain). Available online at http://register.consilium.europa.eu/pdf/en/02/st08/st08831.en02.pdf; police and judicial cooperation measures in accordance with Common Position 2001/931/CUSP (Spain). Available online at http://register.consilium.europa.eu/pdf/en/02/st07/st07756.en02.pdf; new functions for the SIS (Spain). Available online at http://register.consilium.europa.eu/pdf/en/02/st07/st07756.en02.pdf; increased cooperation between national Asset Recovery Offices (Austria, Belgium, Finland). Available online at: http://register.consilium.europa.eu/pdf/en/06/st07/st07259.en06.pdf; the Pram Decision (Belgium, Bulgaria, Germany, Spain, France, Luxembourg, Netherlands, Austria, Slovenia, Slovakia, Italy, Finland, Portugal, Romania, Sweden). Available online at http://register.consilium.europa.eu/pdf/en/07/st06/st06566.en07.pdf; implementation of the Prüm Decision (Germany). Available online at http://data.consilium.europa.eu/doc/document/ST-11563–2007-INIT/en/pdf; increased cooperation between national special forces units (Austria). Available online at http://register.consilium.europa.eu/pdf/en/06/st15/st15437.en06.pdf

61 Joint investigation teams (Belgium, France, Spain, UK). Available online at http://www.statewatch.org/semdoc/assets/files/council/11990–01.pdf; freezing of assets or evidence (France, Spain, Belgium). Available online at http://register.consilium.europa.eu/pdf/en/01/st05/st05126.en01.pdf; confiscation of crime-related proceeds, instrumentalities and property (Denmark). Available online at http://register.consilium.europa.eu/pdf/en/02/st10/st10697.en02.pdf (accessed); mutual recognition of confiscation orders (Denmark). Available online at http://register.consilium.europa.eu/pdf/en/02/st10/st10701.en02.pdf (accessed); simplifying the exchange of information between law enforcement authorities (Sweden). Available online at http://register.consilium.europa.eu/pdf/en/04/st10/st10215.en04.pdf; European enforcement order (Austria, Finland, Sweden). Available online at http://register.consilium.europa.eu/pdf/en/05/st07/st07307.en05.pdf

62 Introduction of new functions for the SIS (Spain). Available online at http://register.consilium.europa.eu/pdf/en/02/st09/st09407.en02.pdf

63 European Commission (2002) *European governance: Better lawmaking*, COM(2002) 275 final, 5 June 2002, pp. 3–4.

interests involved in crafting EU legislation: they are at the 'core of the negotiation process' and 'therefore a political balancing act'.[64] The European Parliament has recently commissioned a number of studies that interrogate the assumptions and processes used by the Commission in specific impact assessments,[65] some of which have questioned the legitimacy and motive of those documents. The report assessing the impact assessment that accompanied the Commission's smart borders package, for example, argued that 'it is difficult to escape the conclusion that having decided to pursue smart borders as a political objective in 2008 . . . the Commission has concentrated on "selling" the policies at the expense of impartially evaluating their necessity, feasibility and impact'.[66] The European Parliament has now established an Ex Ante Impact Assessment Unit to assess the Commission's impact assessments on a more systematic basis.

Participation in the decision-making process

Involvement of the European Parliament

When the Commission publishes a legislative proposal, the European Parliament assigns it to relevant committees and selects a rapporteur for the proposal, and the Council of the EU sends it to one or more working groups (comprised of representatives of the Member States) that are specialized in particular policy areas (e.g. law enforcement, terrorism, internal security, etc.). These two groups of co-legislators are responsible for developing the positions of their institutions, which then negotiate a compromise agreement between them. However, this 'normal' legislative procedure has not always applied to EU proposals in the area of counter-terrorism. On the contrary, whereas the entry into force of the Lisbon Treaty technically abolished the pillar structure of the EU and gave new powers to the Parliament,[67] many CTMs were adopted under the old third pillar rules, meaning that the Parliament had no real power to alter the draft legislation; it 'could do no more than give an opinion on certain acts and was consulted only on the

64 A-K. Bäcklund, 'Impact assessment in the European Commission – a system with multiple objectives' (2009) *Environmental Science & Policy* Vol. 12, p.1085.

65 Issues examined have included control of narcotic drug precursors, measures to prevent counterfeiting of the Euro, the prevention of money laundering and terrorist financing, the conditions of entry into the EU for certain third country-nationals, and the smart borders package.

66 D. Bigo, B. Hayes, J. Jeandesboz and S. Simon, *The Commission's legislative proposals on smart borders: their feasibility and costs*, European Parliament, p.23. Available online at http://www.statewatch.org/news/2013/oct/ep-smart-borders-study.pdf

67 Under the previous pillar structure, the first (or Community) pillar encompassed social, economic and environmental policy; the second the Common Foreign and Security Policy; and the third police and judicial cooperation. While it has been abolished, the 'Third Pillar, retains many of its core features, particularly with respect to decision-making on military, internal security and foreign policy issues.

principal aspects of activities'.[68] Of the eighty-eight legally binding EU counter-terrorism laws adopted since September 2001, seventy (79.5 per cent) were the subject of deliberations by the European Parliament, but the majority of these deliberations (forty-four or 50 per cent) took place as part of the consultation procedure, thus strictly limiting their impact. Co-decision, where the Parliament enjoys full legislative powers, only occurred in respect of twenty-three of the measures (26 per cent).[69] Put another way, our research found that the European Parliament was excluded from what is now the normal EU decision-making process in respect of three-quarters of the eighty-eight pieces of legally-binding counter-terrorism legislation.

Advisory opinions

Article 300 of the Lisbon Treaty states that 'the European Parliament, the Council and the Commission shall be advised by an Economic and Social Committee [ECSC] and a Committee of the Regions [CoR], exercising advisory functions'. The two bodies are independent and obliged to act in 'the Union's general interest'. Under the Lisbon Treaty, the consultation of these two bodies is mandatory when passing legislation; however, if they elect to issue opinions, their advice is not binding. Article 127 of the Lisbon Treaty also obliges consultation of the European Central Bank (ECB) 'on any proposed Union act in its fields of competence' – for the purposes of this study, those relating to money laundering and terrorist financing. Another body that frequently takes an interest in the legislative process is the European Data Protection Supervisor (EDPS), an independent supervisory authority established in line with Regulation (EC) No 45/2001.[70] Consultation of the EDPS is not obligatory and, like the ECSC and CoR, the advice of the EDPS is not binding. The extent to which the recommendations produced by these bodies were taken into account was beyond the scope of our research, but in any case, they were only marginally more involved in the legislative

68 European Commission, *The decision-making process under the third pillar*. Available online at http://europa.eu/legislation_summaries/other/l14543_en.htm

69 Three other procedures were used once each: own-initiative (INI), where MEPs decide to issue a non-binding resolution or opinion on an issue or proposal; non-legislative enactment (NLE), which applied to the EU-US Terrorist Finance Tracking Programme Agreement; and resolution on topical subject (RSP), which applied to a number of EU–US proposals being discussed in the wake of 11 September 2001 in the form of a 'resolution on EU judicial cooperation with the United States in combating terrorism'. See: European Parliament, 2001/2633(RSP). Available online at http://www.europarl.europa.eu/oeil/popups/ficheprocedure.do?reference=2001/2633%28RSP%29&l=en

70 Regulation (EC) No 45/2001 of the European Parliament and of the Council of 18 December 2000 on the protection of individuals with regard to the processing of personal data by the Community institutions and bodies and on the free movement of such data. Available online at https://secure.edps.europa.eu/EDPSWEB/webdav/site/mySite/shared/Documents/EDPS/DataProt/Legislation/Reg_45-2001_EN.pdf

process than the European Parliament as a whole under the old consultation procedure, with the majority of the eighty-eight CTMs not subject to any advisory opinion at all.[71]

Ex post assessment of EU CTMs

Once legislation has been adopted, it must be implemented by the Member States, EU bodies or private actors (or a combination of these stakeholders). Depending on the legislative instrument in question and the provisions made by the legislator, the implementation or transposition of the legislation may be subject to a review by the European Commission, Council of the EU or the expert advisors/contractors.[72] However, as suggested above, the primary concern of reviews of CTMs has tended to be whether or not the Member States have implemented the legislation, rather than how effective that legislation has been in respect to its purported aims. Moreover, whereas – as considered above – the transposition of EU Directives is subject to systematic monitoring by the European Commission, the *ex post* review of other instruments has been much more *ad hoc*. Of the eighty-eight legally binding EU CTMs, fifty-nine (or 67 per cent) contain provisions for review by the European Commission and nine of these provide for further reviews by the Council. One third of the EU's legally binding CTMs contain no provisions for review at all, suggesting little or no concern for their impact or effectiveness. Of the fifty-nine measures that are subject to review by the Commission, only thirty-three of those reviews can be located. Sixteen reviews have either not taken place or cannot be located – suggesting that the European Commission has failed to meet its obligations to review specific CTMs under

71 For the eight international agreements we have identified, the EDPS issued an opinion on four of them. Nobody issued opinions on any of the three Common Positions, nor on the one Joint Action. The twenty-five Decisions received a total of ten opinions (five from the EDPS, three from the ECSC and two from the CoR); the fifteen Directives received thirteen opinions (two from the EDPS, seven from the ECSC, one from the CoR and three from the ECB); the eleven Framework Decisions received one opinion from the EDPS; and the twenty-five Regulations received fourteen opinions (four from the EDPS, nine from the ECSC and one from the ECB).

72 Arguably, some of the most important *ex post* evaluations of the impact, legitimacy and effectiveness of EU counter-terrorism legislation have come from the Court of Justice in the European Union. One Agreement, one Common Position, seven Directives, one Framework Decision and four Regulations of the eighty-eight binding measures we have identified have been the subject of proceedings before the European Court of Justice, either in the form of cases brought against the EU institutions (generally the Council and/or Commission) or references from national courts for preliminary rulings from the ECJ on interpretation of the law. However, despite the importance of many of these cases, they are not analysed here as court proceedings and cannot be considered an assessment method in the same way as those that are established through the decision-making procedure or legislation itself. A list of the relevant legislation and legal cases is included in section 5 of: B. Hayes and C. Jones, *Report on how the EU assesses the impact, legitimacy and effectiveness of its counter-terrorism laws*, (SECILE Consortium, 2013). Available online at http://www.statewatch.org/news/2013/dec/secile-how-does-the-EU-assess-its-counter-terrorism-law.pdf

EU law in as many as 27 per cent of cases – while a further ten are yet to be produced in accordance with the deadline provided for in the legislation.[73]

Reviews of legislation are also occasionally undertaken by contractors and expert groups, although with far less frequency than reviews by the Commission or the Council. The five reviews of this kind that have taken place to date all concerned the establishment of EU agencies or funding programmes, with two further due in future.[74] In terms of legitimacy and effectiveness – as always – the key issue is the terms of reference for such reviews and the way in which the impact of the measures is subsequently assessed. RAND Europe's 250-page 'Evaluation of the implementation of the Europol Council Decision and of Europol's activities',[75] for example, was criticized by researchers at the Centre for European Policy Studies who observed that, 'somewhat surprisingly, an extensive evaluation commissioned by Europol's Management Board and carried out by the consultancy firm RAND Europe makes no mention of the [Organised Crime Threat Assessment] methodology or the quality of Europol's strategic analysis products. This seems a stark omission given the range of critiques levelled at the OCTA by external researchers'.[76]

Substantive reviews of EU counter-terrorism policy

A number of more substantive reviews of EU counter-terrorism policy have also been undertaken, albeit with markedly differing objectives. Peer evaluations by Member States have sought to enhance the efficacy of national counter-terrorism arrangements, the now-abolished Network of Independent Experts on Fundamental Rights attempted to ensure fundamental rights were taken into consideration in counter-terrorism policy, and the EU Counter-Terrorism Coordinator and the Commission have produced insipid reports that have largely served to reinforce the 'necessity' of increased EU activity to counter terrorism.

---

73 See section 3.3 in B. Hayes and C. Jones, *Report on how the EU assesses the impact, legitimacy and effectiveness of its counter-terrorism laws* (SECILE Consortium), pp. 17–20. Available online at http://www.statewatch.org/news/2013/dec/secile-how-does-the-EU-assess-its-counter-terrorism-law.pdf

74 Parliament and Council Regulation (EU) No 1168/2011 of 25 October 2011 amending Council Regulation (EC) No 2007/2004 establishing a European Agency for the Management of Operational Cooperation at the External Borders of the Member States of the European Union is due to be evaluated in 2014; Parliament and Council Regulation (EU) No 100/2013 of 15 January 2013 amending Regulation (EC) No 1406/2002 establishing a European Maritime Safety Agency requires an external review every five years.

75 Available online at https://www.europol.europa.eu/sites/default/files/publications/rand_evaluation_report.pdf

76 J. Parkin, *EU Home Affairs Agencies and the construction of EU internal security* (Centre for European Policy Studies, December 2012). Available online at http://www.ceps.eu/book/eu-home-affairs-agencies-and-construction-eu-internal-security

The peer review mechanism

On 20 September 2001, the JHA Council adopted a set of conclusions calling on the Member States to 'define a procedure for the peer assessment of national anti-terrorist arrangements on the basis of considerations of a legislative (e.g. examination of the legislation in certain Member States making it possible to carry out administrative telephone tapping or to draw up a list of terrorist organisations), administrative and technical nature'.[77] An initial report evaluating 15 Member States in November 2004 was followed by a final report on 25 Member States in September 2005. The result was numerous recommendations to the Member States highlighting 'those elements of good practice which might usefully be applied in all (or most) Member States', with the report noting that this may require 'constitutional, legal or structural changes'.[78] Beyond this, there was no mention of fundamental rights, democratic control or accountability. Concerns over legitimacy and effectiveness were nowhere to be seen, while the process was entirely opaque in terms of public access to information, with many of the relevant documents only declassified in 2011 and 2012. The joint report by the German Presidency and the EU Counter-Terrorism Coordinator issued in 2006 found that 'the peer evaluation process has contributed in a significant way to the reform of counter-terrorism arrangements in the Member States',[79] in stark contrast to the lethargy shown by Member States in transposing EU counter-terrorism measures that our research identified.

This may suggest that non-legislative, operational measures are implemented much more effectively than legislative ones. The 2006 report also claimed that '27 Member States were invited to implement all the general recommendations. Out of the total of 432 (27 x 16 recommendations), 421 have been implemented or are being implemented' and this because '11 recommendations were considered by Member States as not relevant'.[80] A second round of peer evaluations followed in 2010 and was also considered a resounding success, resulting in detailed recommendations to the Member States and EU institutions,[81] many of which also managed to

77 Justice and Home Affairs Council, Council conclusions, 12156/01, 20 September 2001. Available online at http://register.consilium.europa.eu/pdf/en/01/st12/st12156.en01.pdf

78 Presidency in cooperation with the Counter-Terrorism Coordinator, 'Final report on the evaluation of National Anti-Terrorist Arrangements: Improving national machinery and capability for the fight against terrorism', 12168/05, 26 September 2005. Available online at http://register.consilium.europa.eu/doc/srv?l=EN&f=ST%2012168%202005%20INIT

79 Presidency and Counter-Terrorism Coordinator, 'Follow-up report on the implementation of recommendations by the Council of the EU on counter-terrorism measures in the Member States – executive summary', 5356/07, 6 March 2007. Available online at http://register.consilium.europa.eu/pdf/en/07/st05/st05356.en07.pdf

80 Ibid.

81 General Secretariat, 'Second round of peer evaluation: Preparedness and consequence management in the event of a terrorist attack – Final report', 8568/10, 16 April 2010. Available online at http://register.consilium.europa.eu/pdf/en/10/st08/st08568.en10.pdf

find their way into a Council Recommendation on public order adopted in 2011.[82]

The network of independent experts on fundamental rights

The Network of Independent Experts on Fundamental Rights (CFR-CDF) was created by the European Commission in response to a recommendation in the European Parliament's report on the state of fundamental rights in the European Union in 2000.[83] The network was established formally in September 2002 and produced four (very detailed) Annual Reports covering the period 2002–2005,[84] four Thematic Comments, including one on the 'balance between security and freedom in the European Union',[85] and fifteen Opinions,[86] including reports on the 'Requirements of fundamental rights in the framework of the measures of prevention of violent radicalisation and recruitment of potential terrorists',[87] the 'Human Rights responsibilities of the EU Member States in the context of the C.I.A. activities in Europe (extraordinary renditions)',[88] and 'ethnic profiling',[89] which responded directly to an EU Recommendation on terrorist profiling.[90]

While these reports were extremely detailed in their critique of the way specific EU measures affected the fundamental rights of citizens, on the

---

82 Statewatch, 'Security of the spectacle: The EU's guidelines for security at major events', *Statewatch Analysis*, December 2012. Available online at http://www.statewatch.org/analyses/no-207-major-events-public-order.pdf

83 European Parliament resolution on the situation as regards fundamental rights in the European Union (2000), 2000/2231(INI), 5 July 2001. Available online at http://www.europarl.europa.eu/oeil/popups/ficheprocedure.do?lang=en&reference=2000/2231%28INI%29

84 CFR-CDF, *Report on the situation of fundamental rights in the European Union and its Member States in 2002*. Available, respectively, online at http://ec.europa.eu/justice/fundamental-rights/files/cfr_cdf_2002_report_en.pdf; 2003, http://www.statewatch.org/news/2004/may/indexperts-report-2003.pdf; 2004, http://www.statewatch.org/news/2005/jul/net-ind-experts-report-2004.pdf; 2005, http://www.statewatch.org/news/2006/jun/EU-funrights-report05.pdf

85 CFR-CDF, 'The balance between freedom and security in the response by the European Union and its Member States to the terrorist threats', March 31 2003. Available online at http://ec.europa.eu/justice/fundamental-rights/files/cfr_cdf_themcomment1_en.pdf

86 The majority of the network's reports are available online on the European Commission's website: European Commission, 'Fundamental rights', http://ec.europa.eu/justice/fundamental-rights/document/

87 CFR-CDF, 'The requirements of fundamental rights in the framework of the measures of prevention of violent radicalisation and recruitment of potential terrorists – Opinion no 3–2005', 23 August 2005. Available online at http://www.fd.uc.pt/hrc/pdf/eu_fund_rights/CFR-CDF_Avis3–2005.pdf

88 CFR-CDF, 'The human rights responsibilities of the EU member states in the context of the C.I.A. activities in Europe (extraordinary renditions)', 25 May 2005. Available online at http://ec.europa.eu/justice/fundamental-rights/files/cfr_cdfopinion3_2006_en.pdf

89 CFR-CDF, 'Ethnic profiling', December 2006. Available online at http://ec.europa.eu/justice/fundamental-rights/files/cfr_cdf_opinion4_2006_en.pdf

90 Council of the European Union, Draft Council Recommendation on the development of terrorist profiles, 11858/3/02 REV 3, 18 November 2002. Available online at http://register.consilium.europa.eu/pdf/en/02/st11/st11858-re03.en02.pdf

relevance of national and European court rulings to EU counter-terrorism policy, and on recommendations to ensure EU legislation complied with the EU Charter of Fundamental Rights, there was no meaningful consideration of the reports by either the Council of the EU or the European Commission, nor any attempt to act upon their findings. Instead, in 2006, the network was disbanded to make way for the relatively toothless Fundamental Rights Agency, which was denied any competence at all with regard to EU JHA policy. As the authors stated in their final report:

> The Network expresses the hope that, in the future, lessons will be drawn from this experiment. In particular, it would emphasize that independency and legal expertise, rather than being ends in themselves, should be seen as means – albeit indispensable ones – of developing a fundamental rights policy; their potential will only be realized if, on the part of the institutions, there exists a genuine commitment to act on the basis of the opinions and recommendations adopted by any independent body set up in order to monitor the situation of fundamental rights. It is clear that neither the Network of Independent Experts on Fundamental Rights, nor – in the future – the Fundamental Rights Agency, may be recognized [as having] any power to adopt binding opinions or recommendations. These are purely advisory bodies. Nevertheless, more could be done in order to ensure that these opinions and recommendations effectively contribute to the grounding in fundamental rights of Union policies and legislation.[91]

The EU Counter-Terrorism Coordinator

The role of the EU Counter-Terrorism Coordinator (CTC) was established by the European Council in its March 2004 Declaration on Combating Terrorism, which emphasized that 'a comprehensive and strongly coordinated approach is required in response to the threat posed by terrorism'. The European Council agreed to the creation of the post within the Secretariat of the Council of the European Union, with the main responsibility of maintaining 'an overview of all the instruments at the Union's disposal with a view to regular reporting to the Council and effective follow-up of Council decisions'.[92] The CTC's web page further notes that the CTC should also 'closely monitor the implementation of the EU counter-terrorism strategy,

91 CFR-CDF, '*Report on the situation of fundamental rights in the European Union and its member states in 2005: conclusions and recommendations*', p.24. Available online at http://cridho.uclouvain.be/documents/Download.Rep/Reports2005/CFR-CDFConclusions2006EN.pdf

92 Council of the European Union, 'Declaration on combating terrorism', 7906/04, 29 March 2004. Available online at http://register.consilium.europa.eu/doc/srv?l=EN&f=ST%207906%202004%20INIT

fostering better communication between the EU and third countries and ensure that the Union plays an active role in the fight against terrorism'.[93] The first Coordinator, appointed by then-Secretary-General/High Representative Javier Solana, was Gijs de Vries, who reportedly stepped down due to frustration with the mandate,[94] followed in 2007 by Gilles de Kerchove, who remains in the post at the time of writing.

While the CTC has issued fairly regular reports on the state of play with regard to the legislation, policies and activities established through the EU's counter-terrorism strategies and action plans, these publications shed no light on the legitimacy or effectiveness of the EU's myriad counter-terrorism measures. A 2007 report examining the implementation of the EU strategy for combating radicalization and recruitment,[95] for example, made no mention of issues relating to legitimacy or effectiveness, nor any reference to fundamental rights (despite the aforementioned 2005 Opinion of the EU's fundamental rights experts). The accompanying discussion paper took a similar approach, concerning itself largely with how EU institutions and Member States could more rapidly implement various policies and measures. This contained a single reference to fundamental rights in a section on data sharing with third countries.[96]

In December 2011, the CTC issued a paper reporting on the implementation of the EU Action Plan on combating terrorism. The CTC noted that he would not 'repeat the findings of the Commission's implementation report, discussed in the following section, but would update the reporting on the implementation of the overall counter-terrorism strategy in the last 12 months'.[97] In fact, the report did cover the same ground as the Commission's and showed no meaningful concern for fundamental rights and democratic control, despite the by-then extensive critique from civil society organizations, lawyers, journalists and even governments, though any criticism in this respect must be underscored by the fact that the CTC is not actually mandated to consider such issues.

---

93 Council of the European Union, 'EU Counter-Terrorism Coordinator'. Available online at http://www.consilium.europa.eu/policies/fight-against-terrorism/eu-counter-terrorism-co-ordinator?lang=en (accessed 11 January 2015).

94 EurActiv (2007) 'EU anti-terror chief to step down in March', 13 February 2007.

95 EU Counter-Terrorism Coordinator, *The EU strategy for combating radicalisation and recruitment – implementation report*, 15443/07, 23 November 2007. Available online at http://register.consilium.europa.eu/pdf/en/07/st15/st15443.en07.pdf

96 EU Counter-Terrorism Coordinator, *Implementation of the EU counter-terrorism strategy – Discussion paper*, 15448/07, 23 November 2007, p.6. Available online at http://register.consilium.europa.eu/pdf/en/07/st15/st15448.en07.pdf

97 EU Counter-Terrorism Coordinator (CTC), 'EU Action Plan on combating terrorism', 17594/1/11 REV 1, 9 December 2011. Available online at http://register.consilium.europa.eu/doc/srv?l=EN&f=ST%2017594%202011%20REV%201

The 2010 review of EU counter-terrorism policy

In July 2010, the European Commission published The EU Counter-Terrorism Policy: main achievements and future challenges. The aim of the Communication was to 'take stock of the main legislative and policy achievements at the EU level in the fight against terrorism, and to outline some future challenges in this field'.[98] The report contained a section on each of the EU counter-terrorism strategy's four themes – prevent, protect, pursue and respond – and set out major achievements and future challenges. The Communication is a wide-ranging, but largely descriptive, report that essentially lists measures implemented satisfactorily and those which the Commission feels need improving or updating. A section on respect for fundamental rights takes up the issue of the compatibility of EU counter-terrorism measures with fundamental rights standards, but does not do so in any great depth. There are general statements such as 'respect for fundamental rights and the rule of law is at the heart of the EU's approach to countering terrorism' and 'the Commission is therefore dedicated to ensuring that all tools that are deployed in the fight against terrorism fully respect fundamental rights', and a reference to a 2009 Commission report that synthesized Member States' responses to a Commission questionnaire on 'criminal law, administrative law/procedural law and fundamental rights in the fight against terrorism'.[99] However, neither this nor any further issues are examined in any detail. Despite the claim that 'the priority will be to ensure that any EU legislation and actions in this area fully complies with the Charter of Fundamental Rights, including implementing legislation put in place by the Member States',[100] there is no suggestion as to how this will be done, nor any reflection on whether this was the case up to the time the Commission Communication was written.

The shortcomings in the Commission's report were seized upon by the European Parliament (EP) in a report published in December 2011,[101] which noted that 'remarkably little has been done to assess to what degree EU counter-terrorism policies have achieved the stated objectives' despite Parliament 'repeatedly call[ing] for a thorough evaluation of EU counter-terrorism policies, as evaluation and assessment are preconditions for the transparency and accountability of policy-makers'. The EP stated that:

---

98 European Commission, 'The EU Counter-Terrorism Policy: main achievements and future challenges', COM(2010) 386 final, 20 July 2010, p.2. Available online at http://ec.europa.eu/dgs/home-affairs/what-is-new/news/pdf/com_2010_386_en.pdf

99 Ibid., p.11.

100 Ibid.

101 European Parliament resolution, 'EU Counter-Terrorism Policy: main achievements and future chal-lenges', 14 December 2011. Available online at http://www.europarl.europa.eu/sides/getDoc.do?type=TA&reference=P7-TA-2011-0577&language=HR

> [A] proper evaluation of ten years of counter-terrorism policies should focus on examining whether the measures taken to prevent and combat terrorism in the EU have been evidence-based (and not based on assumptions), needs-driven, coherent and part of a comprehensive EU counter-terrorism strategy, based on an in-depth and complete appraisal, to be carried out in line with Article 70 of the TFEU [Treaty on the Functioning of the European Union], with the Commission reporting back to a Joint Parliamentary Meeting of the EP and national parliamentary committees responsible for overseeing counter-terrorism activities within six months of the study being commissioned, drawing upon reports to be requested from relevant organisations and agencies such as Europol, Eurojust, the Fundamental Rights Agency, the European Data Protection Supervisor, the Council of Europe and the United Nations.[102]

The Parliament therefore called for the Commission to produce 'a full and detailed evaluation' that included 'at least the following items': (i) a clear analysis of the response to the terrorist threat, based on the definition laid down in Council Framework Decision 2002/475/JHA on combating terrorism as well as the framework of counter-terrorism measures to address this threat in terms of effectiveness, gaps in security, prevention, prosecution and increased security in Europe, including the effectiveness of the EU agencies and the proportionality thereof; (ii) facts, figures and trends relating to terrorist activity and counter-terrorism activity; (iii) a full overview of the accumulated impact of counter-terrorism measures on civil liberties and fundamental rights, measures by third countries with a direct impact in the EU and all measures taken in this field in connection with external relations, as well as the case law of the ECHR, the ECJ and national courts.[103] Further calls were made for: analysis of 'which measures have objectives other than counter-terrorism', or where mission or function creep had taken place; 'a complete and detailed map of all existing counter-terrorism policies in Europe, with a special focus on EU legislation, and how it has been transposed and implemented at EU level; a 'full and detailed report' on resources spent by the EU, Member States and private companies on counter-terrorism; and a study to establish whether counter-terrorism policies are 'subject to effective democratic scrutiny'.[104]

The Commission did claim in its December 2010 Communication that it would 'launch a study to make a more detailed evaluation of the current policies and priorities', and that it 'should be available in time for the mid-term evaluation of the Stockholm Programme'.[105] The mid-term evaluation

102 Ibid.

103 Ibid.

104 Ibid.

105 European Commission, 'The EU Counter-Terrorism Policy: main achievements and future challenges', COM(2010) 386 final, 20 July 2010, p.15. Available online at http://ec.europa.eu/dgs/home-affairs/what-is-new/news/pdf/com_2010_386_en.pdf

of the Stockholm Programme came and went,[106] but the Commission's 'more detailed evaluation' of counter-terrorism policy is yet to appear.

5. Conclusion: mission creep, cognitive bias and selective blindness

Our research has highlighted the sheer volume of CTMs that have been adopted by the EU and the massive expansion of scope in counter-terrorism policy to encompass many measures that have very little to do with combating terrorism *per se*. This mission creep matters a great deal since it is clear that the counter-terrorism label can often prove sufficient to justify the adoption of measures that were hitherto, or might otherwise, be deemed unacceptable in the light of the EU's legal obligations to protect fundamental rights and other values. We have also provided a great deal of evidence suggesting that a majority of EU CTMs developed since 9/11 have not been subject to either (a) democratic scrutiny or (b) an objective assessment of their impact, legitimacy or effectiveness, or (c) both. While counter-terrorism legislation is now subject to the 'normal' EU decision-making process, albeit with many important operational matters still excluded, our research findings clearly lend support to the European Parliament's calls for an in-depth, comprehensive review of all aspects of EU counter-terrorism policy. Moreover, although we note that if applied in full to the EU law- and policy-making process, the procedures for consultation, impact assessment, expert advice, democratic debate and *ex post* review at the EU institutions' disposal have the *potential* to provide for a competent evaluation of the impact, legitimacy and effectiveness of all EU legislation, three substantial concerns remain.

First, it is clear that these resources have been, at best, underutilized and, at worst, applied in a manner that ignores crucial issues of civil liberty and human rights, necessity and proportionality, accountability and democratic control in the counter-terrorism context. Second, the entire process appears subject to a strong cognitive bias that suggests that all EU CTMs are *a priori* necessary and that the only thing that really matters in respect to implementation is that the measures are expeditiously applied by the Member States. Third, it is difficult to escape the impression that what has happened in practice is that critical voices have been marginalized or sidelined in favour of those actors who are ideologically pre-disposed to the hard-security objectives of EU counter-terrorism policy. What is needed, therefore, is not simply the application of more robust deliberative and assessment procedures, but the giving of greater weight to counter-factual positions. Finally, we note that the agenda-setting (executive) dimension of EU counter-terrorism policy remains largely beyond the scope of any meaningful democratic scrutiny.[107] Unless this changes, it is difficult to envisage the reassessment of priority or practice that our research suggests is required.

---

106 EU Presidency, 'Stockholm Programme mid-term review', 15921/12, 13 November 2012. Available online at http://data.consilium.europa.eu/doc/document/ST-15921–2012-INIT/en/pdf

107 See also Chistyakova, this volume.

3 The institutional framework of EU counter-terrorism

*Josephine Doody**

1. Introduction

A core aim of the European Union (EU) is the creation of an area of freedom, security and justice (AFSJ).[1] Since the establishment of the European Coal and Steel Community in 1952, the free movement of persons, goods and services has been at the heart of the European project.[2] Consistent enlargement and deepening integration have contributed to the achievement of this European objective of openness. Such aspirations are complicated, however, by the security challenge posed by open borders. While counter-terrorism has long been a feature of European policy,[3] in the post-9/11 environment there has been an acceleration in law- and policy-making. Since 2001, 238 specific counter terrorism measures have been introduced.[4] This chapter identifies the key actors involved in developing these measures and their roles in the process of securing Europe through counter-terrorism legislation.

Two factors combine to make this a difficult task. First, while several academic articles exist on the topic, many assume a pre-existing knowledge of

---

* Josephine Doody was a researcher at Durham Law School on the SECILE project. She is currently employed as an Associate Lecturer with The Open University.

1 Article 2(2) states 'The Union shall offer its citizens an area of freedom, security and justice without internal frontiers, in which the free movement of persons is ensured in conjunction with appropriate measures with respect to external border controls, asylum, immigration and the prevention and combating of crime'. European Union, *Treaty of Lisbon Amending the Treaty on European Union and the Treaty Establishing the European Community*, 13 December 2007, 2007/C 306/01. Available online at http://europa.eu/lisbon_treaty/full_text/ (accessed 24 October 2013).

2 *Treaty Establishing the European Coal and Steel Community*, signed 18 April 1951, entered into force 23 July 1952, expired 23 July 2002.

3 The establishment of the terrorism, radicalism, extremism, and violence international (TREVI) group in 1975 marked the beginning of European cooperation in the area of counter-terrorism.

4 B. Hayes and C. Jones, *Catalogue of EU Counter-terrorism Measures Adopted since 11 September 2001* (SECILE Consortium, 2013).

the institutional labyrinth that is the EU.[5] Second, a brief overview of the subject area reveals complexity and impenetrability. In 2003, Monica Den Boer described the EU counter-terrorism architecture as 'a crowded policy area, which harbours a multiplication of actors who may not all be seeking to achieve the same policy objectives, which leads to obstructions along the decision-making process, or – seen from a slightly more optimistic perspective – to duplications and inefficiency regarding the achievement of policy objectives'.[6] Two years later, a European Union Committee at the UK House of Lords conducted an inquiry into the EU's response to terrorism after the Madrid bombings and 'found the structures within the EU for combating terrorism complex and confusing'.[7]

Ten years on, post-Lisbon, how can the EU security structure be characterized? This chapter adopts a descriptive approach organized around a series of questions: (1) Who proposes counter-terrorism legislation? (2) Who adopts it? Who is the decision-maker? What groups contribute to this decision-making process? Who oversees the implementation of the legislation? (3) Reflecting upon the complexity identified by other authors, has this situation has improved over time?

2. Identifying the threat

Early security challenges within Europe came from nationalist groups, left- and right-wing groups and organized crime.[8] Threats that were primarily internal to Member States were managed in the main by those states, but a particular security risk in the form of organized crime and money

---

5 D. Keohane, 'Special report 1: The EU and international terrorism' (2005) *European Policy Analyst*; L. Lugna, 'Institutional framework of the European Union counter-terrorism policy setting' (2006) *Baltic Security and Defence Review* Vol. 8; D. Casale, 'EU institutional and legal counter-terrorism framework' (2008) *Defence against Terrorism Review* Vol. 1 No. 1; C. Kaunert and S. Léonard, 'Supranational governance and European Union security after the Lisbon Treaty – Exogenous shocks, policy entrepreneurs and 11 September 2001' (2012) *Cooperation and Conflict* Vol. 47 No.4; J. Monar, 'The external dimension of the EU's area of freedom, security and justice: Progress, potential and limitations after the Treaty of Lisbon' (2012) *Swedish Institute for European Policy Studies*; T. Renard, 'EU Counterterrorism policies and institutions after the Lisbon Treaty' (2012) *Center on Global Counterterrorism Cooperation Policy Brief*; J. Argomaniz, 'Post-9/11 institutionalisation of European Union counter-terrorism: emergence, acceleration and inertia' (2009) *European Security* Vol.18 No.2; D. Bigo, P. Bondotti, L. Bonelli & C. Olsen, 'Mapping the field of EU internal security agencies', Paper produced for the Changing Landscape of European Liberty and Security (CHALLENGE) Project of the Centre for European Studies (CEPS).

6 M. Den Boer, '9/11 and the europeanisation of antiterrorism policy: a critical assessment' (2003) *Policy Papers No. 6, Notre Europe*, p.22.

7 The House of Lords, *House of Lords, European Union Committee, 5th Report of Session 2004–05, After Madrid: the EU's response to terrorism.* (London: The Stationery Office, 2005), p.27.

8 The key threats stemmed from the Irish Republican Army in the UK and Ireland, the Red Brigades in Italy and the Baader-Meinhof gang in Germany. See D. Keohane, 'Special report 1: The EU and international terrorism' (2005) *European Policy Analyst.*

laundering arose for all Member States from the freedom of movement and resultant open borders. Member States addressed the early external security challenge through the development of compensatory measures such as the Schengen Area Agreement.[9] This Agreement, signed in 1985, hinges on the principle of solidarity whereby all Member States to the Agreement shoulder the burden of security rather than leaving it to be primarily absorbed by those at the external borders of the Union. Similarly, informal networks assisted in addressing the early security challenge posed by open borders. The establishment of the Terrorism, Radicalism, Extremism, and Violence International (TREVI) group in 1975 marked the beginning of European cooperation in the area of counter-terrorism.[10] This was an intergovernmental forum composed of interior and justice ministers working outside formal treaty structures. They used the informal grouping to exchange information and best practice. The grouping emerged as a response to events at the time, most notably the 1972 Munich Olympic Games and various threats from nationalist groups across Europe. Police cooperation did not became a formal EU policy area until the signing of the Treaty on European Union (Maastricht treaty) in 1991 and TREVI was replaced in 1992 by the provisions of the Maastricht Treaty[11] third pillar involving immigration and asylum, policing, customs and legal cooperation.[12]

In contrast, the current threat to Europe from terrorism is presented as being quite different in nature and is described by Europol as strong.[13] According to the latest EU Terrorism Situation and Trend Report (TE-SAT) from Europol, seven people died as a result of terrorist attacks in Europe in 2013, down from seventeen the previous year. A total of 152 terrorist attacks were carried out, leading to the arrest of 535 individuals for terrorism-related offences.[14] The threat is characterized as diffuse and emanating from a variety of sources, including separatist groups and religion-inspired terrorism. The threat is constantly evolving with a trend shifting from 'structured groups and networks to smaller EU-based groups and solo terrorists or lone actors'.[15]

---

9 European Union, *Convention Implementing the Schengen Agreement of 14 June 1985 between the Governments of the States of the Benelux Economic Union, the Federal Republic of Germany and the French Republic, on the Gradual Abolition of Checks at their Common Borders ('Schengen Implementation Agreement')*, 19 June 1990. Available online at http://eurlex.europa.eu/LexUriServ/LexUriServ.do?uri=CELEX:42000A0922(02):en:HTML (accessed 24 October 2013).

10 L. Lugna, 'Institutional framework of the European Union counter-terrorism policy setting' (2006) *Baltic Security and Defence Review* Vol. 8, p.105.

11 European Union, 'Treaty on European Union (Consolidated Version), Treaty of Maastricht', 7 February 1992, *Official Journal of the European Communities* C 325/5; 24 December 2002. Available online at http://eur-lex.europa.eu/en/treaties/dat/11992M/htm/11992M.html (accessed 24 October 2013).

12 D. Casale, 'EU institutional and legal counter-terrorism framework' (2008) *Defence against terrorism review* Vol. 1 No. 1, p.50.

13 Europol, *TE-SAT 2014 EU terrorism situation and trend report.*

14 Ibid

15 Ibid

The internet remains a key factor in the promotion of terrorism-related activities. The role of political developments around the world as a trigger or motivating factor in political violence is recognized in the latest Europol report as is the threat posed by foreign fighters returning from Syria.

Thus, the picture today is one of a diffuse and widespread threat.[16] Early challenges posed by nationalist groupings in various Member States and addressed by informal bilateral cooperation mechanisms such as the TREVI group have been overtaken by transnational networks, both external and internal to the EU, and the even more challenging rise of the 'lone-wolf' terrorist demanding more innovative forms of cooperation.[17] The events of 11 September 2001 saw the focus change to transnational terrorism. Identified by most academics as a key turning point, the events of 9/11 set the EU on an accelerated path of law-making and institution-building.[18] The post-9/11 European security environment is characterized by a complex web of legislative instruments. Since 2001, 238 specific counter-terrorism measures have been introduced, eighty-eight of which are legally binding.[19] The spectrum of measures is vast and exists in different forms in different fields including Regulations, Directives and Decisions[20] in the field of Justice and Home Affairs policy, Conventions, Framework Decisions, Decisions and Common Positions[21] in the field of Common Foreign and Security Policy Common Strategies, Common Positions and Joint Actions, legally binding agreements with third states and bodies and a series of non-binding Recommendations, Resolutions, Conclusions, Opinions and Action Plans.[22]

The process of acceleration can be traced to the Conclusions of the extraordinary EU Justice and Home Affairs Council (JHA) convened on 20 September 2001, in the immediate aftermath of the 9/11 attacks.[23] The Council outlined a series of measures to be taken in order to step up the fight against terrorism within the European Union including, specifically, the creation of the European Arrest Warrant, the establishment of Eurojust, an invitation to Member States to ratify the relevant conventions to prevent and combat the financing of terrorism and a series of measures to improve

---

16 Europol, *TE-SAT 2014 EU terrorism situation and trend report.*

17 Ibid.

18 Kaunert would describe the events of 11 September 2001 as an 'exogenous shock'. C. Kaunert and S. Léonard, 'Supranational governance and European Union security after the Lisbon Treaty – Exogenous shocks, policy entrepreneurs and 11 September 2001' (2012) *Cooperation and Conflict* Vol. 47 No. 4.

19 For a complete listing of counter-terrorism measures introduced in the EU since 2001 see B. Hayes and C. Jones, *supra* note 4.

20 Provided for under Article 288 TFEU.

21 Provided for under Title VI TEU.

22 B. Hayes and C. Jones, *Report on the transposition of EU counter-terrorism measures* (SECILE Consortium, 2013).

23 European Council, *Conclusions adopted by the Council (Justice and Home Affairs)* on 20 September 2001, 12156/01 (Brussels; European Council, 2001).

cooperation with the United States. The European Council met the following day in an extraordinary session 'in order to analyse the international situation following the terrorist attacks in the United States and to impart the necessary impetus to the actions of the European Union'.[24] It adopted Conclusions and a plan of action. The plan of action focused on five key areas: enhancing police and judicial cooperation; developing international legal instruments; putting an end to the funding of terrorism; strengthening air security; and coordinating the EU's global action. This was supplemented by an EU Anti-terrorism Roadmap adopted on 26 September 2001 listing 46 measures.[25] The roadmap was updated, with significant progress having been achieved, in November 2002.[26]

Accelerated policy developments associated with 9/11 slowed over the following years and subsequent developments in the area of counter-terrorism policy can be linked to specific attacks. The Declaration on Combating Terrorism, for example, was introduced by the Council following the Madrid bombings in 2004.[27] The position of EU Counter-Terrorism Coordinator (CTC) was also established in 2004 in the aftermath of the Madrid bombings.[28] Gijs de Vries was the first incumbent and was succeeded by Gilles de Kerchove in 2007. The CTC is situated in the Council's General Secretariat and works under the authority of the High Representative of the Union for Foreign Affairs and Security Policy/Vice-President of the European Commission, but takes instruction from and reports to the JHA Council. The role of the CTC is to coordinate counter-terrorism activities within the Council, monitor the implementation of measures, communicate and ensure cooperation. The importance of this position was reaffirmed in the Stockholm Programme.[29] A Revised EU Plan of Action on Combating Terrorism outlining the seven strategic objectives to combat terrorism was adopted in June 2004, replacing the earlier roadmap.[30] In 2005, the 7/7 London bombings were followed by the adoption of the EU Counter-terrorism

---

24 European Council (2001) *Conclusions and plan of action of the extraordinary European Council meeting on 21 September 2001*. SN 140/01. Brussels, European Council.

25 European Council, *Anti-terrorism Roadmap*. SN 4019/01 (Brussels: European Council, 2001).

26 European Council, *European Union action plan to combat terrorism – Update of the roadmap*, 13909/1/02 (Brussels: European Council, 2002).

27 European Council (2004) *Declaration on Combating Terrorism*, 25 March 2004. Brussels: European Council.

28 European Council (2004) *Declaration on combating terrorism adopted by the European Council at its meeting on 25 March 2004*. Doc. 7906/04, p.14. Brussels: European Council.

29 European Council, The Stockholm Programme – An open and secure Europe serving and protecting citizens', *Official Journal* C 115 of 4.5.2010, p. 85: 'The European Council reaffirms the importance of the role of the EU Counter Terrorism Coordinator in ensuring implementation and evaluation of the Counter Terrorist strategy, coordinating Counter Terrorist work within the Union, and fostering better communication between the Union and third countries'.

30 Council of the European Union (2004) *EU Plan of Action on Combating Terrorism*. 10010/3/04, 11 June, Brussels, Council of the European Union.

Strategy introducing the 'prevent, protect, pursue, respond' approach.[31] In the intervening years, further strategies were added to the mix, including the EU Strategy for Combating Radicalisation and Recruitment in 2005[32] and the Revised Strategy on Terrorist Financing in 2008.[33] The next section will explore how European institutions make law in response to the perceived terrorist threat.

3. The proposal phase

The European Commission is the executive arm of the EU and acts as the driving force within the EU's institutional system.[34] It is responsible for proposing legislation, policies and programmes of action to Parliament and Council, and for implementing the decisions of the European Parliament and European Council.[35] The Commission is composed of twenty-eight Commissioners each responsible for a particular policy area. These Commissioners are drawn from the Member States but act on behalf of the Union and not on behalf of national interests.[36] The Commission is answerable to Parliament.[37] The staff are organized into departments known as Directorates-General. In 2010, the former Directorate-General (DG) for Justice, Liberty and Security was divided into two Directorate-Generals (DGs): one for Home Affairs and one for Justice, Fundamental Rights and Citizenship. Counter-terrorism sits within the crisis and terrorism policy in Home Affairs (DG Home).[38] A large part of the Commission's activity in the field of counter-terrorism takes place within DG Home although, given the complex nature of counter-terrorism, activities can be spread across multiple DGs. For example, the EU Data Retention Directive implicated DG Information Society and Media and DG Internal Market and Services.[39]

---

31 Council of the European Union (2005) *The European Union Counter-Terrorism Strategy*, 14469/4/05, 30 November, Brussels, Council of the European Union.

32 Council of the European Union (2005) *The European Union Strategy for Combating Radicalisation and Recruitment to Terrorism*. 14781/1/05, 24 November, Brussels, Council of the European Union.

33 Council of the European Union (2008) *Revised Strategy on Terrorist Financing*. 11778/1/08, 17 July, Brussels: Council of the European Union. For a complete listing of counter-terrorism measures introduced in the EU since 2001 see B. Hayes and C. Jones, *supra* note 4.

34 European Union, *The European Union Explained, How the European Union Works*, July 2012, p.19. Brussels: European Commission.

35 Ibid.

36 Ibid.

37 Ibid.

38 Available online at http://ec.europa.eu/dgs/home-affairs/what-we-do/policies/crisis-and-terrorism/index_en.htm

39 Directive 2006/24/EC of the European Parliament and of the Council of 15 March 2006 on the retention of data generated or processed in connection with the provision of publicly available electronic communications services or of public communications networks and amending Directive 2002/58/EC. 2006/24, 2006 O.J. (L 105) 54 (EC).

The general role of the Commission in the context of counter-terrorism is to draft legislation implementing the EU Action Plan on Combating Terrorism.[40] To this end, it is involved in developing targeted actions and initiatives, primarily within the 'prevent' and 'protect' strands of the plan. The Commission has played an important role in developing the legislative framework within which counter terrorism policies and actions operate at EU level. A key example is the Council Framework Decision on Combating Terrorism, which provides a common definition of terrorist and terrorist-linked offences.[41] Drafting legislation follows a series of methodical steps including identifying the problem, defining objectives, developing policy options, analysing and comparing the impacts of each option, and monitoring and evaluating the measures.[42] The Commission has developed policies in all sectors related to the prevention of terrorist attacks and the management of their consequences, e.g., in countering terrorist financing,[43] and hindering access to explosives[44] and chemical, biological, radiological and nuclear materials.[45] The Commission is also responsible for the European Programme for the Protection of Critical Infrastructure[46] and the EU-US Agreement on the Terrorist Finance Tracking Programme.[47] It is currently developing a European equivalent of the latter programme.[48] Other important roles that the Commission is involved in include providing assistance to victims of terrorism, supporting security research projects and coordinating European crisis management.

---

40 Council of the European Union, *EU Action Plan on Combating Terrorism*, 7233/1/07 REV 1, 29 March 2007.

41 Commission of the European Communities, *Proposal for a Council Framework Decision on Combating Terrorism*, Brussels, 19.9.2001, COM(2001) 521 final. 2001/0217 (CNS).

42 Commission of the European Communities, *Impact Assessment Guidelines*, Brussels, 15.1.2009, SEC (2009)92.

43 Commission of the European Communities, *Communication from the Commission to the Council and the European Parliament on the Prevention of and the Fight against Terrorist Financing through measures to improve the exchange of information, to strengthen transparency and enhance the traceability of financial transactions*, Brussels, 20.10.2004, COM(2004) 700 final.

44 Commission of the European Communities, *Communication from the Commission on Measures to Ensure Greater Security in Explosives, Detonators, Bomb-Making Equipment and Fire-Arms*, Brussels, 18.07.2005, COM(2005) 329 final.

45 Commission of the European Communities, *Communication from the Commission to the European, Parliament and the Council on Strengthening Chemical, Biological, Radiological and Nuclear Security in the European Union – An EU CBRN Action Plan*. Brussels, 24.6.2009, COM(2009) 273 final.

46 Commission of the European Communities, *Communication from the Commission on a European Programme for Critical Infrastructure Protection*, Brussels, 12.12.2006 COM (2006) 786 final.

47 Agreement between the European Union and the United States of America on the processing and transfer of Financial Messaging Data from the European Union to the United States for the purposes of the Terrorist Finance Tracking Program.

48 European Commission, *Communication from the Commission to the European Parliament and the Council – A European Terrorist Finance Tracking System: Available Options*. Brussels, 13.7.2011 Com(2011) 429 Final. For further information on the role of the Commission in relation to terrorism see http://ec.europa.eu/dgs/home-affairs/what-we-do/policies/crisis-and-terrorism/index_en.htm

4. Adoption and decision-making phase

The decision-making and adoption of legislation phases involve the European Council, the Council of Ministers and the European Parliament. The European Council is the overarching authority in relation to strategies involving external area of freedom and security and justice issues.[49] Article 68 of The Treaty on the Functioning of the European Union outlines the role of the European Council to 'define the strategic guidelines for legislative and operational planning within the area of freedom, security and justice'.[50] The European Council consists of heads of state or government from each Member State joining with the President of the European Council and the President of the European Commission. Together, they represent the highest level of political cooperation between Member States. Based in Brussels, the role of the European Council is to define the political direction and priorities of the EU, but it has no powers to pass laws per se. It does, however, issue Council Conclusions, which form a very substantial part of the EU's body of counter-terrorism measures[51] and are highly influential in the creation of *both* legislative measures within the EU *and* operational agreements and arrangements concluded by Member States, often with the coordinating assistance of agencies such as Europol. The Council meets every six months and a number of its organizations and working groups are involved in counter-terrorism.[52]

The second decision-making actor, the Council of Ministers, also known as the Council, is composed of government ministers from all Member States. Based in Brussels and Luxembourg, the role of the Council is to decide on proposals from the Commission and, in collaboration with the Parliament, to adopt decisions.[53] There are ten different Council configurations within the Council of Ministers including, for example, Foreign Affairs, Agriculture and Fisheries, and Competitiveness. The configurations of interest with relation to terrorism are the Justice and Home Affairs Council, the Foreign Affairs Council and the General Affairs Council.

The third key actor in decision-making is the European Parliament, the directly elected legislative arm of the EU. Members of the European Parliament (MEPs) are elected every five years and there are currently 751 members

---

49 J. Monar, '*The External Dimension of the EU's Area of Freedom, Security and Justice: Progress, Potential and Limitations after the Treaty of Lisbon* (2012) Swedish Institute for European Policy Studies, p.35.

50 European Union Article 68, *Consolidated Version of the Treaty on the Functioning of the European Union*, 13 December 2007, 2008/C 115/01. Available online at http://eur-lex.europa.eu/JOHtml.do?uri=OJ:C:2012:326:SOM:EN:HTML (accessed 24 October 2013).

51 For more information about Council Conclusions see http://www.european-council.europa.eu/council-meetings/conclusions

52 See section below, 'The Role of Advisory Groups'.

53 For more information on the Council of Ministers see http://www.consilium.europa.eu/council

across twenty-eight countries. The Parliament has three main roles. It shares with the Council the power to legislate; it exercises democratic supervision over all EU institutions; and it manages the EU budget alongside the Council.[54] Much of the work of the Parliament is organized by committee. The Civil Liberties, Justice and Home Affairs Committee (LIBE) is in charge of most of the legislation and democratic oversight for policies linked to the transformation of the European Union in the area of freedom, security and justice (AFSJ). Current work themes of the Committee include voting on the EU Data Protection Package and a hearing on the situation of fundamental rights in the EU, both reflecting the Parliament's traditional role of human rights and civil liberties monitor.[55] The second relevant committee is the Committee on Foreign Affairs, which helps to formulate and monitor a foreign policy that addresses the interests of the Union, the security expectations of its citizens and the stability of its neighbours while ensuring overall coherence and effectiveness.[56] At the time of writing, this committee was absorbed in the issue of transatlantic spying and implications for citizens' privacy.

Post-Lisbon, the European Parliament now has full co-decision powers.[57] The Parliament flexed its new-found muscle in February 2010 when it rejected The Society for Worldwide Interbank Financial Telecommunication (SWIFT) Interim Agreement between the EU and US intended to facilitate the transfer of financial data. The agreement was rejected by the LIBE committee on the grounds of inadequate data protection provision, lack of requirement of judicial authorization, and lack of rules on retention and oversight.[58] The Agreement was subsequently renegotiated and passed by Parliament in July 2010, leaving some to suggest that its earlier recalcitrance was more about 'affirming institutional prerogatives than substantive policy reasons'.[59] Regardless, the SWIFT case established a precedent for future negotiations involving the Parliament.

---

54 European Union, *supra* note 34, p.10.

55 For more information about the LIBE committee see http://www.europarl.europa.eu/committees/en/libe/home.html

56 For more information about the Committee on Foreign Affairs see http://www.europarl.europa.eu/committees/en/afet/home.htm

57 European Union Article 294 *Consolidated Version of the Treaty on the Functioning of the European Union*, 13 December 2007, 2008/C 115/01. Available online at http://eur-lex.europa.eu/JOHtml.do?uri=OJ:C:2012:326:SOM:EN:HTML (accessed 19 August 2014).

58 European Parliament: Draft Recommendation on the proposal for a Council decision on the conclusion of the Agreement between the European Union and the United States of America on the processing and transfer of Financial Messaging Data from the European Union to the United States for purposes of the Terrorist Finance Tracking Program, Committee on Civil Liberties, Justice and Home Affairs, Rapporteur: Jeanine Hennis-Plasschaert, PE438.440v01–00,3.2.2010.

59 See, for example, the discussion on the SWIFT case in J. Monar, *supra* note 49, p.42.

The role of advisory groups

A number of advisory groups assist with the decision-making process. The work of the Council of Ministers is prepared by the Permanent Representatives Committee (COREPER).[60] This Committee is composed of Member States' ambassadors and works in two configurations: COREPER I consists of deputy permanent representatives and deals with technical matters, while COREPER II consists of ambassadors and deals with political, commercial, economic and institutional matters. There are over 150 different working groups and parties assisting COREPER in its work.[61]

The Political and Security Committee (PSC) is a permanent structure of the Council of the European Union, the creation of which is provided for by Article 38 of the Treaty on the European Union (formerly Article 25 of the EU Treaty).[62] The PSC contributes to the drafting and implementation of the Common Foreign and Security Policy (CFSP), and the Common Security and Defence Policy (CSDP). In particular, it defines and follows up the EU's response in the event of a crisis. The mission of the PSC is to monitor the international situation in the areas covered by the CFSP. Thus, it delivers opinions to the Council in order to help define policies, coordinates, supervises and monitors the work led by the different Council working groups in the area of the CFSP and examines the draft conclusions of the General Affairs Council.[63]

The Council meets in a number of configurations. This section describes the Council configurations with a particular focus on terrorism, namely JHA, Foreign Affairs and General Affairs, and the corresponding working groups that assist the Council.

Justice and home affairs

The JHA Council is the principal decision-making institution. It comprises ministers of interior and of justice. The JHA Council is responsible for a

---

60 European Union Article 240 *Consolidated Version of the Treaty on the Functioning of the European Union,* 13 December 2007, 2008/C 115/01.

61 For a full list of council preparatory bodies please see Council of the European Union, *Note from General Secretariat of the Council to Delegations,* 5581/13, 22 January 2013.

62 Article 38 states: 'Without prejudice to Article 240 of the Treaty on the Functioning of the European Union, a Political and Security Committee shall monitor the international situation in the areas covered by the common foreign and security policy and contribute to the definition of policies by delivering opinions to the Council at the request of the Council or of the High Representative of the Union for Foreign Affairs and Security Policy or on its own initiative. It shall also monitor the implementation of agreed policies, without prejudice to the powers of the High Representative'. European Union, 'Treaty on European Union (Consolidated Version), Treaty of Maastricht', 7 February 1992, *Official Journal of the European Communities* C 325/5; 24 December 2002. Available online at http://eur-lex.europa.eu/LexUriServ/LexUriServ.do?uri=OJ:C:2010:083:0013:0046:en:PDF (accessed 24 October 2013).

63 For more information on the PSC see http://europa.eu/legislation_summaries/foreign_and_security_policy/cfsp_and_esdp_implementation/r00005_en.htm

number of key tasks. This grouping is required 'to approve all programming documents for the JHA external dimension . . . adopt all relevant legislative acts, take the decisions on the opening, signing and conclusion of international agreements in the AFSJ domain, approve the Commission's negotiation mandates, decide on external risk assessments and define action priorities regarding specific third-countries or – regions'.[64] Within the JHA Council configuration, there are five working groups of interest from a counter-terrorist perspective: the Article 36 Committee (CATS), the Terrorism Working Group, the Working Party on Civil Protection, the Strategic Committee on Immigration, Frontiers and Asylum (SCIFA) and the Standing Committee on Internal Security (COSI).

The role of CATS (or the Article 36 Committee in honour of the article of the Treaty on European Union (Maastricht Treaty) that established it) is to assist COREPER in relation to law enforcement and judicial cooperation in criminal matters. It acts as a useful network for senior officials in the field and focuses in particular on 'horizontal or cross cutting issues in the field of law enforcement and judicial cooperation in criminal matters and on politically important legislative proposals and non-legislative initiatives'.[65] Its role is to:

- be involved in in-depth discussions on relevant multi-annual programmes and their respective evaluation;
- facilitate work in the field of law enforcement and judicial cooperation matters by clearing the number of outstanding questions and thus narrowing down the issues to be examined by COREPER and Council;
- serve as a forum for an initial exchange of views in case of politically important legislative proposals and initiatives in order to set the direction for work at expert level in the relevant working parties;
- serve as a complementary forum for the purpose of informing and/or consulting Member States by the Commission in relation to important forthcoming initiatives;
- be a forum for the exchange of information on developments of interest in the areas of its mandate, in particular pending cases and developments in the case law of the Court of Justice/European Court of Human Rights.[66]

The Terrorism Working Group comprises interior ministry representatives and law enforcement agencies of Member States focusing on internal terrorism threats. This group meets three times per Presidency and deals with

---

64 J. Monar, *supra* note 49, p.37.

65 Council of the European Union, *'I' item note from the General Secretariat of the Council to COREPER, The Future of CATS*, 17187/11, 18 November 2011.

66 Ibid.

internal threat assessments, practical cooperation, and coordination among EU bodies.[67] The Working Party on Civil Protection works on early-warning mechanisms and consequence-management as a whole.[68] SCIFA coordinates the work of the various working groups in the field of migration, visa, borders and asylum.[69] COSI was created by the Lisbon Treaty in order to 'ensure that operational cooperation on internal security is promoted and strengthened' within the EU.[70] It is composed of representatives from national security services who coordinate operational cooperation in criminal matters in internal security. If the situation requires it, expertise can be sought from the working group on external JHA issues (JAIEX).

General affairs

The second Council configuration of interest in relation to counter-terrorism is the General Affairs Council. It deals with dossiers that affect more than one of the Union's policies, such as negotiations on EU enlargement, preparation of the Union's multi annual budgetary perspective, and institutional and administrative issues. It also coordinates preparation for and follow-up to meetings of the European Council, and has a role in coordinating work on different policy areas carried out by the Council's other configurations. The Security Committee is the key working group assisting the General Affairs Council in its work for the Council of Ministers. It examines and assesses any security matter and makes recommendations to the Council when appropriate. The Security Committee has established three expert sub-groups within the areas of Information Assurance, GNSS (Global Navigation Satellite System) and Security Accreditation.

Foreign affairs

Within the Foreign Affairs configuration of the Council there are three working groups that contribute to the preparation of counter-terrorism legislation: the Working Party on Terrorism (International aspects) (COTER),

---

67 The Council of the European Union (05.2004), *Working Structures of the Council in terrorism matters – Options paper, Note from EU Counter-Terrorism Coordinator to COREPER.* Doc. 9791/04,25.05.2004, p.2.

68 Ibid., p.2.

69 Ibid., p.2.

70 Article 71 states, 'A standing committee shall be set up within the Council in order to ensure that operational cooperation on internal security is promoted and strengthened within the Union. Without prejudice to Article 240, it shall facilitate coordination of the action of Member States' competent authorities. Representatives of the Union bodies, offices and agencies concerned may be involved in the proceedings of this committee. The European Parliament and national Parliaments shall be kept informed of the proceedings.' European Union, *Consolidated Version of the Treaty on the Functioning of the European Union*, 13 December 2007, 2008/C 115/01. Available online at http://eur-lex.europa.eu/LexUriServ/LexUriServ.do?uri=OJ:C:2010:083:0047:0200:en:PDF (accessed 24 October 2013).

the Working Party on the Application of Specific Measures to Combat Terrorism (COCOP), and the Working Party of Foreign Relations Counsellors (RELEX). COTER is composed of foreign ministry representatives working on external aspects of counter-terrorism. This group meets once a month and deals with issues relating to external matters, threat assessments and policy recommendations as regards third countries and regions, implementation of UN Conventions and coordination of work, in particular in the UN, and seminars on the financing of terrorism.[71] RELEX deals with legal, financial and institutional issues in the external field with the main focus being on the Common Foreign and Security Policy (CFSP). Priorities include the financing of external activities, EU crisis management operations, non-proliferation, sanctions, EU Special Representatives and other cross-cutting issues. The role of the working party on the application of specific measures to combat terrorism is to implement Common Position 2001/931/CFSP.[72] In particular, its mandate is to:

- Examine and evaluate information with a view to listing and de-listing of persons, groups and entities pursuant to Common Position 2001/931/CFSP;
- Assess whether the information meets the criteria set out in Common Position 2001/931/CFSP and in the Council's statement agreed when the Common Position was adopted;
- Prepare the regular review of the list as foreseen in Article 1(6) of the Common Position; and
- Make recommendations for listings and de-listings to be reflected in the necessary legal instruments, which will be endorsed by the Permanent Representatives Committee with a view to their adoption by the Council.[73]

The role of EU agencies

Along with the various advisory groups that contribute to the decision-making process, there are a number of EU agencies that play a role. The

71 The Council of the European Union (05.2004), *Working Structures of the Council in terrorism matters – Options paper, Note from EU Counter-Terrorism Coordinator to COREPER*. Doc. 9791/04,25.05.2004, p.2.

72 Council of the European Union, *Fight Against the Financing of Terrorism: Implementation of Common Position 2001/931/CFSP*, Doc. 10826/1/07, Rev. 1, 28 June 2007. Available at http://register.consilium.europa.eu/pdf/en/07/st10/st10826-re01.en07.pdf (accessed 24 October 2013).

73 Ibid. Although not their core business, a number of other entities under Foreign Affairs may engage to some degree with counter-terrorism, such as the European Union Military Committee (which directs all EU military activity and advises the Political and Security Committee), the Politico-Military Group (which handles politico-military aspects of the Common Security and Defence Policy) and the European Union Military Committee Working Group (which prepares materials relating to many of the issues dealt with by the EUMC).

European Defence Agency (EDA) supports the Council and Member States in improving EU defence capabilities as part of the CSDP. It was established under a joint action of the Council of Ministers in 2004.[74] The head of the EDA is also the High Representative of the Union for Foreign Affairs and Security Policy and Vice-President of the European Commission.

Europol is the European Union's law enforcement agency assisting Member States in, among other things, their fight against terrorism.[75] Established by the Maastricht Treaty in 1992, it became operational in 1998, is based at The Hague, and has a staff of almost 800. Europol officers are drawn from national law enforcement agencies. They take part in Joint Investigation Teams conducting over 13,500 cross-border investigations each year. A Joint Investigation Team is established between two or more Member States for a specific task and for limited duration.[76] It gathers, analyses and disseminates information and coordinates intelligence. Europol does not have direct powers of arrest but rather works closely with law enforcement agencies across the twenty-eight Member States and with non-EU partner states such as Australia, Canada, USA and Norway. It relies heavily on national security and intelligence services to share information with it but has no power to oblige them to cooperate.

Europol is accountable to the JHA Council, which appoints the Director and Deputy Directors. The Council, together with the Parliament, approves the budget for Europol. Within Europol, the two key counter-terrorism bodies are the Counter-Terrorism Unit and the Counter-Terrorism Task Force.[77] Europol publishes TE-SAT, an annual detailed account of the state of terrorism in the EU.[78]

Europol's work in the field of counter-terrorism is conducted through the negotiation of international agreements with third countries or third-country authorities.[79] There are two types of agreement. Operational agreements are far-reaching, permitting the exchange of personal data between cooperation partners. These agreements have been signed with twelve non-EU states: Albania,[80]

74 Council Joint Action 2004/551/CFSP of 12 July 2004 on the establishment of the European Defence Agency and later Council Decision 2011/411/CFSP of 12 July 2011 defining the statute, seat and operational rules of the European Defence Agency and repealing Joint Action 2004/551/CFSP.

75 Legal basis is Article 23 of the Council Decision of 6 April 2009 establishing the European Police Office (Europol) (2009/371/JHA), OJ L 121/37–66 of 15.5.2009.

76 Council of the European Union 'Note from Council Secretariat to Delegations', *Joint Investigations Team Manual*, 15790/1/11, Rev 1, Brussels 4 November 2011.

77 D. Casale, *supra* note 12, p.55.

78 See for example, Europol, *TE-SAT 2013 EU Terrorism Situation and Trend Report.*

79 Current list (August 2014) taken from Europol website https://www.europol.europa.eu/content/page/external-cooperation-31 (accessed 17 August 2014).

80 Agreement on Operational and Strategic Co-operation between the Republic of Albania and the European Police Office. Available online at https://www.europol.europa.eu/sites/default/files/publications/agreement_on_operational_and_strategic_co-operation_between_the_republic_of_albania_and_the_european_police_office_english_version_0.pdf(accessed 17 August 2014).

Australia,[81] Canada,[82] Colombia,[83] the former Yugoslav Republic of Macedonia,[84] Iceland,[85] Norway,[86] Republic of Serbia,[87] Switzerland,[88] The Principality of Lichtenstein,[89] The Principality of Monaco,[90] the United States of America[91] and one international organization, Interpol.[92]

Less far-reaching strategic agreements permit the exchange of strategic and technical information and provide for training but they do not permit the exchange of personal data. These agreements have been signed with six non-EU states: Ukraine,[93] Montenegro,[94] Moldova,[95] Bosnia and Herzegovina,[96]

---

81 Agreement on Operational and Strategic Co-operation between Australia and the European Police Office, https://www.europol.europa.eu/sites/default/files/flags/australia.pdf (accessed 17 August 2014).

82 Cooperation Agreement between the Government of Canada and the European Police Office. Available online at https://www.europol.europa.eu/sites/default/files/flags/canada.pdf (accessed 17 August 2014).

83 Agreement on Operational and Strategic Co-operation between the Republic of Colombia and the European Police Office. Available online at https://www.europol.europa.eu/sites/default/files/publications/agreement_on_operational_and_strategic_co-operation_between_colombia_and_the_european_police_office_2.pdf (accessed 17 August 2014).

84 Agreement on Operational and Strategic Co-operation between the Former Yugoslav Republic of Macedonia and the European Police Office. Available online at https://www.europol.europa.eu/sites/default/files/operationala.pdf (accessed 17 August 2014).

85 Agreement between the Republic of Iceland and the European Police Office. Available online at https://www.europol.europa.eu/sites/default/files/flags/iceland.pdf (accessed 17 August 2014).

86 Agreement between the Kingdom of Norway and the European Police Office. Available online at https://www.europol.europa.eu/sites/default/files/flags/norway.pdf (accessed 17 August 2014).

87 Agreement on Operational and Strategic Co-operation between the Republic of Serbia and the European Police Office. Available online at https://www.europol.europa.eu/sites/default/files/publications/edoc-663978-v10-agreement_on_operational_and_strategic_co-operation_between_the_republic_of_serbia_and_the_european_police_office_english_version.pdf (accessed 17 August 2014).

88 Agreement between the Swiss Confederation and the European Police Office. Available online at https://www.europol.europa.eu/sites/default/files/flags/switzerland.pdf (accessed 17 August 2014).

89 Agreement on Operational and Strategic Co-operation between the Principality of Lichtenstein and the European Police Office. Available online at https://www.europol.europa.eu/sites/default/files/agreement_on_operational_and_strategic_co-operation_between_the_principality_of_liechtenstein_and_the_european_police_office_en.pdf (accessed 17 August 2014).

90 Agreement on Operational and Strategic Co-operation between the Government of HSH The Sovereign Prince of Monaco and the European Police Office. Available online at https://www.europol.europa.eu/sites/default/files/principalityofmonaco.pdf (accessed 17 August 2014).

91 Agreement between the United States of America and the European Police Office. Available online at https://www.europol.europa.eu/sites/default/files/flags/united_states_of_america.pdf (accessed 17 August 2014).

92 Agreement between Interpol and Europol. Available online at https://www.europol.europa.eu/sites/default/files/flags/interpol_.pdf (accessed 17 August 2014).

93 Agreement between the European Police Office and Ukraine on Strategic Co-operation. Available online at https://www.europol.europa.eu/sites/default/files/flags/ukraine.pdf (accessed 17 August 2014).

94 Agreement on Strategic Cooperation between Montenegro and the European Police Office. Available online at https://www.europol.europa.eu/sites/default/files/flags/montenegro.pdf (accessed 17 August 2014).

95 Strategic Co-operation Agreement between the Republic of Moldova and the European Police Office. Available online at https://www.europol.europa.eu/sites/default/files/flags/moldova.pdf (accessed 17 August 2014).

96 Cooperation Agreement between Bosnia and Herzegovina and the European Police Office. Available online at https://www.europol.europa.eu/sites/default/files/flags/bosniaherzegovia.pdf (accessed 17 August 2014).

the Russian Federation,[97] and Turkey.[98] They have been signed with two international organizations: UN Office on Drugs and Crime[99] and the World Customs Organization.[100]

Eurojust was established in 2002 replacing its forerunner Pro-Eurojust.[101] Acting as a cross-border judicial coordination unit, its mission is 'to support and strengthen coordination and cooperation between national investigating and prosecuting authorities in relation to serious crime affecting two or more Member States [. . .]'.[102] Based at The Hague, it works with Member States, assisting them in dealing with cross-border threats such as those posed by terrorism. It is staffed by lawyers, judges and other legal experts seconded from each Member State. Each Member State designates a National Correspondent for terrorism.[103] Eurojust's competencies have expanded and strengthened with various Council amendments in 2003 and 2008.[104] The Lisbon Treaty envisaged further development of Eurojust with Article 86 calling for the establishment of a European Public Prosecutor's Office.[105] The European Parliament confirmed its support for this new office in March 2014. This new office envisages delegated European prosecutors integrated into national systems conducting investigations and prosecutions, and national courts conducting judicial review.[106]

97 Agreement on Cooperation between the European Police Office and the Russian Federation. Available online at https://www.europol.europa.eu/sites/default/files/flags/russia.pdf (accessed 17 August 2014).

98 Agreement on Cooperation between the European Police Office and the Republic of Turkey. Available online at https://www.europol.europa.eu/sites/default/files/flags/turkey_.pdf (accessed 17 August 2014).

99 Cooperation Agreement between the United Nations Office on Drugs and Crime and the European Police Office (Europol). Available online at https://www.europol.europa.eu/sites/default/files/flags/united_nations_office_on_drugs_and_crime_.pdf (accessed 17 August 2014).

100 Cooperation Agreement between the World Customs Organization (WCO) and the European Police Office (Europol). Available online at https://www.europol.europa.eu/sites/default/files/flags/world_customs_organization_.pdf (accessed 17 August 2014).

101 Eurojust was established by Council Decision 2002/187/JHA of 28 February 2002. This was subsequently amended in 2003 (Council Decision 2003/659/JHA of 18 June 2003 and 2008 (Council Decision 2009/426/JHA of 16 December 2008).

102 European Union Article 85, *Treaty of Lisbon Amending the Treaty on European Union and the Treaty Establishing the European Community*, 13 December 2007, 2007/C 306/01. Available online at http://eur-lex.europa.eu/JOHtml.do?uri=OJ:C:2007:306:SOM:EN:HTML (accessed 24 October 2013).

103 Article 3 of Council Decision of 19 December 2002 on the implementation of specific measures for police and judicial cooperation to combat terrorism in accordance with article 4 of the Common Position 2001/931/CSFP.

104 2003 (Council Decision 2003/659/JHA of 18 June 2003) and 2008 (Council Decision 2009/426/JHA of 16 December 2008).

105 European Union Article 86, *Treaty of Lisbon Amending the Treaty on European Union and the Treaty Establishing the European Community*, 13 December 2007, 2007/C 306/01

106 European Commission, 'European Parliament confirms its support', Strasbourg, European Public Prosecutors Office, 12 March 2014.

Similar to Europol, Eurojust has a legal personality permitting it to enter into international agreements. Eurojust has been active in negotiating cooperation agreements and memoranda of understanding with third States and other EU agencies, allowing the exchange of judicial information and personal data.[107] Agreements were concluded with a number of EU partners including Europol,[108] the European Commission,[109] the European Police College (CEPOL),[110] the European Anti-Fraud Office (OLAF),[111] the European Agency for the Management of Operational Cooperation at the External Borders of the Member States of the European Union (Frontex),[112] the European Monitoring Centre for Drugs and Drug Addiction[113] and the European Judicial Training Network.[114] Third States agreements have been entered into with Lichtenstein,[115] the Swiss

107 List taken from Eurojust website at http://www.eurojust.europa.eu/doclibrary/Eurojust-framework/Pages/agreements-concluded-by-eurojust.aspx?Page=1 (accessed 17 August 2014).

108 Agreement between Eurojust and Europol. Available online at http://www.eurojust.europa.eu/doclibrary/Eurojust-framework/agreements/Agreement%20between%20Eurojust%20and%20Europol%20(2010)/Eurojust-Europol-2010–01–01-EN.pdf (accessed 17 August 2014).

109 Memorandum of Understanding between the European Commission and Eurojust. Available online at http://www.eurojust.europa.eu/doclibrary/Eurojust-framework/agreements/Memorandum%20of%20Understanding%20between%20the%20European%20Commission%20and%20Eurojust%20(2012)/Eurojust-Commission-2012–07–20_EN.PDF (accessed 17 August 2014).

110 Memorandum of Understanding on Cooperation between Eurojust and the European Police College (CEPOL). Available online at http://www.eurojust.europa.eu/doclibrary/Eurojust-framework/agreements/MoU%20between%20Eurojust%20and%20CEPOL%20(2009)/Eurojust-CEPOL-2009–12–07-EN.pdf (accessed 17 August 2014).

111 Practical Agreement on Arrangements of Cooperation between Eurojust and OLAF. Available online at http://www.eurojust.europa.eu/doclibrary/Eurojust-framework/agreements/Practical%20Agreement%20on%20arrangements%20of%20cooperation%20between%20Eurojust%20and%20OLAF%20(2008)/Eurojust-OLAF-2008–09–24-EN.pdf (accessed 17 August 2014).

112 Memorandum of Understanding on Cooperation between Frontex and Eurojust. Available online at http://www.eurojust.europa.eu/doclibrary/Eurojust-framework/agreements/Memorandum%20of%20Understanding%20between%20Eurojust%20and%20Frontex%20(2013)/Frontex-Eurojust-2013–12–18_EN.pdf (accessed 17 August 2014).

113 Memorandum of Understanding on Cooperation between Eurojust and the European Monitoring Centre for Drugs and Drug Addiction (EMCDDA). Available online at http://www.eurojust.europa.eu/doclibrary/Eurojust-framework/agreements/Memorandum%20of%20Understanding%20between%20Eurojust%20and%20the%20European%20Monitoring%20Centre%20for%20Drugs%20and%20Drug%20Addiction%20(2014)/EUROJUST-EMCDDA-2014–07–15-EN.pdf (accessed 17 August 2014).

114 Memorandum of Understanding on Cooperation between Eurojust and the European Judicial Training Network. Available online at http://www.eurojust.europa.eu/doclibrary/Eurojust-framework/agreements/Memorandum%20of%20Understanding%20between%20Eurojust%20and%20the%20European%20Judicial%20Training%20Network%20(2008)/Eurojust-EJTN-2008–02–07-EN.pdf (accessed 17 August 2014).

115 Agreement on Co-operation between Eurojust and the Principality of Lichtenstein. Available online at http://www.eurojust.europa.eu/doclibrary/Eurojust-framework/agreements/Agreement%20on%20Cooperation%20between%20Eurojust%20and%20the%20Principality%20of%20Liechtenstein%20(2013)/Eurojust-Liechtenstein_2013–06–07_EN.pdf (accessed 17 August 2014).

Confederation,[116] the Former Yugoslav Republic of Macedonia,[117] Croatia,[118] the USA,[119] Iceland,[120] the Republic of Moldova[121] and Norway.[122] Agreements have been reached with a number of international organizations including Interpol,[123] the UN Office on Drugs and Crime[124] and Ibero-American Network of International Legal Cooperation.[125] Liaison prosecutors from Norway and the USA are now permanently based at Eurojust. In addition to cooperation agreements, Eurojust also maintains a network of contact points worldwide.

The European Agency for the management of operational cooperation at the external borders of the Member States of the European Union (Frontex)

---

116 Agreement between Eurojust and Switzerland. Available online at http://www.eurojust.europa.eu/doclibrary/Eurojust-framework/agreements/Agreement%20between%20Eurojust%20and%20Switzerland%20(2008)/Eurojust-Switzerland-2008–11–27-EN.pdf (accessed 17 August 2014).

117 Agreement on Co-operation between Eurojust and the Former Yugoslav Republic of Macedonia. Available online at http://www.eurojust.europa.eu/doclibrary/Eurojust-framework/agreements/Agreement%20on%20cooperation%20between%20Eurojust%20and%20the%20former%20Yugoslav%20Republic%20of%20Macedonia%20(2008)/Eurojust-fYROM-2008–11–28-EN.pdf (accessed 17 August 2014).

118 Agreement between Eurojust and the Republic of Croatia. Available online at http://www.eurojust.europa.eu/doclibrary/Eurojust-framework/agreements/Agreement%20between%20Eurojust%20and%20the%20Republic%20of%20Croatia%20(2007)/Eurojust-Croatia-2007–11–09-EN.pdf (accessed 17 August 2014).

119 Agreement between Eurojust and the United States of America. Available online at http://www.eurojust.europa.eu/doclibrary/Eurojust-framework/agreements/Agreement%20Eurojust-USA%20(2006)/Eurojust-USA-2006–11–06-EN.pdf (accessed 17 August 2014).

120 Agreement between Eurojust and the Republic of Iceland. Available online at http://www.eurojust.europa.eu/doclibrary/Eurojust-framework/agreements/Agreement%20Eurojust-Iceland%20(2005)/Eurojust-Iceland-2005–12–02-EN.pdf (accessed 17 August 2014).

121 Agreement on Cooperation between Eurojust and the Republic of Moldova. Available online at http://www.eurojust.europa.eu/doclibrary/Eurojust-framework/agreements/Agreement%20on%20cooperation%20between%20Eurojust%20and%20the%20Republic%20of%20Moldova%20(2014)/Eurojust-Republic-of-Moldova-2014–07–10-EN.pdf (accessed 17 August 2014).

122 Agreement between the Kingdom of Norway and Eurojust. Available online at http://www.eurojust.europa.eu/doclibrary/Eurojust-framework/agreements/Agreement%20Eurojust-Norway%20(2005)/Eurojust-Norway-2005–04–28-EN.pdf (accessed 17 August 2014).

123 Memorandum of Understanding on Cooperation between Eurojust and the International Criminal Police Organisation (ICPO-Interpol). Available online at http://www.eurojust.europa.eu/doclibrary/Eurojust-framework/agreements/Memorandum%20of%20Understanding%20between%20Eurojust%20and%20ICPO-INTERPOL%20(2013)/Eurojust-Interpol_2013–07–15_EN.pdf (accessed 17 August 2014).

124 Memorandum of Understanding between Eurojust and the United Nations Office on Drugs and Crime (UNODC). Available online at http://www.eurojust.europa.eu/doclibrary/Eurojust-framework/agreements/MoU%20between%20Eurojust%20and%20the%20United%20Nations%20Office%20on%20Drugs%20and%20Crime%20(2010)/Eurojust-UNODC-2010–02–26-EN.pdf (accessed 17 August 2014).

125 Memorandum of Understanding between Eurojust and the Ibero-American Network of International Legal Co-operation. Available online at http://www.eurojust.europa.eu/doclibrary/Eurojust-framework/agreements/Memorandum%20of%20Understanding%20between%20Eurojust%20and%20Iber-RED%20(2009)/Eurojust-IberRED-2009–05–04-EN.pdf (accessed 17 August 2014).

was established in 2004.[126] Based in Warsaw, Frontex aims to balance the freedoms associated with the eradication of internal borders within the Schengen area with the potential security issues that such an arrangement can invite. Described as 'compensatory measures',[127] Frontex focuses on cooperation and coordination of police and judicial authorities' work. Similar to Europol and Eurojust, Frontex has a legal personality and can enter into international agreements.[128] Frontex has the authority to enter into working arrangements with third countries and as of June 2012 has concluded seventeen such arrangements with: the Russian Federation,[129] Ukraine,[130]Moldova,[131] Georgia,[132] the Former Yugoslav Republic of Macedonia,[133] Serbia,[134]

---

126 Frontex was established by Council Regulation (EC) 2007/2004/ (26.10.2004, OJ L 349/25.11.2004) having regard to the Treaty establishing the European Community. It was later amended by the Regulation (EC) No 863/2007 of the European Parliament and of the Council of 11 July 2007 and last amended by the Regulation (EU) No 1168/2011 of the European Parliament and of the Council of 25 October 2011.

127 For more see the Frontex website at http://frontex.europa.eu/about-frontex/origin (Accessed 17 August 2014).

128 List taken from Frontex website: http://www.frontex.europa.eu/partners/third-countries (Accessed 17 August 2014).

129 Terms of Reference on the Establishment of Operational Co-operation between the European Agency for the Management of Operational Co-operation at the External Borders of the Member States of the European Union (Frontex) and the Border Guard Service of the Federal Security Service of the Russian Federation. Available online at http://frontex.europa.eu/assets/Partners/Third_countries/WA_with_Russia.pdf (Accessed 17 August 2014).

130 Working Arrangement on the establishment of Operational Cooperation between the European Agency for the Management of Operational Cooperation at the External Borders of the Member States of the European Union (Frontex) and the Administration of the State Border Guard Service of Ukraine. Available online at http://frontex.europa.eu/assets/Partners/Third_countries/WA_with_Ukraine.pdf (Accessed 17 August 2014).

131 Working Arrangement on the establishment of Operational Cooperation between the European Agency for the Management of Operational Cooperation at the External Borders of the Member States of the European Union (Frontex) and the Border Guard Service of the Republic of Moldova. Available online at http://frontex.europa.eu/assets/Partners/Third_countries/WA_with_Moldova.pdf (Accessed 17 August 2014).

132 Working Arrangement on the establishment of Operational Cooperation between the European Agency for the Management of Operational Cooperation at the External Borders of the Member States of the European Union (Frontex) and the Ministry of Internal Affairs of Georgia. Available online at http://frontex.europa.eu/assets/Partners/Third_countries/WA_with_Georgia.pdf (Accessed 17 August 2014).

133 Working Arrangement establishing Operational Cooperation between the European Agency for the Management of Operational Cooperation at the External Borders of the Member States of the European Union (Frontex) and the Ministry of Internal Affairs of the Former Yugoslav Republic of Macedonia. Available online at http://frontex.europa.eu/assets/Partners/Third_countries/WA_with_former_Yugoslav_Republic_of_Macedonia.pdf (Accessed 17 August 2014).

134 Working Arrangement establishing Operational Cooperation between the European Agency for the Management of Operational Cooperation at the External Borders of the Member States of the European Union (Frontex) and the Ministry of the Interior of Republic of Serbia. Available online at http://frontex.europa.eu/assets/Partners/Third_countries/WA_with_Serbia.pdf (Accessed 17 August 2014).

Albania,[135] Bosnia and Herzegovina,[136] the United States,[137] Montenegro,[138] Belarus,[139] Canada,[140] Cape Verde,[141] Nigeria,[142] Armenia,[143] Turkey[144] and Azerbaijan[145] as well as with the Commonwealth of Independent States (CIS)

---

135 Working Arrangement establishing Operational Cooperation between the European Agency for the Management of Operational Cooperation at the External Borders of the Member States of the European Union (Frontex) and the Ministry of Interior of Republic of Albania. Available online at http://frontex.europa.eu/assets/Partners/Third_countries/WA_with_Albania.pdf (Accessed 17 August 2014).

136 Working Arrangement establishing Operational Cooperation between the European Agency for the Management of Operational Cooperation at the External Borders of the Member States of the European Union (Frontex) and the Ministry of Security of Bosnia and Herzegovina. Available online at http://frontex.europa.eu/assets/Partners/Third_countries/WA_with_BiH.pdf (Accessed 17 August 2014).

137 Working Arrangement establishing Cooperation between the European Agency for the Management of Operational Cooperation at the External Borders of the Member States of the European Union and the United States Department of Homeland Security. Available online at http://frontex.europa.eu/assets/Partners/Third_countries/WA_with_US.pdf (Accessed 17 August 2014).

138 Working Arrangement establishing Operational Cooperation between the European Agency for the Management of Operational Cooperation at the External Borders of the Member States of the European Union (Frontex) and the Police Directorate of Montenegro. Available online at http://frontex.europa.eu/assets/Partners/Third_countries/WA_with_Montenegro.pdf (Accessed 17 August 2014).

139 Working Arrangement on the establishment of Operational Cooperation between the European Agency for the Management of Operational Cooperation at the External Borders of the Member States of the European Union (Frontex) and the State Border Committee of the Republic of Belarus. Available online at http://frontex.europa.eu/assets/Partners/Third_countries/WA_with_Belarus.pdf (Accessed 17 August 2014).

140 Working Arrangement establishing Cooperation between the European Agency for the Management of Operational Cooperation at the External Borders of the Member States of the European Union and the Canada Border Services Agency. Available online at http://frontex.europa.eu/assets/Partners/Third_countries/WA_with_Canada.pdf (Accessed 17 August 2014).

141 Working Arrangement establishing Operational Cooperation between the European Agency for the Management of Operational Cooperation at the External Borders of the Member States of the European Union (Frontex) and the Policia Nacional de Cabo Verde. Available online at http://frontex.europa.eu/assets/Partners/Third_countries/WA_with_Cape_Verde.pdf (Accessed 17 August 2014).

142 Working Arrangement establishing Operational Cooperation between the European Agency for the Management of Operational Cooperation at the External Borders of the Member States of the European Union (Frontex) and the Nigerian Immigration Service. Available online at http://frontex.europa.eu/assets/Partners/Third_countries/WA_with_Nigeria.pdf (Accessed 17 August 2014).

143 Working Arrangement establishing Operational Cooperation between the European Agency for the Management of Operational Cooperation at the External Borders of the Member States of the European Union (Frontex) and the National Security Council of the Republic of Armenia. Available online at http://frontex.europa.eu/assets/Partners/Third_countries/WA_with_Armenia.pdf (Accessed 17 August 2014).

144 Memorandum of Understanding on establishing Cooperation between the European Agency for the Management of Operational Cooperation at the External Borders of the Member States of the European Union and the Ministry of Foreign Affairs of the Republic of Turkey. Available online at http://frontex.europa.eu/assets/Partners/Third_countries/WA_with_Turkey.pdf (Accessed 17 August 2014).

145 Working Arrangement establishing Operational Cooperation between the European Agency for the Management of Operational Cooperation at the External Borders of the Member States of the European Union (Frontex) and the State Border Service of the Republic of Azerbaijan. Available online at http://frontex.europa.eu/assets/Partners/Third_countries/WA_with_Azerbaijan.pdf (Accessed 17 August 2014).

Border Troop Commanders Council[146] and the MARRI Regional Centre in the Western Balkans.[147] It is in various stages of negotiations with the authorities of a further seven countries: Libya, Morocco, Senegal, Mauritania, Egypt, Brazil and Tunisia.

The European External Action Service (EEAS) was introduced by the Lisbon Treaty and started to function in 2011.[148] The HR/VP heads this service and the staff is drawn from the Commission, the Council and Member States' foreign ministries. The EEAS is the EU's diplomatic arm assisting the High Representative of the European Union for Foreign Affairs and Security Policy/Vice-President of the European Commission HR/VP in the coordination of EU external action. There are two agencies and services within EEAS that are relevant to counter-terrorism: EU SITCEN and EUMS Intelligence Directorate (EUMS INT). They were previously located within the Council's General Secretariat but were transferred to EEAS by the Lisbon Treaty. Within EEAS lies the EU Situation Centre (SITCEN), a strategic analytical body of eighty analysts who prepare intelligence reports on the basis of intelligence collected by Member States, EU delegations, CSDP missions and open sources. It produces assessments of the internal and external security threat.[149] Also within EEAS is EUMS INT, which has a staff of forty analysts producing intelligence reports for the EEAS.[150]

---

146 Memorandum on the establishment of Operational Cooperation in border related matters between the European Agency for the Management of Operational Cooperation at the External Borders of the Member States of the European Union (Frontex) and the Coordination Service of the Commonwealth of Independent States Border Commandants' Council (SKPV Coordination Service). Available online at http://frontex.europa.eu/assets/Partners/Third_countries/WA_with_CIS.pdf (Accessed 17 August 2014).

147 Working Arrangement in the Form of an Exchange of Letters between the European Agency for the Management of Operational Cooperation at the External Borders of the Member States of the European Union (Frontex) and Migration, Asylum, Refugees, Regional Initiative (Marri) Regional Centre. Available online at http://frontex.europa.eu/assets/Partners/Third_countries/WA_with_MARRI.pdf (Accessed 17 August 2014).

148 European Union, *Treaty of Lisbon Amending the Treaty on European Union and the Treaty Establishing the European Community*, 13 December 2007, 2007/C 306/01. Available online at http://eur-lex.europa.eu/JOHtml.do?uri=OJ:C:2007:306:SOM:EN:HTML (accessed 24 October 2013). Article 13 (a) (3) states 'In fulfilling his mandate, the High Representative shall be assisted by a European External Action Service. This service shall work in cooperation with the diplomatic services of the Member States and shall comprise officials from relevant departments of the General Secretariat of the Council and of the Commission as well as staff seconded from national diplomatic services of the Member States. The organization and functioning of the European External Action Service shall be established by a decision of the Council. The Council shall act on a proposal from the High Representative after consulting the European Parliament and after obtaining the consent of the Commission.' A Council Decision of 26 July 2010 established the organization and functioning of the European External Action Service.

149 T. Renard, 'EU counterterrorism policies and institutions after the Lisbon Treaty' (2012) *Center on Global Counterterrorism Cooperation Policy Brief*, p.9.

150 Ibid., p.10.

The role of external agencies

The Counter-Terrorism Group facilitates cooperation between European internal intelligence services outside EU structures, bringing together counter-terrorist experts of the intelligence services on a regular basis to facilitate cooperation.[151] This cooperation is based on mutual trust and flexibility. The group focuses specifically on Islamic extremist terrorism. Police services do not participate in this group but rather cooperate in the Police Chiefs Task Force and the Police Working Group on Terrorism.[152]

The European Police Chiefs Task Force is a forum for the Heads of States' police forces where they meet to agree on targets for action in the area of terrorism.[153] It was established at an EU Council Decision meeting in Tampere in 1999 and began to meet from 2000.[154] Since the Lisbon Treaty, the Task Force meets under the European Police Chiefs Convention. It is not accountable to the Union as it has no Treaty basis but rather was formed on the basis of a Council Recommendation.[155]

The Police Working Group on Terrorism was established in 1979 by the UK, Netherlands, Germany and Belgium following the assassination of the British Ambassador to Ireland in 1976.[156] Other countries followed suit by joining the group and formal cooperation was achieved in 1986 with the 'Political Declaration by the Governments of the Member States on the Free Movement of Persons'.[157]

In addition to the above-mentioned working groups of the Council, there is a Contact Group (network of focal points) of persons from the Member States' Brussels Permanent Representations dealing with all aspects of terrorism. It is, as the title suggests, a contact group of focal points for preparing the meetings of the Council preparatory bodies. It is not a Council working group. Its purpose is to act as a central contact point on issues related to counter-terrorism, guaranteeing the flow of information to the relevant competent authorities in the Member States.[158]

---

151 D. Keohane, *supra* note 8, p. 44.

152 The Commission of the European Communities (05.2004), *Communication from the Commission to the European Parliament and the Council. Enhancing Police and Customs Cooperation in the European Union.* Doc. COM(2004) 376 final, 18.05.2004, p.27.

153 D. Keohane, *supra* note 8, p. 44.

154 Tampere European Council 15 and 16 October 1999, Presidency Conclusions, Conclusion No. 44.

155 M. Deflem, 'Europol and the policing of international terrorism: Counter-terrorism is a global perspective' (2006), *Justice Quarterly* Vol. 23 No. 3, p.350.

156 Ibid., p.341.

157 The Political Declaration states 'In order to promote the free movement of persons, the Member States shall cooperate, without prejudice to the powers of the Community, in particular as regards the entry, movement and residence of nationals of third countries. They shall also cooperate in the combating of terrorism, crime, the traffic in drugs and illicit trading in works of art and antiques'. Available online at http://www.eurotreaties.com/seafinalact.pdf (Accessed 24th October 2013).

158 L. Lugna, *supra* note 10, p.108.

5. Conclusion

Since 2001, 238 specific EU counter-terrorism measures have been introduced.[159] The legislative and institutional response to the events of 11 September, 2001 and subsequent events, most importantly the London and Madrid bombings, have led some authors to describe the EU structures for countering terrorism as overcrowded, complex and confusing.[160] This chapter set out to investigate whether, almost ten years on, the situation had improved or not. It began by exploring the evolution of the terrorist threat in Europe. Over the last forty years, the threat has mutated in terms of actor, motivation and tactics. There has been a shift from left- and right-wing groups motivated by nationalist and separatist ideologies to more disparate groups and lone actors motivated by extremist religious-based ideology. The threat itself has ebbed and flowed and appears strongest at times of attack, what Kaunert and Léonard call 'exogenous shocks'[161] or what Argomaniz calls 'critical junctures'.[162] They are critical in the sense that they shock the political system into a legislative and institutional response, thus ensuring the institutionalization of counter-terrorism as a distinct policy area.

This chapter examined the institutional response through a detailed examination of the EU organizational chart. It described how measures are developed, who proposes the measure, who makes the decision, and who implements the measures. It described the work of the Council, the Commission and the Parliament and the way in which they are assisted by an army of internal working groups and external agencies. It focused in particular on the three Council configurations related to Terrorism, Justice and Home Affairs, Foreign Affairs and General Affairs who alone have nine working groups supporting their work. They in turn are supported by an array of internal agencies and external agencies. The continuous supplementation of groups, organizations and agencies following particular events without the removal of existing structures contributes to what has quickly become a formidable and sprawling framework.[163] This combination of political response to terrorist attacks and the continual aggrandizement of the security architecture has meant that the simplification promised by the de-pillarization introduced with Lisbon has failed to deliver the anticipated simplicity required for EU citizens and researchers alike to negotiate policy-making pathways and to comprehend fully how decisions are made in the counter-terrorist context.

159 B. Hayes and C. Jones, *supra* note 4.

160 See for example M. Den Boer, *supra* note 6, p.22, and The House of Lords, *supra* note 7, p.27.

161 C. Kaunert and S. Léonard, *supra* note 18.

162 J. Argomaniz, *supra* note 5, pp. 151–172.

163 Argomaniz talks about institutional bricolage and layering in this context. See Ibid.

Part II

Disciplinary perspectives on EU counter-terrorism

4 Assessing counter-terrorism as a matter of human rights

Perspectives from the European Court of Human Rights

Mathias Vermeulen

1. Introduction

This chapter will analyse (a) how the European Court of Human Rights has assessed the compatibility of European counter-terrorism measures with the European Convention of Human Rights in order to determine the impact of counter-terrorism measures, and (b) the extent to which this Court has taken into account the perceived effectiveness of counter-terrorism measures in this assessment. Following earlier work, I distinguish a *direct* negative impact of a counter-terrorism measure—which results in decreased (procedural) safeguards for terrorist suspects subjected to the measure(s) in question—from an *indirect* negative impact of a counter-terrorism measure (which manifests itself only over a longer period of time in that these decreased safeguards can become standard outside an emergency context and, as such, slowly erase a particular human right). Section 2 will analyse how the European Court of Human Rights has assessed the legality of three particularly controversial counter-terrorism measures, which have both a direct and indirect impact on the protection of human rights: terrorist listings, public provocation laws and the use of diplomatic assurances. Section 3 analyses how the Court assesses the effectiveness of a specific counter-terrorism measure, and analyses whether the European Court of Human Rights has taken into account considerations of effectiveness in determining the legality of a counter-terrorism measure. This chapter argues that the Court focuses on the direct – rather than indirect – impacts of counter-terrorism measures on the procedural dimension of a human right, and that it does not take into account the perceived or actual effectiveness of a counter-terrorism measure. Instead, the Court grants states a wide margin of appreciation in deciding which counter-terrorism measures to take. It analyses whether the measure in question (a) infringes upon a protected right and (b) is accompanied by sufficient safeguards to make that infringement proportionate.

2. Assessing the impact of counter-terrorism measures

Terrorist listings

Since the adoption of UN Resolution 1373, many individuals and organizations have been put on terrorist 'blacklists', which have been created by international and regional organizations, and at the national level. In June 2014, the UN's Al-Qaida Sanctions List consisted of 211 individuals and sixty-six entities;[1] the EU's own terrorist list consists of eleven persons and twenty-five entities.[2] The UK's consolidated list of financial sanctions targets consists of twenty-three persons, and twenty-seven entities as of June 2014.[3] The individuals and members of these organizations typically not only face restrictions on their financial transactions but also on their freedom of movement. From the outset, the listing practice and procedure has been controversial, and many organizations and academics have criticized the lack of due-process guarantees in the listing procedure, notably the lack of an effective complaint mechanism and the political and open-ended nature of the listing decision.[4]

The practice of terrorist listings has also been denounced for its broader impact on the rule of law. The European Centre for Constitutional and Human Rights has pointed to the broader impact of the listings practice, which includes the 'externalisation and expansion of (unaccountable) executive powers'.[5] Essentially, it is claimed that states have deliberately circumvented the evidentiary and procedural requirements of the criminal justice system in exchange for 'easier' administrative law measures, which face less judicial and democratic control. This practice also allows states to criminalize

1 United Nations Security Council Committee, *The List established and maintained by the 1267 Committee with respect to individuals, groups, undertakings and other entities associated with Al-Qaida.* Available online at http://www.un.org/sc/committees/1267/aq_sanctions_list.shtml (accessed 11 January 2015).

2 EU Council Implementing Regulation (EU) No 125/2014 of 10 February 2014, *Implementing Article 2(3) of Regulation (EC) No 2580/2001 on specific restrictive measures directed against certain persons and entities with a view to combating terrorism, and repealing Implementing Regulation (EU) No 714/2013.*

3 Consolidated list of financial sanctions targets in the UK, available online at: https://www.gov.uk/government/uploads/system/uploads/attachment_data/file/207736/terrorism.pdf (accessed 11 January 2015).

4 Council of Europe Parliamentary Assembly, *Resolution 1597 (2008) United Nations Security Council and European Union blacklists*, 23 January 2008. European Data Protection Supervisor, *Opinion on the Communication from the Commission to the European Parliament and the Council – 'The EU Counter-Terrorism Policy: main achievements and future challenges'*, 24 November 2010. See also the contributions in the *Yearbook of European Law*, (2009) vol. 28(1) on 'Challenging EU Counter-Terrorism Measures before the Courts: An Assessment of the Kadi Judgment', pp. 533–697.

5 B. Hayes and G. Sullivan, 'BLACKLISTED: Targeted sanctions, preemptive security and fundamental rights' in *European Center for Constitutional Human Rights newsletter*, December 2010, p.79. Available online at http://www.statewatch.org/news/2010/dec/eu-ecchr-blacklisted-report.pdf (accessed 11 January 2015).

and delegitimize popular resistance movements with ease, which in turn has impacted on the work of international development organizations and conflict resolution processes.[6]

Last, but not least, the lists also have a direct and indirect impact on the human rights of third parties, particularly female family members. According to the UN Special Rapporteur on the protection of human rights while countering terrorism in 2009, listings 'directly impact women, who, for example may have their bank accounts separately monitored and experience limits on their normal family life through conditions such as those that restrict who can enter the family home'.[7]

This last impact was indirectly addressed by the European Court of Human Rights in an important case lodged by Mr Youssef Nada, who was placed on the United Nations Sanctions Committee's list in 2001. Switzerland implemented the sanctions regime, and applied an entry and transit ban to all individuals put on the list. Nada lived in Campione d'Italia, an Italian enclave of about 1.6 km^2 surrounded by the Swiss Canton of Ticino and separated from the rest of Italy by Lake Lugano. Nada complained that the travel ban had breached his Article 8 right to 'respect for his private life, including his professional life, and his family life'.[8] He contended that this ban had prevented him from seeing his doctors in Italy or Switzerland, and from visiting his friends and family, including for important events such as funerals or weddings. He further claimed that the addition of his name to the list annexed to the Taliban Ordinance had impinged on his honour and reputation.[9] In September 2009, Nada was delisted.

The European Court of Human Rights did not denounce the listings practice as such, nor the long-term impact of the use of the terrorist listing, but instead focused solely on the direct impact of the listing on Mr Nada and his family. After pointing out that investigations conducted by the Swiss and Italian authorities concluded in 2005 that suspicions about Nada's participation in terrorist activities were clearly unfounded, the Court was 'surprised' that the Swiss authorities only informed the Sanctions Committee in 2009 of this decision. The Court found that 'a more prompt communication of the investigative authorities' conclusions might have led to the deletion of the applicant's name from the United Nations list at an earlier stage, thereby considerably reducing the period of time in which he was subjected to the restrictions of his rights under Article 8'.[10] The Court stressed that it was important in the present case to consider the measures that the national

6 Ibid., p.89.

7 UN General Assembly, *Protection of human rights and fundamental freedoms while countering terrorism: note by the Secretary-General*, 3 August 2009, A/64/211, para. 16.

8 ECHR Case of *Nada v. Switzerland*, 10593/08 – HEJUD [2012] ECHR 1691, para. 149 (12 September 2012).

9 Ibid., para. 146.

10 Ibid., para. 188.

authorities actually took, or sought to take, in response to the applicant's very specific situation. The Court argued in particular that the Swiss authorities in their implementation of the Security Council Resolution 'did not sufficiently take into account the realities of the case, especially the unique geographical situation of Campione d'Italia, the considerable duration of the measures imposed or the applicant's nationality, age and health'.[11] The Court found unanimously a violation of Article 8, since the restrictions imposed on the applicant's freedom of movement for a considerable period of time had not struck a fair balance between his right to the protection of his private and family life and the legitimate aims pursued.

Public provocation laws

Counter-terrorism legislation in European states increasingly allows law enforcement agencies to take a more pre-emptive approach in order to counter terrorist threats. A crucial element to this has been the creation of inchoate offences such as incitement or provocation of terrorist activities. Spain, for instance, has criminalized the 'praising or justification, through any means, of public expression or broadcasting' of terrorist offences.[12] The UK's 2006 Terrorism Act provided for similar 'glorification' offences that criminalize the publication of a statement that 'intends members of the public to be directly or indirectly encouraged or otherwise induced by the statement to commit, prepare or instigate acts of terrorism' or 'is reckless as to whether members of the public will be directly or indirectly encouraged or otherwise induced by the statement to commit, prepare or instigate such acts or offence'.[13] The Act then clarifies that this provision includes 'every statement which – (a) glorifies the commission or preparation (whether in the past, in the future or generally) of such acts or offences'.[14]

The International Commission of Jurists (ICJ) has correctly pointed out that such provisions weaken the causal link normally required in law between the original speech (or other forms of expression) and the risk that criminal acts may be committed.[15] Such wide-ranging laws can have a substantial impact on legitimate political debate, 'particularly within immigrant or minority communities'.[16] The following statement of the Islamic Human Rights Commission at the hearing of the Eminent Jurist Panel of the ICJ was telling:

---

11 Ibid., para. 195.

12 Article 578 of the Spanish Penal Code.

13 UK Terrorism Act 2006, part 1, 1(2)(b).

14 UK Terrorism Act 2006, part 1, 1(3)(a).

15 International Commission of Jurists (ICJ) (2009) *Assessing Damage, Urging Action.* Report of the Eminent Jurists Panel on Terrorism, Counter-terrorism and Human Rights. (p.129). Available at http://www.un.org/en/sc/ctc/specialmeetings/2011/docs/icj/icj-2009-ejp-report.pdf (accessed 11 January 2015).

16 Ibid., p.130.

"Certain statements made by Muslims will be regarded as 'glorification' due to its delivery to a Muslim audience; similar comments made by members of other communities will not be held to the same standard".[17]

Glorification laws also have an impact on the ability of journalists to gather and disseminate information. Under the Council of Europe Convention on the Prevention of Terrorism, states are obliged to criminalize the distribution of or otherwise making available a message to the public advocating terrorist offences, and notes that 'whether this is done directly or indirectly is irrelevant for the application of this provision'.[18] It is easy to see how such laws could be abused. In Azerbaijan, for example, opposition editor Eynulla Fatullayev was convicted of incitement to terrorism in 2007 and sentenced to an eight-and-a-half-year custodial sentence for an article opposing Azerbaijan's support of US policies relating to Iran. In particular, Fatullayev had noted that the country's continued close alliance with the US was likely to lead to Azerbaijan's involvement in a possible US-Iran war. The author further proposed a hypothetical scenario of such a war, according to which, Iran would respond by bombing a number of facilities on the territory of Azerbaijan, and he distributed a potential list of terrorist targets. A domestic court found that the publication of the article had pursued the aim of creating panic among the population and constituted a terrorist threat. Fatullayev spent four years in jail before being pardoned in May 2011.[19]

In respect of Turkey, the UN Human Rights Committee has expressed its concerns about 'the high number of cases in which human rights defenders, lawyers, journalists and even children are charged under anti-terrorism law for the free expression of their opinions and ideas, in particular in the context of non-violent discussions of the Kurdish issue'.[20] Article 7.2 of Turkey's anti-terrorism law is particularly broad, and allows jail sentences for any person 'who makes propaganda in connection with' a terrorist organization.[21] According to Turkey, these provisions were needed 'with a view to prevent gaining strength of terrorist organisations by way of propaganda'.[22]

17 Ibid., p.130.

18 Explanatory Report to the Council of Europe Convention on the Prevention of Terrorism (2006), p.85. Available online at http://conventions.coe.int/Treaty/EN/Reports/Html/196.htm (accessed 11 January 2015).

19 Amnesty International USA, 'Jailed Azerbaijani journalist pardoned', 26 May 2011. Available online at http://www.amnestyusa.org/our-work/latest-victories/jailed-azerbaijani-journalist-pardoned (accessed 11 January 2015).

20 UN Human Rights Committee, Concluding observations on the initial report of Turkey adopted by the Committee at its 106th session, 15 October to 2 November 2012, UN Doc. CCPR/C/TUR/CO/1, para. 16.

21 Article 7.2 Turkish Counter-terrorism Law no. 3713.

22 UN Human Rights Committee, Concluding observations on the initial report of Turkey adopted by the Committee at its 106th session, 15 October to 2 November 2012, UN Doc. CCPR/C/TUR/CO/1, at p.14.

The European Court of Human Rights has considered the impact of incitement provisions on freedom of speech in a number of cases, including the Fatullayev case above. The judgment of the Court is illustrative of its general, rather permissive, approach to incitement issues. Despite the wide application of anti-terrorism legislation to demonstrably political speech, the Court stated that it was not its task 'to rule on the constituent elements of the offences under domestic law of terrorism and threat of terrorism, by reviewing whether the corpus delicti [i.e., the facts and circumstances constituting a crime] of "threat of terrorism" actually arose from the applicant's actions'.[23] Instead, the Court's task is 'merely to review under Article 10 the decisions they delivered pursuant to their power of appreciation'.[24]

The European Court of Human Rights has dealt with glorification laws in two cases. In *Leroy v. France* (which will be dealt with in more detail below), the Court agreed with a local court in Pau that a cartoon that portrayed the Twin Towers with a caption that parodied the advertising slogan of Sony, 'We have all dreamt of it . . . Hamas did it', amounted to 'the support and glorification of the violent destruction of the United States'.[25] The court in Pau had held that:

> [B]y making a direct allusion to the massive attacks on Manhattan, by attributing these attacks to a well-known terrorist organisation and by idealising this lethal project through the use of the verb 'to dream', [thus] unequivocally praising an act of death, the cartoonist justifies the use of terrorism, identifies himself through his use of the first person plural ('We') with this method of destruction, which is presented as the culmination of a dream and, finally, indirectly encourages the potential reader to evaluate positively the successful commission of a criminal act.[26]

In the *Batasuna v. Spain* case, the Court referred to *Leroy* and the international 'concern to universally condemn justification for terrorism', in order to come to the conclusion that the actions and speeches of the Basque political parties, 'taken together, give a clear picture of a model of society

---

23 ECHR Case of *Fatullayev v. Azerbaijan*, 40984/07, Council of Europe: European Court of Human Rights, 22/04/2010, para. 121.

24 Ibid. (para. 123–124). The court did find that the domestic courts' finding that the applicant threatened the state with terrorist acts was 'nothing but arbitrary' and that the domestic courts overstepped the margin of appreciation afforded to them for restrictions on debates on matters of public interest. Ibid. (para. 129):

25 ECHR Case of *Leroy v. France*, 36109/03, Council of Europe: European Court of Human Rights, 02/10/2008 para. 43.

26 Ibid., para. 14.

conceived and advocated . . . which is incompatible with the concept of a "democratic society" '.[27] The court noted that Batasuna's conduct[28]

> bears a strong resemblance to explicit support for violence and the commendation of people seemingly linked to terrorism. It can also be considered to be capable of provoking social conflict between supporters of the applicant parties and other political organisations, in particular those of the Basque country. In that connection, the Court reiterates that in the actions and speeches to which the Supreme Court referred, the members and leaders of the applicant parties had not ruled out the use of force with a view to achieving their aims. In those circumstances, the Court considers that the national courts sufficiently established that the climate of confrontation created by the applicant parties risked provoking intense reactions in society capable of disrupting public order, as has been the case in the past.[29]

In neither case did the Court address the compatibility of the criminalization of glorification of terrorism per se with the European Convention on Human Rights; it instead reviewed only whether convictions on the grounds of the glorification of terrorism were compatible with freedom of expression.

Diplomatic assurances

In May 2007, the interior ministers of France, Germany, Italy, Poland, Spain and the United Kingdom discussed the difficulties faced by states in seeking to implement an 'effective expulsion policy', which was defined as 'the need to protect national security and the human rights of those who pose a threat'.[30]

> To that aim, they decided to analyse better the different mechanisms that exist, including a case by case approach, diplomatic contacts or assurances, that could be useful under certain circumstances for promoting, in repatriation states, pattern of conduct compliant with the international obligations as to the safeguard of human rights.[31]

This practice of seeking 'diplomatic assurances' in order to be able to deport foreign terrorist suspects to countries with dubious human rights

27 ECHR Case of *Batasuna v Spain*, 25803/04 and 25817/04, Council of Europe: European Court of Human Rights, 30 June 2009, para. 91.

28 Ibid., para. 85.

29 Ibid., para. 86.

30 Conclusion of G-6 Meetings in Venice 11–12 May 2007, Italian Interior Ministry (12/05/07). Available online at http://www.statewatch.org/news/2007/may/05venice-g7-may-2007.htm (accessed 11 January 2015).

31 Ibid.

records, even where such a person might face a real risk of being subjected to treatment contrary to Article 3 of the European Convention, has been explicitly defended by the United Kingdom, Lithuania, Portugal and Slovakia in the *Ramzy v. Netherlands* case at the European Court of Human Rights,[32] and by Italy in the *Saadi v. Italy* case.[33] The governments argued that there needed to be a new balance that afforded 'proper weight to the fundamental rights of the citizens of contracting states who are threatened by terrorism'.[34]

The practice of diplomatic assurances has been widely denounced by human rights organizations and international bodies. These bodies argue against this 'rebalancing' of rights not only because the measure has a direct impact on the suspect who could be subjected to torture or inhuman and degrading treatment, but also because this practice has a potentially devastating long-term impact on the absolute nature of the prohibition against torture. Louise Arbour, speaking at the time in her capacity as United Nations High Commissioner for Human Rights, described diplomatic assurances as having an 'acutely corrosive effect on the global ban on torture and cruel, inhuman or degrading treatment',[35] while in 2005, a group of human rights organizations stated that 'the use of such assurances violates the absolute prohibition against torture and other ill-treatment and is eroding a fundamental principle of international human rights law'.[36]

The European Court of Human Rights has recognized that a state is allowed to deport non-nationals whom they consider to be threats to national security. The European Convention of Human Rights even allows states to apply more abbreviated procedures on national security grounds in cases of deportation.[37] Despite this flexibility, the European Court of Human Rights made it clear that the prohibition of deportation to face treatment contrary to Article 3 is absolute.[38] In *Saadi v. Italy*, the Court

---

32 ECHR Case of *Ramzy v. the Netherlands*, 25424/05, 27/05/2008.

33 ECHR Case of *Saadi v. Italy*, 37201/06, 28/02/2008.

34 ECHR Case of *Ramzy vs Netherlands* in The European Court of Human Rights, 'Observations of the Governments of Lithuania, Portugal, Slovakia, and the United Kingdom', para.1. Available online at http://www.redress.org/Government_intervenors_observations_in_Ramzy_case%20_21November.pdf (accessed 11 January 2015).

35 Louise Arbour, High Commissioner for Human Rights, *Human Rights Day statement – On Terrorists and Torturers*, New York: United Nations, 7 December, 2005. Available online at http://www.ohchr.org/EN/NewsEvents/Pages/DisplayNews.aspx?NewsID=2117&LangID=E (accessed 11 January 2015).

36 Amnesty International *et al.* Call for Action Against the Use of Diplomatic Assurances in Transfers to Risk of Torture and Ill-Treatment, 12 May 2005. Available online at http://www.statewatch.org/cia/documents/ai-hrw-joint-statement.pdf (accessed 11 January 2015).

37 Council of Europe Convention for the Protection of Human Rights and Fundamental Freedoms Article 1, Protocol No. 7 as amended by Protocol No. 11 (1984).

38 ECHR Case of *Chahal v. The United Kingdom*, Appl. No. 22414/93 para. 79–80, Council of Europe: European Court of Human Rights, 15 November 1996.

explicitly rejected the balance argument presented by the UK and others, holding that

> The Court cannot accept the argument . . . that distinction must be drawn under Article 3 between treatment inflicted directly by a signatory State and treatment that might be inflicted by the authorities of another State, and that protection against this latter form of ill-treatment should be weighed against the interests of the community as a whole. Since protection against the treatment prohibited by Article 3 is absolute, that provision imposes an obligation not to extradite or expel any person who, in the receiving country, would run the real risk of being subjected to such treatment. As the Court has repeatedly held, there can be no derogation from that rule[39]

However, the Court did not explicitly reject the practice of diplomatic assurances as such, but noted that it would assess whether, 'in their practical application', such assurances provided a sufficient guarantee that the applicant would be protected against the risk of treatment prohibited by the Convention. The weight to be given to assurances from the receiving State depended, 'in each case, on the circumstances obtaining at the material time'.[40] The Court had already found that the extradition of applicants based on an assurance by the Uzbek government that they would not be subjected to torture, did not violate Article 3.[41] In 2012, the Court offered a more detailed ruling on the practice of diplomatic assurances. In the controversial case of *Othman v. UK*, the Court listed eleven factors it takes into account to assess the quality of assurances given and whether, in light of the receiving state's practices, they can be relied upon.[42] The Court repeated that it 'never laid down an absolute rule that a State which does not comply with multilateral obligations cannot be relied on to comply with bilateral assurances', and argued that,

> [T]he United Kingdom and Jordanian Governments have made genuine efforts to obtain and provide transparent and detailed assurances to ensure that the applicant will not be ill-treated upon return to Jordan. The product of those efforts, the MOU, is superior in both its detail and its formality to any assurances, which the Court has previously examined. . .[43]

39 ECHR Case of *Saadi v. Italy*, Appl. No 37201/06, para. 138, Council of Europe: European Court of Human Rights, 28 February 2008.

40 Ibid., para. 148.

41 ECHR Case of *Mamatkulov and Askarov v. Turkey*, 46827/99 and 46951/99, para. 72, Council of Europe: European Court of Human Rights, 4 February 2005.

42 ECHR Case of *Othman (Abu Qatada) v. The United Kingdom*, Application No. 8139/09, para. 189, Council of Europe: European Court of Human Rights, 17 January 2012.

43 Ibid., para. 194.

While the Court made a clear principled statement against the abstract idea that Article 3 would apply to a lesser degree to non-nationals in *Saadi v. Italy*, its judgment in *Othman v. UK* demonstrates the Court's pragmatic approach to diplomatic assurances as a practical measure to address the *non-refoulement* obligation in concrete cases. In other words, the Court refuses the practice of a sending state delegating its responsibility for the absolute prohibition on torture to the receiving state alone, but accepts that the sending state can seek assurances from the receiving state to respect its Article 3 obligations.

This section highlighted the indirect, potential long-term negative impact of three particular counter-terrorism measures. These included (a) the corrosive effect of the use of terrorist listings on the ordinary criminal justice system by expanding unaccountable executive powers at the expense of the evidentiary and procedural requirements of the criminal justice system, (b) the long-term impact of glorification laws on legitimate political debates, especially within minority communities and (c) the corrosive effect of the practice of diplomatic assurances on the global ban on torture and cruel, inhuman or degrading treatment. The three case studies suggest that the European Court of Human Rights does not take the long-term negative effects of specific counter-terrorism measures into account in deciding on their lawfulness. Rather than making normative statements on specific counter-terrorism measures, the Court takes an individual, contextualized, case-by-case approach in order to determine the proportionality of a specific counter-terrorism measure as applied in the particular case before it. The Court therefore only focuses on the direct impact of a counter-terrorism measure. In hindsight, this is not entirely surprising, given the fact that the Court has given a rather large margin of appreciation to states' counter-terrorist measures, stressing on numerous occasions that it is aware that States face 'particular challenges posed by terrorism and terrorist violence'.[44] Thus, the breadth of this margin varies depending on a number of factors, including the nature of the Convention right in issue, its importance for the individual and the nature of the interference.[45]

A counter-terrorism measure can be said to be effective if it is successful in producing an intended, positive result, which in this context would mean the improved prevention or prosecution of terrorist activities.[46] Some of

44 See ECHR Case of *Brogan and Others v. the United Kingdom*, 29 November 1988, § 61, Series A no. 145-B; ECHR Case of *Öcalan v. Turkey* [GC], no. 46221/99, §§ 104, 192–196, ECHR 2005-IV; *Ramirez Sanchez v. France* [GC], no. 59450/00, §§ 115–116, ECHR 2006-IX; and ECHR Case of *Finogenov and Others v. Russia*, cited above, § 212.

45 It could be argued that national courts would be less deferential to governments in anti-terrorism cases because they are not subsidiary courts. A similar claim has been made in F. de Londras, *Detention in the 'War on Terror': Can human rights fight back?* (Cambridge: Cambridge University Press, 2011), Chapters 5–6.

46 M. Vermeulen, D. Deering and S. McCarthy (with research assistance from Carolin Möller), *Report on legal understandings of impact, legitimacy and effectiveness in counter-terrorism*, (SECILE Consortium, 2013).

these measures are deliberately intended to limit directly the (procedural) rights of terrorist suspects, and are justified by governments as a necessary response to a terrorist threat. However, this justification requires that there is a reasonable relationship between the security objective to be achieved and the means used to achieve it. Assessing the effectiveness of a specific measure can therefore influence the necessity, and hence the legality, test applied by the European Court of Human Rights. The following section will analyse the extent to which the European Court of Human Rights has taken into account considerations of effectiveness in determining the legality of a counter-terrorism measure.

3. Assessing the effectiveness of counter-terrorism legislation

From the outset, it is important to note that the Court makes a distinction between actions that were taken when a state of emergency was declared, and actions undertaken in 'ordinary' times. Article 15(1) of the European Convention of Human Rights allows states to derogate from a number of obligations under the Convention 'in time of war or other public emergency threatening the life of the nation'. Not every disturbance or catastrophe qualifies as such an emergency; the term refers to 'an exceptional situation of crisis or emergency which affects the whole population and constitutes a threat to the organised life of the community of which the State is composed'[47] insofar as normal measures or restrictions, permitted by the Convention for the maintenance of public safety, health and order, are deemed to be 'plainly inadequate'.[48] The purpose of Article 15 is to permit states to take derogating measures to protect their populations from 'future risks'.[49] The Court has ruled that a major terrorist attack – and even a terrorist threat – would allow a state to derogate from a number of rights under the Convention.[50] In this context, it is interesting to note that the European Court of Human Rights has ruled that a terrorist threat does not have to be 'imminent' and can exist for many years.[51] Contrary to the findings of the UN Human Rights Committee, for instance, the Court's case law has never explicitly incorporated the requirement that the emergency be temporary. The Court has stated that the applicability of a derogation regime is limited to the geographical area that is explicitly named in the notice of derogation.[52]

47 ECHR Case of *Lawless v. United Kingdom* Application no. 332/57, Council of Europe: European Court of Human Rights, 1 July 1961, para. 28.

48 ECHR *Greek Case* (1969) 12 YB 1, § 153.

49 ECHR Case of *A and Others v. United Kingdom* Application no. 3455/05, Council of Europe: European Court of Human Rights, 19 February 2009, para. 177.

50 ECHR Case of *A and Others v. United Kingdom* Application no. 3455/05, Council of Europe: European Court of Human Rights, 19 February 2009.

51 Ibid., para. 177–178.

52 ECHR Case of *Sakik and others v. Turkey* (87/1996/67/897–902) 26 November 1997, para. 39.

In a way, this derogation mechanism suggests an inverse relationship between impact and effectiveness: a country can intentionally decrease legal safeguards for terrorist suspects in order to allow for an effective investigation and/or prosecution. This does not mean, however, that all bets are off; such 'effective' measures can only be taken to the extent strictly required by the exigencies of the situation, provided that such measures are not inconsistent with its other obligations under international law. These provisions act as safeguards to prevent emergency measures from taking place in a legal vacuum. Last but not least, Article 15(2) explicitly states that no derogations can be made from Articles 2 (right to life), 3 (prohibition of torture), 4(1) (prohibition of slavery) and 7 (no punishment without law). Interrogation techniques that amount to torture or degrading treatment are therefore never allowed, even in times of emergency or when a government claims that the particular measure has led to the acquisition of a 'considerable quantity of intelligence information'.[53]

While many European countries have faced serious terrorist threats in recent decades, it is interesting to note that only three countries have derogated from the European Convention of Human Rights by referring to a terrorist threat: the United Kingdom, Ireland and Turkey. The following sub-sections outline how states have explained the effectiveness of these derogating measures, and whether the European Court of Human Rights has taken their perceived effectiveness into account when determining the legality of such a derogating measure. Section 3.2 undertakes the same exercise in relation to determining the legality of a counter-terrorism measure in 'ordinary' times. The last section analyses around fifty cases the court has deemed to be most important in its fact sheet on terrorism cases.[54]

Effectiveness of counter-terrorism measures taken in times of emergency

Ireland

In 1957, Ireland announced a derogation from the Convention – without explicitly mentioning any Articles from which it was derogating – after it adopted a law that conferred on Ministers of State special powers of detention without trial.[55] The Irish Government expressly stated that, 'the detention of persons under the Act is considered necessary to prevent the commission of offences against public peace and order and to prevent the maintaining of military or armed forces other than those authorised by

53 ECHR Case of *Ireland v. United Kingdom, (5310/71,) 18 January 1978,* para. 98.

54 For further information see the ECHR factsheet on terrorism. Available at: http://www.echr.coe.int/Documents/FS_Terrorism_ENG.pdf (accessed 11 January 2015).

55 Part II of the Offences against the State Act, 1940 (No. 2).

the Constitution'.[56] The European Commission on Human Rights found at the time that the situation in Ireland could be characterized as a 'public emergency threatening the life of the nation' because of

> the existence in the territory of the Republic of Ireland of a secret army engaged in unconstitutional activities and using violence to attain its purposes; secondly, the fact that this army was also operating outside the territory of the State, thus seriously jeopardising the relations of the Republic of Ireland with its neighbour; thirdly, the steady and alarming increase in terrorist activities from the autumn of 1956 and throughout the first half of 1957.[57]

The Commission assessed the necessity of the administrative detention regime in light of possible alternatives that Ireland could have adopted to address this emergency, with or without derogating from the European Convention, such as the application of the ordinary criminal law, the institution of special criminal courts of the type provided for by the Offences against the State Act 1939 or of military courts, or the sealing of the border between the Republic of Ireland and Northern Ireland.[58] According to the Court, these alternatives would not have made it possible 'to deal with the situation existing in Ireland in 1957'. The administrative detention appeared therefore, 'despite its gravity, to be a measure required by the circumstances'.[59] The Court also noted the existence of safeguards in Irish law designed to prevent abuses in the operation of the system of administrative detention.[60]

The United Kingdom

In the 1970s, Ireland alleged that the UK's extrajudicial detention powers in Northern Ireland were not in line with Article 5 since they failed to meet in full the requirements of Article 15. The United Kingdom had sent six notices of derogation to the Secretary-General of the Council of Europe, which enabled the UK to derogate from Article 5 in order to effect what the Court called 'extrajudicial deprivation of liberty' in three

56 ECHR Case of *Lawless v. Ireland* (332/57) 1 July 1961, para. 16 and 24.

57 Ibid., para. 28.

58 Ibid., para. 35–36.

59 Ibid., para. 36.

60 Ibid., para. 37. The court noted that (1) the act was subject to constant supervision by Parliament, which received precise details of its enforcement at regular intervals, and which could also at any time annul the Act, (2) any person detained under the Act could refer his case to a Detention Commission, which was able to decide the release of the person, and (3) the government guaranteed that a person would be released if they gave an undertaking to 'observe the law and refrain from activitites contrary to the 1940 Act'.

basic categories: initial arrest for interrogation, detention for further interrogation, and preventive detention.[61] The Court accepted that the crisis in Northern Ireland was a public emergency threatening the life of the nation. This was 'perfectly clear', according to the Court, given the statistics provided by the UK government, which claimed that 'over 1,100 people had been killed, over 11,500 injured and more than £140,000,000 worth of property destroyed during the recent troubles in Northern Ireland'.[62] From 9 August 1971 until 7 November 1972, the authorities in Northern Ireland decided to introduce four extrajudicial detention powers: (a) arrest for interrogation purposes for up to forty-eight hours (under Regulation 10); (b) arrest and remand in custody (under Regulation 11 (1)); (c) detention of an arrested person (under Regulation 11 (2)); and (d) internment (under Regulation 12 (1)).[63]

The UK government had quoted three principal reasons to introduce these measures: (a) normal procedures of investigation and criminal prosecution had become inadequate to deal with Irish Republican Army (IRA) terrorists, (b) the population was intimidated, which made it 'impossible to obtain sufficient evidence to secure a criminal conviction against a known IRA terrorist', and (c) the ease of escape across the territorial border between Northern Ireland and the Republic of Ireland presented difficulties of control.[64] Interestingly, in addition to the three 'security' reasons, there was, in the judgement of both the Northern Ireland Government and the United Kingdom Government, 'no hope of winning over the terrorists by political means', after a 'reform programme' had failed in 1969.[65] The Court agreed with the UK that it was 'reasonably entitled to consider that normal legislation offered insufficient resources for the campaign against terrorism and that recourse to measures outside the scope of the ordinary law, in the shape of extrajudicial deprivation of liberty, was called for'.[66] The Court found that the limits of its review powers are 'particularly apparent' where Article 15 is concerned.

---

61 ECHR Case of *Ireland v. United Kingdom,* (5310/71) 18 January 1978, para. 78–79. The Special Powers Act empowered the Minister of Home Affairs for Northern Ireland, until 30 March 1972, or, thereafter and until 8 August 1973, the Secretary of State for Northern Ireland to take all such steps and issue all such orders as might be necessary for preserving peace and maintaining order. It was an enabling Act whose substantive provisions were contained in Regulations made thereunder. The number and scope of the Regulations in force varied over the years; they could be brought into use without any legislative act or proclamation. Those relevant to the present case were made in 1956 (Regulations 11 and 12) and 1957 (Regulation 10). They were utilized to implement the policy of internment introduced on 9 August 1971 and advice of their use was given to the Secretary-General by the United Kingdom Government's notice of derogation of 20 August 1971.

62 Ibid., para. 12.

63 Ibid., para. 81–84.

64 Ibid., para. 36.

65 Ibid., para. 36.

66 Ibid., para. 212.

> By reason of their direct and continuous contact with the pressing needs of the moment, the national authorities are in principle in a better position than the international judge to decide both on the presence of such an emergency and on the nature and scope of derogations necessary to avert it. In this matter Article 15 para. 1 (Art. 15–1) leaves those authorities a wide margin of appreciation.[67]

The Court judges only whether states have gone beyond the extent strictly required by the exigencies of the crisis. This type of European supervision does not include an assessment of the effectiveness of a counter-terrorism measure. In this case, statistics proved that the extrajudicial deprivation of liberty had been ineffectual. The policy introduced on 9 August, 1971 not only failed to put a brake on terrorism, but actually aligned with an increase in terrorist activity. From August 1971 until 30 March 1975 there were 1,130 bomb explosions and well over 2,000 shooting incidents in Northern Ireland, with 158 civilians, fifty-eight soldiers and seventeen police officers killed, and 2,505 civilians, 306 soldiers and 107 police officers injured.[68] Consequently, the British Government abandoned the policy. According to the Irish government, this proved 'that extrajudicial deprivation of liberty was not an absolute necessity'.[69]

The Court's response to this claim is its most clear statement on how it assesses the effectiveness of counter-terrorism measures:

> The Court cannot accept this argument. It is certainly not the Court's function to substitute for the British Government's assessment any other assessment of what might be the most prudent or most expedient policy to combat terrorism. The Court must do no more than review the lawfulness, under the Convention, of the measures adopted by that Government from 9 August 1971 onwards. For this purpose the Court must arrive at its decision in the light, not of a purely retrospective examination of the efficacy of those measures, but of the conditions and circumstances reigning when they were originally taken and subsequently applied. Adopting, as it must, this approach, the Court accepts that the limits of the margin of appreciation left to the Contracting states by Article 15 para. 1 (Art. 15–1) were not overstepped by the United Kingdom when it formed the opinion that extrajudicial deprivation of liberty was necessary from August 1971 to March 1975.[70]

The Court then specifically analysed how the UK legislation included or failed to include safeguards in the form of the availability of judicial

67 Ibid., para. 207.
68 Ibid., para. 42, 44, 47–48.
69 Ibid., para. 114.
70 Ibid., para. 214.

remedies.[71] It ultimately concluded that although insufficient safeguards were initially included in the legislation, Article 15 must leave space for progressive adaptations. Since the UK constantly modified its emergency legislation to include more safeguards for individuals, it did not overstep its margin of appreciation.[72] The court is not willing to consider the effectiveness of a measure in its necessity and proportionality test, but instead considers the effectiveness of *safeguards* against the use of a measure – even if statistical evidence shows that a counter-terrorism measure has not been effective.

In 1984, the UK government had withdrawn its derogation when it arrested Brogan and others without a warrant under section 12 of the Prevention of Terrorism (Temporary Provisions) Act 1984. This law allowed the Secretary of State to extend the period of arrest without a warrant for up to five days. While the derogation to Article 5 did not apply to this Act any more, the Court held that this did not 'preclude proper account being taken of the background circumstances of the case',[73] which consisted of a situation where 'organised terrorism continued to thrive'.[74] The Court agreed with the UK that the fact that the complainants were neither charged nor brought before a court during their detention did not necessarily mean that the purpose of their detention was not in accordance with Article 5.1.c of the European Convention.

> Article 5 para. 1 (Art. 5–1-c) does not presuppose that the police should have obtained sufficient evidence to bring charges, either at the point of arrest or while the applicants were in custody. Such evidence may have been unobtainable or, in view of the nature of the suspected offences, impossible to produce in court without endangering the lives of others.[75]

The Court accepted further that – subject to the existence of adequate safeguards – the context of terrorism in Northern Ireland had the effect of prolonging the period during which the authorities may, without violating Article 5(3), keep a person suspected of serious terrorist offences in custody before bringing him before a judge or other judicial officer. The Court accepted that the difficulties of judicial control over decisions to arrest and detain suspected terrorists may call for 'appropriate procedural precautions',[76] but it questioned the need to dispense altogether with 'prompt judicial control'.[77] Even the legitimate aim of 'protecting the community as a whole

71 Ibid., para. 216–219.
72 Ibid., para. 220.
73 ECHR Case of *Brogan and Others v. the United Kingdom*, 29 November 1988, § 48.
74 Ibid., para. 25.
75 Ibid., para. 51.
76 Ibid., para. 61.
77 Ibid.

from terrorism' was not seen by the Court as 'on its own sufficient' to interpret and apply a flexible notion of 'promptness'.[78]

The decision was accompanied by five dissenting opinions from ten judges (out of nineteen), in which much more weight was given to the exceptional nature of the situation in Northern Ireland. Judges Vilhjálmsson, Bindschedler-Robert, Gölcüklü, Matscher and Valticos stressed that

> The nature and organisation of terrorism, the fear it inspires and the secrecy surrounding it make it difficult, having regard also to the applicable criminal procedure (which does not provide for the swift intervention of an investigating judge), to bring detainees promptly before a court.[79]

Judge Evans dissented along the same lines, arguing that the 'special factors', which underlined the provisions of the law, justified a flexible interpretation of the notion of 'promptness' in Article 5.3. Those factors included:

> [T]he difficulty faced by the security forces in these cases in obtaining evidence which is admissible and usable particularly in consequence of the training received by terrorists in anti-interrogation techniques, the highly sensitive nature of information on which suspicion is based in many such cases making impossible its production in court in the presence of the detained person or his legal adviser, and the extra time needed for examining and correlating evidence and for liaison with other security forces.[80]

Judge Evans quoted statistics to justify the need for a flexible interpretation of Article 5.3.:

> The need for the exceptional powers under section 12 to which such factors give rise is supported by the statistics quoted in the same paragraph of the judgment – that in 1987, for instance, of some 83 persons detained in excess of five days, 39 were charged with serious terrorist offences during the extended period[. . .] My conclusion is that the provisions in question are justified by the need to strike a fair balance in the circumstances and that they are consonant with what must also be the aim under the Convention of protecting human rights against the continuing inhumanity of terrorism in Northern Ireland.[81]

The most elaborate dissenting opinion came from Judge Martens, who argued that it was not the task of the Court to 'excessively clip the wings'

78 Ibid., para. 62.
79 Ibid., p.25.
80 Ibid., p.32.
81 Ibid., p.32.

of the executive, especially since '. . . terrorism – and particularly terrorism on the scale obtaining in Northern Ireland – is the very negation of the principles the Convention stands for and should therefore be combated as vigorously as possible'.[82] As a result, 'It seems obvious that to suppress terrorism the executive needs extraordinary powers, just as it seems obvious that Governments should to a large extent be free to choose the ways and means which they think most efficacious for combating terrorism'.[83]

Therefore, a wide margin of appreciation should be given to the actions of a country in this context in order to counter terrorism effectively. On the other hand, Judges Walsh and Carrillo Salcedo believed that the Convention did not afford *any* margin of appreciation to the State regarding Article 5, since this 'would change the whole nature of this all-important provision which would then become subject to executive policy'.[84] They also quoted statistics, in order to make the point that

> [T]he arrests in the present cases were for the purpose of interrogation at a time when there was no evidential basis for the bringing of any charge against them. No such evidence ever emerged and eventually they had to be released. That the legislation in question is used for such a purpose is amply borne out by the fact that since 1974 15,173 persons have been arrested and detained in the United Kingdom pursuant to the legislation yet less than 25% of those persons, namely 3,342, have been charged with any criminal offence arising out of the interrogation including offences totally unconnected with the original arrest and detention. Still fewer of them have been convicted of any offence of a terrorist type. The Convention embodies the presumption of innocence and thus enshrines a most fundamental human right, namely the protection of the individual against arbitrary interference by the State with his right to liberty. The circumstances of the arrest and detention in the present cases were not compatible with this right and accordingly we are of the opinion that Article 5.1 has been violated.[85]

Interestingly, the judges assessed very differently the effectiveness of the safeguards against arbitrary detentions. While Judges Walsh and Carrillo Salcedo seemed to suggest that charging only 25 per cent of the detainees between 1974 and 1984 amounted to an arbitrary interference by the State with the right to liberty, Judge Evans focused on the fact that 45 per cent of those who were detained in excess of five days in 1987 were ultimately charged with serious terrorist offences during the extended period. One month after the judgment in *Brogan v. the UK*, the UK renewed its

82 Ibid., p.34.
83 Ibid.
84 Ibid., p.28.
85 Ibid., pp. 28–29.

derogation from Article 5 in order to continue to be able to detain suspects for up to seven days in some cases without judicial intervention, because of the special difficulties associated with the investigation and prosecution of terrorist crime.[86] As expressed in the derogation, it remained the view of the UK that this was 'essential to prevent the disclosure to the detainee and his legal adviser of information on the basis of which decisions on the extension of detention are made and that, in the adversarial system of the common law, the independence of the judiciary would be compromised if judges or other judicial officers were to be involved in the granting or approval of extensions'.[87]

The Court said again that it is not its role to substitute 'its view as to what measures were most appropriate or expedient at the relevant time in dealing with an emergency situation for that of the Government which have direct responsibility for establishing the balance between the taking of effective measures to combat terrorism on the one hand, and respecting individual rights on the other'.[88]

The Court stated that it was satisfied that sufficient safeguards were present against arbitrary and/or incommunicado detention, i.e., the availability of the remedy of habeas corpus, and the absolute right detainees had to consult a solicitor after forty-eight hours from the time of arrest.[89] Again, there were dissenting opinions that questioned the effectiveness of the safeguards. Judge Walsh highlighted the fact that 'out of 1,549 persons arrested in 1990 only 30 were subsequently charged', which in his mind indicated 'a paucity of proof rather than any deficiency in the operation of the judicial function'.[90] Judge Makarczyk dissented along the same lines, saying that he would only accept the legality of the derogation if the government had been able 'to prove that extended detention without any form of judicial control does in fact contribute both to the punishment and prevention of the crime of terrorism'.[91]

On 11 November 2001, the UK derogated from Article 5(1)(f) of the European Convention on Human Rights, which permits the detention of a person against whom action is being taken 'with a view to deportation or extradition'.[92] Part 4 of the UK's Anti-Terrorism Crime and Security Act 2001, which was introduced in the House of Commons one day later and quickly passed into law, set out powers that enabled the detention

---

86 ECHR Case of *Brannigan & McBride v. UK*, 14553/89 14554/89, 26/05/1993 para. 51. (For a more detailed argument see Letter written to Secretary-General, quoted in para. 31.)

87 Ibid., para. 58.

88 Ibid.

89 Ibid., para. 62–66.

90 Ibid., Judge Walsh dissenting opinion, at p.9.

91 Ibid., Judge Makarczyk dissenting opinion at p.3.

92 Council of Europe, *European Convention for the Protection of Human Rights and Fundamental Freedoms, as amended by Protocols Nos. 11 and 14*, 4 November 1950.

of non-nationals suspected of being international terrorists, where their deportation was, for the time being, impossible. The government argued that such a measure was needed, because in some cases it could not deport terrorist suspects since there existed a real risk that the person would suffer treatment contrary to Article 3 of the Convention.

Doubts arose about the effectiveness of this discriminatory measure in addressing the terrorist threat, since the threat coming from UK citizens appeared to be as substantive as threats coming from non-UK citizens.[93] When a Committee of Privy Counsellors recommended that powers which allow foreign nationals to be detained potentially indefinitely should be replaced with new legislation that deals 'with all terrorism, whatever its origin or the nationality of its suspected perpetrators',[94] the UK government answered that applying counter-terrorism measures to all persons within the UK's jurisdiction would be a 'draconian' measure which would be 'difficult to justify'. [95] 'Experience has demonstrated the dangers of such an approach and the damage it can do to community cohesion and thus to support from all parts of the public that is so essential to countering the terrorist threat'.[96]

In 2004, the House of Lords assessed Part 4 of the 2001 Act, and concluded that it did not *rationally* address the threat to security and that it was a disproportionate response to that threat. The House of Lords focused inter alia on two effectiveness arguments to come to this conclusion: (a) the detention scheme applied only to non-nationals suspected of international terrorism and did not address the threat that came from United Kingdom nationals who were also suspected; (b) the scheme left suspected international terrorists at liberty to leave the United Kingdom and continue their threatening activities abroad.[97] As a result, the European Court of Human Rights also focused *en passant* on the effectiveness of the measure, but only because the House of Lords had done so in its judgment.[98]

> Part 4 of the 2001 Act was designed to avert a real and imminent threat of terrorist attack which, on the evidence, was posed by both nationals and non-nationals. The choice by the Government and Parliament of an immigration measure to address what was essentially a security issue had the result of failing *adequately* to address the problem, while imposing a disproportionate and discriminatory burden of indefinite detention on one group of suspected terrorists.[99]
>
> (*emphasis added*)

93 ECHR Case of *A & Others vs. UK* (3455/05), 19 February 2009, para. 98.

94 Privy Counsellor Review Committee, Anti-terrorism, Crime and Security Act 2001 Review: Report. Presented to Parliament pursuant to Section 122(5) of the Anti-terrorism, Crime and Security Act 2001, para. 203.

95 ECHR Case of *A & Others vs. UK* (3455/05), 19 February 2009, para. 99.

96 Ibid.

97 Ibid., para. 20–21.

98 Ibid., para. 182.

99 Ibid., para. 186.

The Court then further stressed that it had not been provided with any evidence that persuaded it to overturn the House of Lords' conclusion that the difference in treatment was unjustified. Again, the Court stressed its subsidiary role, and noted that national courts, being in direct and continuous contact with the realities of their countries, can better assess the effectiveness of a counter-terrorism measure. It will only disagree with the national court when it can be shown that the latter misinterpreted the Convention or the Court's case law, or reached a conclusion that was manifestly unreasonable.[100] Therefore, the Court, like the House of Lords, found that the derogating measures were disproportionate in that they discriminated unjustifiably between nationals and non-nationals.

Turkey

The Court dealt in detail with the Turkish governments' justifications to derogate from Article 5 in south-east Turkey in the case of *Aksoy v. Turkey.*[101] Mr Aksoy, an alleged Partiya Karkerên Kurdistani (PKK) member, had been detained on suspicion of aiding and abetting PKK terrorists for at least fourteen days without being brought before a judge or other judicial officer. According to the Turkish government, such detention was needed because

> the members of terrorist organisations were expert in withstanding interrogation, had secret support networks and access to substantial resources. A great deal of time and effort was required to secure and verify evidence in a large region confronted with a terrorist organisation that had strategic and technical support from neighbouring countries. These difficulties meant that it was impossible to provide judicial supervision during a suspect's detention in police custody.[102]

While the Court acknowledged the difficulties of a terrorist investigation, it did not comment on the effectiveness of the prolonged detention in this case. It did focus, however, on the absence of judicial supervision, especially since this absence left the applicant vulnerable 'not only to arbitrary interference with his right to liberty but also to torture'.[103] The Court failed to see how judicial intervention would have an effect on the effectiveness of the investigation.[104]

Effectiveness of counter-terrorism measures in 'ordinary' times

The Court has accepted that, in limited circumstances, the effective investigation of terrorist cases requires far-reaching measures, and the context in

100 Ibid., para. 182.

101 ECHR Case of *Aksoy v. Turkey* (21987/93) 18/12/1996.

102 Ibid., para. 72.

103 Ibid., para. 78.

104 Ibid., para. 78. See also ECHR Case of *Demir and Others v. Turkey* (21380/93, 21381/93, 21383/93) 23–09–1998, para. 52.

which these measures are taken can affect its assessment of their necessity. The Court takes into account the timing and location in which anti-terrorism measures are being used in order to assess their necessity, even when a state party does not derogate from the Convention.[105] As outlined above, in times of emergency the Court does not want to substitute the assessment of the national authorities for any other assessment of what might be the best policy in this field, while stressing that states do not enjoy an 'unlimited discretion' to choose 'whatever measures they deem appropriate'.[106] In this section, we will assess whether the Court uses the same reasoning in cases where there is no derogation under Article 15, i.e. in 'ordinary' times.

Use of force against terrorist suspects

In *McCann v. UK*[107] the Commission had to decide whether the killing, by members of the British Army, of three IRA members suspected of involvement in a car-bombing mission in Gibraltar constituted a breach of Article 2 of the Convention. The three IRA members turned out to be unarmed, and not in possession of a radio-controlled device that could detonate the car bomb. The Court accepted, however, that the soldiers honestly believed, in light of the information that they had been given, that it was necessary to shoot the suspects in order to prevent them from detonating a bomb and causing serious loss of life. The Court considered that

> the use of force by agents of the State in pursuit of one of the aims delineated in paragraph 2 of Article 2 (Art. 2–2) of the Convention may be justified under this provision (Art. 2–2) where it is based on an honest belief which is perceived, for good reasons, to be valid at the time but which subsequently turns out to be mistaken. To hold otherwise would be to impose an unrealistic burden on the State and its law-enforcement personnel in the execution of their duty, perhaps to the detriment of their lives and those of others.[108]

Despite this statement, the Court found that the counter-terrorism operation as a whole was not organized in a way that was absolutely necessary under Article 2(2). Here, the Court questioned details of the UK's plan to arrest the suspects at an appropriate stage, which had always been its main intention. The Court went through an alternative option with the UK government, namely, the possibility of arresting suspects at the border upon

105 See for instance ECHR Case of *Leroy v. France*, 36109/03, 2 October 2008, para. 41; ECHR Case of *Batasuna v. Spain* 25803/04, 30/06/2009, para 89; ECHR Case of *Nada v. Switzerland*, 10593/08, 12 September 2012, para. 186.

106 ECHR Case of *Klass v. Germany*, 15473/89, 22/09/1993, para. 49.

107 ECHR Case of *McCann and Others v. the UK*, 18984/91, 27/09/1995.

108 Ibid., para. 200.

arrival to Gibraltar. The absence of such a measure 'set the scene' in which the fatal shooting happened and, hence, was a 'relevant factor' that the Court took into account in assessing the complete counter-terrorism operation.[109] The Court, de facto, commented upon what it saw as the most effective measure to protect the population of Gibraltar:

> In sum, having regard to the decision not to prevent the suspects from travelling into Gibraltar, to the failure of the authorities to make sufficient allowances for the possibility that their intelligence assessments might, in some respects at least, be erroneous and to the automatic recourse to lethal force when the soldiers opened fire, the Court is not persuaded that the killing of the three terrorists constituted the use of force which was no more than absolutely necessary in defence of persons from unlawful violence within the meaning of Article 2 para. 2 (a) (Art. 2–2-a) of the Convention.[110]

A significant minority (nine out of nineteen judges) disagreed, however, with the majority's assessment, and were satisfied that no failings had been shown in the organization and control of the operation by the authorities that could justify a conclusion that force was used against the suspects disproportionately for the purpose of defending innocent persons from unlawful violence. The following remark in particular stood out:

> It would be wrong to conclude in retrospect that a particular course would, as things later transpired, have been better than one adopted at the time under the pressures of an ongoing anti-terrorist operation and that the latter course must therefore be regarded as culpably mistaken. It should not be so regarded unless it is established that in the circumstances as they were known at the time another course should have been preferred.[111]

Level of suspicion required to arrest a terrorist suspect

Mr Fox and Ms Campbell had been arrested in 1986 under section 11(1) of the Northern Ireland (Emergency Provisions) Act 1978, which allowed any constable to execute the warrantless arrest of any person who was suspected of being a terrorist. According to the applicants, they had not been arrested and detained on 'reasonable' suspicion of having committed an offence and, as Article 5(1)(c) of the Convention speaks of a 'reasonable suspicion' rather than a genuine and bona fide suspicion, their rights had thus been violated.

---

109 Ibid., para. 203–204.
110 Ibid., para. 203.
111 Ibid., para. 8, p.57.

The Court argued that 'what may be regarded as reasonable will depend upon all the circumstances'.[112] In this regard, the Court claimed that terrorism in Northern Ireland falls into a special category, and therefore the 'reasonableness of the suspicion justifying such arrests cannot always be judged according to the same standards as are applied in dealing with conventional crime'.[113] The Court acknowledged that states cannot be asked to establish the reasonableness of the suspicion grounding the arrest of a suspected terrorist by disclosing the confidential sources of supporting information or even facts that would indicate such sources or their identity. Nevertheless, the Court argued that its main task – within this context – was to ensure that 'the essence of the safeguard afforded by Article 5.1.c' had been secured.[114] Without commenting on the necessity of the lower threshold of suspicion in the law itself, the Court ruled that in this particular case there were not sufficient elements to support the conclusion that there was 'reasonable suspicion'. The Court applied the same reasoning[115] in *Murray v. the UK*, but here reached the conclusion that the 'level of factual justification required at the stage of suspicion and the special exigencies of investigating terrorist crime' provided sufficient facts to justify a suspicion against Mrs Murray.[116] In *O'Hara v. UK* the Court admitted that there may be 'a fine line' between those cases where the suspicion grounding the arrest is not sufficiently founded on objective facts and those cases where it is. The Court continued that 'whether the requisite standard is satisfied and whether the guarantee against arbitrary arrest laid down by Article 5.1(c) is thereby satisfied depends on the particular circumstances of each case'.[117]

Suspected terrorists' right to remain silent

Heaney and McGuinness had been arrested and detained after a large explosion killed six people at a checkpoint in Derry/Londonderry. Both men were suspected members of the IRA and thought to be involved in the bombing. They refused to answer questions about their movements on the day of the bombing.[118] At a trial before a Special Criminal Court they were acquitted of the charge of membership of the IRA, but convicted of failing to provide an account of their movements during a specified period, contrary to

112 ECHR Case of *Fox, Campbell and Hartley v. the UK*, 12244/86, 12245/86, 12383/86, 13 July 1989, para. 32.

113 Ibid.

114 Ibid., para. 34.

115 ECHR Case of *Murray v. the UK*, 14310/88, 28 October 1994, para. 47.

116 Ibid., para. 63.

117 ECHR Case of *O'Hara v. the UK*, 37555/97, 16 October 2001, para. 41.

118 Offences against the State Act (1939) Section 51. Available online at http://www.irishstatutebook.ie/1939/en/act/pub/0013/print.html#sec51 (accessed 11 January 2015).

section 52 of the 1939 Offences against the State Act. They complained that section 52 of the Act violated their rights to silence and against self-incrimination guaranteed by Article 6(1) of the Convention and inverted the presumption of innocence guaranteed by Article 6(2). The Irish government contended that section 52 was a proportionate response to the subsisting terrorist and security threat given the need to ensure the proper administration of justice and the maintenance of public order and peace.[119] The Court, however, relying on its previous judgment in *Brogan*, found that these concerns could not justify a provision 'which extinguishes the very essence of the applicants' rights to silence and against self-incrimination guaranteed by Article 6.1 of the Convention'.[120] The Court considered that these rights were an essential safeguard to protect an accused person against improper compulsion by the authorities, thereby contributing to the avoidance of miscarriages of justice and to the fulfilment of the aims of Article 6.[121]

Powers to stop and search terrorist suspects

The UK's Terrorism Act 2000[122] gave a constable the power to stop and search a vehicle or pedestrian (including anything carried by the pedestrian) in a specified area. Section 45 of the Act gave the constable the power for the purpose of 'searching for articles of a kind which could be used in connection with terrorism' whether or not the constable had grounds for suspecting the presence of articles of that kind. The constable could require a person to remove headgear, footwear, an outer coat, a jacket or gloves. The Court was 'struck by the statistical and other evidence showing the extent to which resort is had by police officers to the powers of stop and search under section 44 of the Act'.[123]

> The Ministry of Justice recorded a total of 33,177 searches in 2004/5, 44,545 in 2005/6, 37,000 in 2006/7 and 117,278 in 2007/8. In his Report into the operation of the Act in 2007, Lord Carlile noted that while arrests for other crimes had followed searches under section 44, none of the many thousands of searches had ever related to a terrorism offence; in his 2008 Report, Lord Carlile noted that examples of poor and unnecessary use of section 44 abounded, there being evidence of cases where the person stopped was so obviously far from any known terrorism profile that, realistically, there was not the slightest possibility of him/her being a terrorist, and no other feature to justify the stop.[124]

119 ECHR Case of *Heaney and McGuinness v. Ireland*, 34720/97, 21 December 2000, para. 56.
120 Ibid., para. 58.
121 Ibid., para. 40.
122 The Terrorism Act 2000 [United Kingdom of Great Britain and Northern Ireland].
123 Ibid., p.25.
124 ECHR Case of *Gillan and Quinton*, 4158/05, 12/01/2010, para. 84.

Nevertheless, the Court did not comment upon the effectiveness of the measure; instead it focused on the powers of authorization and confirmation as well as those of stop and search under sections 44 and 45 of the 2000 Act, which it deemed to be neither sufficiently circumscribed nor subject to adequate legal safeguards against abuse.

From this analysis it is clear that the European Court of Human Rights defers to both national courts and states in assessing the effectiveness of counter-terrorism measures. While the court recognizes the specific difficulties counter-terrorism operations pose, it rarely discusses the effectiveness of a given counter-terrorism measure, nor does it take measures of effectiveness explicitly into account to determine the legality, necessity or proportionality of a counter-terrorism measure. In *Ireland v. UK* the Court admitted that the limits of its review powers are 'particularly apparent' where article 15 is concerned. The Court gives a great margin of appreciation to national authorities to decide both on the presence of such an emergency and on the nature and scope of derogations necessary to avert it. It does not want to second-guess governments' assessments of what might be the most prudent or expedient policy to combat terrorism, even if it is presented with statistical evidence that at least suggests that a measure is highly ineffective. Only in *Lawless v. Ireland* in the 1950s did the Court directly assess the effectiveness of the derogation by comparing it to other alternatives the Irish government could have taken to counter the terrorist threat it was facing. In *A and Others v. UK* the Court referred to the effectiveness of the discriminatory detention of non-nationals suspected of being international terrorists only because the House of Lords had questioned the effectiveness of this measure. The Court stressed here that national courts, being in direct and continuous contact with the forces of their countries, can better assess the effectiveness of a counter-terrorism measure than it can.

The Court only refers in a limited amount of cases directly or indirectly to the effectiveness of a counter-terrorism measure in 'ordinary' times. Only in *McCann v. UK* did the Court question directly the effectiveness of the UK's methods, and this assessment influenced its decision on whether the killing of the three terrorist suspects was absolutely necessary. However, this line of reasoning was highly controversial. Nine out of nineteen judges disagreed with the majority's assessment, and were satisfied that no failings had been shown in the organization and control of the operation by the authorities that could justify a conclusion that force was used against the suspects disproportionately. Instead of analysing the effectiveness of a particular counter-terrorism measure, the Court assesses the effectiveness of the safeguards that accompany extraordinary counter-terrorism powers. In *Brogan v. UK* for instance, judges focused on different sets of statistics to assess the effectiveness of the safeguards against arbitrary detentions. The Court has further held that the exigencies of dealing with terrorist crime cannot justify stretching the notion of 'reasonableness' to the point where the safeguard secured by Article 5 § 1(c) is impaired. Similarly, it ruled in *Heaney and*

McGuinness that the situation in Northern Ireland did not justify erosion of the very essence of the applicants' rights to silence and against self-incrimination guaranteed by Article 6 § 1 of the Convention.

4. Conclusion

In this chapter, the indirect, potentially long-term negative impacts of three particular counter-terrorism measures were highlighted. These included (a) the corrosive effect of the use of terrorist listings on the ordinary criminal justice system by expanding unaccountable executive powers at the expense of the evidentiary and procedural requirements of the criminal justice system, (b) the long-term impact of glorification laws on legitimate political debates especially within minority communities and (c) the corrosive effect of the practice of diplomatic assurances on the global ban on torture and cruel, inhuman or degrading treatment. While NGOs and other international human rights bodies tend to focus on both the indirect and direct impact of a specific measure, an analysis of the most relevant judgments of the European Court of Human Rights suggests that this subsidiary court rarely makes comments on the indirect impact of counter-terrorism measures. Rather than making normative statements on specific counter-terrorism measures, the Court takes an individual, contextualized, case-by-case approach in order to determine the proportionality of a specific counter-terrorism measure as applied in the particular case before it. The Court therefore only focuses on the direct impact of a counter-terrorism measure. In hindsight, this is not entirely surprising, given the fact that the Court has given a rather large margin of appreciation to states in respect of counter-terrorist measures, stressing on numerous occasions that it is aware that states face 'particular challenges posed by terrorism and terrorist violence'.[125] Thus, the breadth of this margin varies depending on a number of factors including the nature of the Convention right in issue, its importance for the individual and the nature of the interference.

Similarly, it was clear the European Court of Human Rights rarely discusses the effectiveness of a given counter-terrorism measure, nor does it take measures of effectiveness explicitly into account to determine the legality, necessity or proportionality of a counter-terrorism measure. The Court is reticent to second-guess governments' assessments of what might be the most prudent or expedient policy to combat terrorism, even if it is presented with statistical evidence that at least suggests that a measure is highly ineffective. Instead of analysing the effectiveness of a particular counter-terrorism measure, the Court assesses the effectiveness of the safeguards that accompany

125 See: ECHR Case of *Brogan and Others v. the United Kingdom*, 29 November 1988, § 61, Series A no. 145-B; ECHR Case of *Öcalan v. Turkey* [GC], no. 46221/99, §§ 104, 192–196, ECHR 2005-IV; *Ramirez Sanchez v. France* [GC], no. 59450/00, §§ 115–116, ECHR 2006-IX; and ECHR Case of *Finogenov and Others v. Russia*, cited above, § 212.

extraordinary counter-terrorism powers. The jurisprudence of the ECHR does not elaborate much on the direct relationship between the direct and indirect human rights impact and effectiveness of a counter-terrorism measure. The ECHR could give more weight to effectiveness considerations of national courts in counter-terrorism cases, and even explicitly encourage these courts to thoroughly assess the effectiveness of a counter-terrorism measure in order to determine the proportionality, and hence the impact, of a measure. However, as might be expected of a subsidiary international court, the ECHR is hesitant to engage in such an exercise.

5 The societal impact of European counter-terrorism

Médéric Martin-Mazé and J. Peter Burgess

1. Introduction

The rise of global terrorism has been accompanied by a range of strategic and in-kind counter-terrorism measures, many of which have weakened civil liberties and strengthened illiberal practices in Western democracies. The aim of this chapter is to set out an appropriate framework for measuring and assessing the impact on society of such counter-measures.

The question of the societal impact of counter-terrorism measures can best be situated in the debate that played out in the literature on international relations and that was launched in the early 1990s by the Copenhagen School. For these scholars, societal security is distinct from the more traditional and conventional notions of state security insofar as it regards society not as a specific sector of state security, but rather as a referent object and an actor in its own right. Whereas state security refers to the upholding of sovereignty in its territorial integrity, societal security refers to the ability of a human community to preserve its cultural identity, as 'the ability of a society to persist in its essential character under changing conditions and possible as well as actual threats'.[1] This theoretical background shifts the focus from the preservation of identity over time to the interrelation of security and society.[2] It presumes that the impact of security measures on societies must be gauged against the fact that the latter are made up of a set of settled social contexts resulting from a long-term process of historical differentiation: an observation that constitutes the bedrock of sociology.[3] It is thus crucial to recognize that measures taken in the name of security will

1 O. Wæver, 'Societal Security: The Concept' in O. Wæver, B. Buzan, M. Kelstrup and P. Lemaître (Eds.) *Identity, Migration, and the New Security Agenda in Europe*, (New York: St. Martin's Press 1993), p. 23; B. Buzan, O. Wæver and J. de Wilde, *Security: A New Framework for Analysis*, (Boulder, Colorado and London: Lynne Rienner, 1997), pp. 119–140.

2 O. Waever, 'The Changing Agenda of Societal Security' in *Globalization and Environmental Challenges*, in H. G. Brauch, Ú. Oswald Spring, C. Mesjasz, J. Grin, P. Dunay, N. Chadha Behera, B. Chourou, P. Kameri-Mbote, and P. H. Liotta (Eds.), Hexagon Series on Human and Environmental Security and Peace 3 (Berlin: Springer). Available online at http://link.springer.com/chapter/10.1007/978-3-540-75977-5_44.

3 B. Lahire, *Monde Pluriel: Penser L'unité Des Sciences Sociales*, (Paris: Seuil 2012) pp. 59–141.

play out differently in uneven social contexts, where economic well-being, political systems, and cultural traditions are unequally distributed.

While security measures may have value added in one specific societal sector, they may also have detrimental impact in others.[4] Beneficial impact can be defined as an increase in the level of security in society; detrimental impact refers to undesired or negative consequences. In particular, some measures taken in the name of security can provoke unease or insecurity amongst bystanders; they may be experienced as too intrusive or as having a disproportionate impact upon a given social group. This chapter aims to clarify the character and dynamic of societal impact, and its reciprocal dependency upon both the effectiveness of the security value added it produces and the political and social legitimacy required to sustain it. How can beneficial and detrimental societal impact be consistently assessed and compared?

Democratic legitimacy comprises a range of criteria that are usually derived from different and sometimes divergent political theories of democracy. Amongst these, one can underline the importance of democratic accountability. It requires that those exercising public office remain under the control of the people, their elected representatives or some oversight mechanism. It presumes that participation of citizens ought to be ensured at the different phases of decision-making processes. The political consent of the people is indeed key and entails a clear delegation of sovereignty from the voters to administrative bodies, a clear budgetary control by the parliament as well as ministerial accountability.[5] Checked against these criteria, the European Union seems to be lacking democratic legitimacy. This matter is usually described under the label of 'democratic deficit'.[6]

Fritz Scharpf has made a specific and influential contribution to this debate by underlining that, even if the EU lacks formal legitimacy as far as participation of the people is concerned, it is able to derive legitimacy from the effectiveness of the public policies that it supports.[7] This argument echoes

4 P. Burgess, 'The Societal Impact of Security Research', *PRIO Policy Brief* (Oslo: PRIO 2012).

5 S. Kröger, 'The End of Democracy as We Know It? The Legitimacy Deficits of Bureaucratic Social Policy Governance' (2007) *Journal of European Integration* Vol. 29 No. 5, pp. 567–570; S. Borrás and T. Conzelmann, 'Democracy, Legitimacy and Soft Modes of Governance in the EU: The Empirical Turn' (2007) *Journal of European Integration* Vol. 29 No. 5, pp. 540–543; M. Den Boer, C. Hillebrand and A. Nölke, 'Legitimacy under Pressure: The European Web of Counter-Terrorism Networks' (2008) *Journal of Common Market Studies* Vol. 46 No. 1, pp. 105–107.

6 G. Majone, 'Europe's "Democratic Deficit": The Question of Standards' (1998) *European Law Journal* Vol. 4 No. 1; F. Decker, 'Governance beyond the Nation-State. Reflections on the Democratic Deficit of the European Union' (2002) *Journal of European Public Policy* Vol. 9 No. 2; C. Crombez, 'The Democratic Deficit in the European Union: Much Ado about Nothing?' (2003) *European Union Politics* Vol. 4 No.1; See also Chistyakova in this volume.

7 F.W. Scharpf, 'Legitimate Diversity: The New Challenge of European Integration' (2003) *Zeitschrift Für Staats-Und Europawissenschaften* Vol. 1 No. 1; F.W. Scharpf, *Governing in Europe: Effective and Democratic?* (Oxford: Oxford University Press 1999); See also V.A. Schmidt, 'Democracy and Legitimacy in the European Union Revisited: Input, Output, and "Throughput"' (2013) *Political Studies* Vol. 61 No. 1.

the above-mentioned pluralization of repertoires of legitimization, and the emergence of new forms of organizational legitimacy codified inter alia by the new public management discourses.[8] Power is no longer solely presented as power over, but also and increasingly as power to.[9] In other words, legitimacy becomes a Janus-faced concept, where the input of procedural validation meets the output of effective results. Legitimacy is increasingly drawn and derived from the consequences of public policy-making whose effectiveness is attested to by pervasive methods of result-based evaluation.[10]

2. Counter-terrorism and legitimacy in Europe

To what extent does counter-terrorism transform benchmarks of acceptability in EU societies? The rule of law ranks high amongst the societal values most at risk of being destabilized by anti-terrorist measures.[11] Indeed, counter-terrorism relies extensively on illiberal practices that pave the way for the re-enactment of arbitrary exceptionalism. As we discuss below, some scholars suspect that this exceptional claim lies at the core of the modern, liberal and democratic societal orders.

The exceptionalist argument usually starts by taking stock of the fact that 9/11 and subsequent events (such as the 2004 Madrid and 2005 London bombings) have raised awareness of the new vulnerability of contemporary societies in the face of 'new' or 'hyper-terrorism'. Draconian counter-terrorist measures are thereafter legitimized as appropriate responses to what is perceived as the radical novelty and outright violence of these terrorists of a new generation. The latter are widely branded as fanatic combatants, driven by a deep-seated hatred of Western values, unwilling to reason and negotiate, and solely interested in inflicting grave damage upon innocent civil populations. According to this narrative, they disregard taboos on the choice of their instruments or targets, and represent an existential threat to democratic and liberal societies. States are thus prompted – the argument continues – to take drastic and decisive measures in order to continue providing security for their population.[12] This discourse simultaneously works as a way to delegitimize terrorist groups,

8 See also Oliveria, this volume.

9 P. Duran, 'Légitimité, Droit et Action Publique' (2009) *L'Année Sociologique* Vol. 59 No. 2.

10 G. Skogstad, 'Legitimacy and/or Policy Effectiveness?: Network Governance and GMO Regulation in the European Union' (2003) *Journal of European Public Policy* Vol. 10 No. 3.

11 W. Webster, C. Leleux, J. Sterbik-Lamina, J. Cas, W. Peissl, D. Fischer, W. Bonss, et al.. *Increasing Resilience in Surveillance Societies – The Social Perspective* (2013) p. 12. Available online at http://irissproject.eu/wp-content/uploads/2013/04/Social-perspectives-of-surveillance-and-democracy-report-D2.1-IRISS.pdf (5 February 2015); E. P. Guittet, 'Ne pas leur faire confiance serait leur faire offense: Antiterrorisme, solidarité démocratique et identité politique' (2006) *Cultures & Conflits* No. 61 (March).

12 J. Stock and A. Herz, 'The Threat Environment Created by International Terrorism from the German Police Perspective' (2007) *European Journal on Criminal Policy & Research* Vol. 13 No. 1, pp. 85–92; C. Pantazis and S. Pemberton, 'Trading Civil Liberties for Greater Security?: The Impact on Minority Communities' (2008) *Criminal Justice Matters* Vo. 73 No. 1, pp. 12–14; D. Bigo, S. Carrera, E. Guild and R. B. J. Walker (Eds.) *Europe's 21st Century Challenge: Delivering Liberty* (Farnham, Surrey, [England]; Burlington, VT: Ashgate Pub. Co. 2010), pp. 388–391.

a move that is key when put into perspective with the legitimacy struggle that transnational political violence necessarily entails.[13]

But the terrorist acts of 9/11 are not new, nor are the measures adopted in the name of 9/11 and the exceptionalist rhetoric that justifies them.[14] Thus, previous experiences (such as in Northern Ireland) ought to be interpreted not as models to be replicated, but as meaningful metaphors of the contemporary reconfiguration of security practices.[15] But, more to the point, the claim of radical novelty, although not new in itself, needs to be grasped as a threshold whose crossing opens up an era marked by exceptionalism. Indeed what makes the post-9/11 political period remarkable is not the expansion, intensification or radicalization of transnational violence as such, but its politicization as an event that is out of the ordinary.[16] The exception argument goes on; exceptional times require exceptional measures.[17] This line of argument informs the legitimization of counter-terrorism as an exception to the norm. Illiberal antiterrorist laws are adopted under conditions of emergency. Extraordinary renditions, electronic surveillance and blacklisting are justified as derogations from the norm necessary to protect the legal order.[18] The ticking-bomb argument is brought in as the most basic justification for exceptions to ordinary criminal justice procedures.[19] Under an imminent and existential threat, regular rules of the game no longer apply. Interestingly, the argument works both ways. The same logic dictates that, when a political or religious community is on the edge of eradication or enslavement, the immunity of non-combatants ought to be lifted.[20]

13 D. Hermant, 'Guerre et Terrorisme' (1986) *Cultures & Conflits* (2005) available online at http://conflits.revues.org/1146?lang=en (accessed 11 January 2015); M. Hechter, 'Legitimacy in the Modern World' (2009) *American Behavioral Scientist* Vol. 53 No. 3, p. 280.

14 M. Perier and E. P. Guittet, 'Editorial. Suspicion et exception' (2005) Edited by Didier Bigo. *Cultures & Conflicts*, No. 58 (June) pp. 6–12; A. Tsoukala, 'La légitimation des mesures d'exception dans la lutte antiterroriste en Europe' (2006) *Cultures & Conflits* No. 61 (March) pp. 25–27.

15 D. Bigo and E. P. Guittet, 'Northern Ireland as Metaphor: Exception, Suspicion and Radicalization in the "war on terror" (2011) *Security Dialogue* Vol. 42 No. 6, pp. 483–498.

16 J. Huysmans, 'International Politics of Exception: Competing Visions of International Political Order between Law and Politics' (2006) *Alternatives: Global, Local, Political* Vol. 31 No. 2, pp. 12.

17 C.A.S.E. Collective, 'Critical Approaches to Security in Europe: A Networked Manifesto' (2006) *Security Dialogue* Vol. 37 No. 4, pp. 464–467; A. Neal, 'Foucault in Guantánamo: Towards an Archaeology of the Exception' (2006) *Security Dialogue* Vol. 37 No. 1, pp. 31–32; M. Neocleous, 'The Problem with Normality: Taking Exception to 'Permanent Emergency' (2006) *Alternatives: Global, Local, Political* Vol. 31 No. 2; A.W. Neal, *Exceptionalism and the Politics of Counter-Terrorism: Liberty, Security, and the War on Terror*, Routledge Studies in Liberty and Security (Abingdon, Oxon and New York, NY: Routledge, 2010), pp. 7–8.

18 F. Allhoff, 'The War on Terror and the Ethics of Exceptionalism' (2009) *Journal of Military Ethics* Vol. 8 No. 4; C. Aradau and R. van Munster, 'Exceptionalism and the "war on Terror": Criminology Meets International Relations' (2009) *British Journal of Criminology* Vol. 49 No. 5, pp. 686–701.

19 L. Zedner, 'Terrorism, the Ticking Bomb, and Criminal Justice Values' (2008) *Criminal Justice Matters* Vol. 73 No. 1.

20 S. Kaplan, 'Unraveling Emergency Justifications and Excuses for Terrorism' (2011) *Journal of Social Philosophy* Vol. 42 No. 2, p.220.

The degree of legitimation achieved by counter-terrorist practices thus seems to depend on their perception as necessary steps exceptionally taken to ensure the survival of that from which they derogate. Yet, analysis of parliamentary debates either preceding or directly following the adoption of counter-terrorist legislation in France, the United Kingdom and Italy shows that the exception argument does not tally with consensus within these political arenas. However, it represents an increasing part in the overall talking points tackled during parliamentary discussion dealing with anti-terrorist legislation.[21]

Prior to 9/11, considerations of whether counter-terrorism should derogate from regular rules do not feature prominently during the few sessions of the European Parliament Civil Liberties, Justice and Home Affairs (LIBE) Committee dedicated to this issue. In the immediate aftermath of 9/11, however, arguments against or in defence of emergency rules are voiced by 12.2 per cent of the speakers. Those who are in favour of exceptional measures affirm that terrorism is linked to immigration, demand tighter control of the Internet and disregard protection of human rights as facilitating terrorism. Yet, even during this highly sensitive period, the majority of the speakers recall that the upholding of human rights represents an imperative from which no derogation can be tolerated.[22]

3. The balance between security and liberty

The particular phrasing of this exceptionalist claim draws on the Lockean argument that security is only one value amongst other societal values.[23] According to this point of view, security must be kept in check so as to avoid the destruction of the very object that it is set to protect, namely liberal democratic principles. In other words, for a political order to remain at the same time safe and democratic, a proper balance between security and liberty must be struck. Thus, the balance metaphor emerges as a response to the exception argument.[24] It assumes that liberty and security are variables that can be adjusted in response to the changing threat environment in which liberal states are embedded. In order to explain this, Vermeule and Posner borrow the image of a 'frontier' from Pareto's classical economics in

21 A. Tsoukala, 'Democracy in the Light of Security: British and French Political Discourses on Domestic Counter-Terrorism Policies' (2006) *Political Studies* Vol. 54 No. 3.

22 Ibid. and Tsoukala (2006) *supra* note 14.

23 T. Meisels, *The Trouble with Terror: Liberty, Security, and the Response to Terrorism* (Cambridge, UK and New York: Cambridge University Press 2008), pp. 61–82; C. Kantner and A. Liberatore, 'Security and Democracy in the European Union: An Introductory Framework' (2006) *European Security* Vol. 15 No. 4, p.367; A. Amicelle, J. Bus, T. El-Baba, C. Fuchs, E. Mordini, A. Rebera, N. Robinson, D. Trottier, S. Venier and S. Wright, *Public Perception of Security and Privacy: Assessing Knowledge, Collecting Evidence, Translating Research into Action – Report on Theoretical Frameworks and Previous Empirical Research.* (Brussels: European Commission, 2012), p.34.

24 D. Bigo *et al.*, *supra* note 12, p.390.

order to convey the idea that security and liberty can be concomitantly enhanced up to a point. Beyond that limit, security can only be increased at the expense of liberty and vice-versa. In this context, decision-makers must not minimize but rather optimize the security costs that bear on civil liberties.[25]

Although in Vermeule's and Posner's eyes, the balance model is uncontroversial because it simply reflects the fact that people attach relative values to security and liberty, criticism has been leveled against this pragmatist and consequentialist interpretation of the relationship between liberty and security in particular, and against the balance metaphor in general. In order to assess these, one needs to take stock of the consensus regarding the balance metaphor. The balance metaphor has come to epitomize, encapsulate and frame a great deal of the public debate pertaining to counter-terrorism practices in the post 9/11 era. The idea that the new threat environment, as revealed by the events of 9/11, prompts the need to forego some liberties in the pursuit of security has readily become common-sensical.[26]

Although the debate about the balance between liberty and security has mainly been about US practices in the war on terror, it has also had a sizable impact on the European Union.[27] Moreover, the changing balance between security and liberty has its origins in deep social and political changes that largely pre-date 9/11.[28] Indeed, the notions of balance and trade-off have a rather long history, as do counter-terrorism and transnational political violence. These features make it necessary to historicize the

---

25 E. A. Posner, *Terror in the Balance: Security, Liberty, and the Courts* (New York: Oxford University Press, 2007); A. Vermeule, 'Emergency Lawmaking after 9/11 and 7/7' (2008) *The University of Chicago Law Review* Vol. 75 No. 3; A. Vermeule, 'Security and Liberty: Critiques of the Tradeoff Thesis' (2011) SSRN Scholarly Paper ID 1888334. Rochester, NY: Social Science Research Network. Available online at http://papers.ssrn.com/abstract=1888334 (accessed 11 January 2015).

26 C. Aradau, 'Forget Equality? Security and Liberty in the "War on Terror"' (2008) *Alternatives: Global, Local, Political* Vol. 33 No. 3, pp. 295–296; T. Dragu, 'Is There a Trade-off between Security and Liberty? Executive Bias, Privacy Protections, and Terrorism Prevention' (2011) *American Political Science Review* Vol. 105 No. 1, p.64; B. J. Goold and L. Lazarus, 'Introduction Security and Human Rights: The Search for a Language of Reconciliation' in B. J. Goold and L. Lazarus (Eds.) *Security and Human Rights* (Oxford and Portland, OR: Hart, 2007), p.17; M. Neocleous, 'Security, Liberty and the Myth of Balance: Towards a Critique of Security Politics' (2007) *Contemporary Political Theory* Vol. 6 No. 2, pp. 132–133; J. Waldron, 'Security and Liberty: The Image of Balance' (2003) *Journal of Political Philosophy* Vol. 11 No. 2, p.191; L. Zedner, 'The Concept of Security: An Agenda for Comparative Analysis' (2003) *Legal Studies* Vol. 23 No. 1, pp. 153–176.

27 M. L. Wade, 'Fear vs Freedom Post 9/11 – A European Debate: Introduction' (2007) *European Journal on Criminal Policy & Research* Vol. 13 No. 1/2, pp. 3–4.

28 B. J. Goold, 'Privacy, Identity and Security' in B.J. Goold and L. Lazarus (Eds.) *Security and Human Rights* (Oxford and Portland, OR: Hart, 2007); S. Gutwirth, R. Bellanova, R. Gellert, M. Friedewald, P. Schütz, D. Wright, E. Mordini and S. Venier, *Privacy and Emerging Fields of Science and Technology: Towards a Common Framework for Privacy and Ethical Assessment – Legal, Social, Economic and Ethical Conceptualisations of Privacy and Data Protection* (Brussels: European Commission, 2011), pp. 29–31.

relationships between security and liberty.[29] Furthermore, the direction in which the balance tilts depends closely on cultural conditions that may facilitate or hamper the overriding of liberty by security.[30] Indeed, 'balancing' is a key move of liberal politics, central to the rationality of the political Western discourse.[31] It is so well entrenched in the public debate that liberty is used both to oppose illiberal security practices and to legitimatize them.[32] In this connection, democratic societies are supposed to be pursuing a proper balance between security and liberty at all times.[33]

Construing the relationship between security and liberty as a balanced one entails a number of assumptions that one needs to bring to the fore. To begin with, the need for a new balance implies that the balance was unsettled in the first place. Adjusting civil liberties in the face of greater and/or new risk supposes that it is possible to evaluate this risk objectively. Indeed, balancing security and liberty assumes a form of metrics that makes it possible to measure and range both values.[34] The metaphor furthermore implies that, once restruck, the balance will remain stable.[35] In addition, balancing is taken to be an appropriate and reasonable act in itself, regardless of what is being balanced and under what conditions. But most importantly, trading liberty against security presumes that security and liberty are homogeneous, equal and antithetical values that vary independently from one another but according to an inversed proportionate reason.[36]

The balancing metaphor, and the cost-benefit calculus that it implies, have been subjected to a number of criticisms. It has been suggested, for example, that while comforting at first glance, this image is deeply misleading and over simplistic.[37] First, it is often unclear what tipped the balance in the first place. Even more so since terrorist risks are, by their very definition, rather impossible to evaluate with any certainty.[38] Second, since the

---

29 D. Bigo, R. B. J. Walker and C. Elise, 'Liberté et Sécurité en Europe: enjeux contemporains' (2006) *Cultures & Conflits* No. 61 (March), pp. 108–109; D. Bigo, R. B. J. Walker, S. Carrera and E. Guild, *The Changing Landscape of European Liberty and Security: Mid-Term Report on the Results of the CHALLENGE Project*. Research Paper 4 (2007), pp. 1–2.

30 I. Loader, 'The cultural lives of security and rights' in B.J. Goold and L. Lazarus (Eds.) *Security and human rights* (Oxford and Portland, OR, Hart, 2007).

31 A. Amicelle *et al.*, *supra* note 23, pp. 34–35; M. Neocleous, *supra* note 26, p.132; J. Waldron, *supra* note 26, p.192.

32 A. W. Neal, *supra* note 17, p.2; C. Aradau, *supra* note 26, p.295.

33 C. Kantner and A. Liberatore, *supra* note 23, p.368.

34 J. Waldron, *supra* note 26, pp. 192–193.

35 A. Ashworth, 'Security, Terrorism and the Value of Human Rights' in B.J. Goold and L. Lazarus (Eds.) *Security and Human Rights* (Oxford and Portland, OR: Hart, 2007).

36 M. Gani, P. Mathew and S. Bronitt (Eds.) 'Balancing Security and Liberty: Critical Perspectives on Terrorism Law Reform' in *Fresh Perspectives on the 'War on Terror'* (Canberra: ANU E Press, 2008), pp. 69–72.

37 A. Amicelle *et al.*, *supra* note 23, p.6.

38 L. Zedner, 'Securing Liberty in the Face of Terror: Reflections from Criminal Justice' (2005) *Journal of Law and Society* Vol. 32 No. 4, p.512.

balance holds value in itself, striking one amounts to a goal that has to be achieved on its own terms, thus being substituted for a real, sound and open argument.[39] Third, the balance metaphor hypothesizes that liberty and security are commensurable goods. However, this commensurability is in tension with the uneven distribution of security and liberty amongst different segments of the population. It is furthermore destabilized by temporal dissonances between the rights that have to be relinquished in the present for perceived insecurities pertaining to the possibility (as opposed to the probability) of future risks. These hurdles arguably complicate the task of attaching relative worth to security and liberty.[40]

The balance metaphor also overlooks the possibility that security agencies, which are given more latitude to operate, may also be a source of insecurity. There are no reasons to think that the possibility of a terrorist attack will diminish the threat that liberals have historically identified in state bureaucracies.[41] Furthermore, one needs to unpack the concept of liberty that is encapsulated in this metaphor since liberties are heterogeneous and may play out differently in relation to increased or decreased levels of security. If one distinguishes between rights to physical integrity, such as the freedom from torture or political imprisonment, on the one side, and empowerment rights, such as free speech or assembly, on the other, it would appear that counter-terrorist policies curtail the former but not the latter.[42] Therefore, instead of a balancing act, one would need to carefully define a hierarchy amongst rights because some are more sensitive to security claims than others.

A further flaw in the balancing metaphor regards the distribution of security and liberty in society. Even though this point has been hinted at in earlier comments, a more nuanced and detailed discussion is required here. The balance discourse implicitly relies on a homogeneous account of society insofar as it presumes the even distribution of both values across its different segments. Simply put, according to this discourse, everyone should see their liberties curtailed and their security enhanced when the balance is readjusted. But this assumption overlooks two inescapable facts. First, the differentiation inherent to complex and modern societies weakens this claim. For instance, since security is increasingly commoditized, wealthy social groups may be in a position to afford more of it, whilst the disenfranchised may have less. Similarly, other cleavages, such as ethnicity or/ and nationality, readily become relevant to the extent that only some

39 M. Neocleous, *supra* note 26, p.132.

40 M. Gani *et al.*, *supra* note 36, p.68.

41 J. Waldron, *supra* note 26, pp. 194–195, 204–206; L. Zedner, *supra* note 38, p.532; C. Kantner and A. Liberatore, *supra* note 23, p.365.

42 J. A. Piazza and J. I. Walsh, 'Transnational Terror and Human Rights' (2009) *International Studies Quarterly* Vol. 53 No. 1, pp. 144–145.

categories (foreigners and immigrants, for instance) of the population are targeted for further scrutiny by counter-terrorist policies.[43] These difficulties are illustrated by the search for 'balance' between privacy and surveillance, as we discuss below.

4. The trade-off between privacy and surveillance

As a precondition for democratic life, privacy is a backbone of the constitutional architecture of liberal states. It is enshrined in the European Convention on Human Rights (art. 8) as well as in the Charter of Fundamental Rights of the European Union (art. 7) as a fundamental right from which derogations are nonetheless legally possible if, and only if, they are proportionate and necessary.[44] Beyond this legal aspect, which is not our focus here, privacy should also be construed as a contextual value that evolves over time. It has thus become increasingly problematic since private firms and security agencies have been more and more interested in accessing personal data. One could even suspect that, from being the object of security which must be protected, privacy has turned into a hurdle, if not a threat to security. Therefore, those states that do not follow the surveillance enhancing path become weak links posing a threat to other states.[45]

If surveillance largely predates the counter-terrorist policies that were justified by 9/11,[46] increased technical capacities have arguably excited the imagination of policy-makers eager to make complicated matters simple by the means of surveillance technologies.[47] The computerization of social life presents ever-growing possibilities to encroach upon privacy for security reasons.[48] For instance, life-logging technologies record and stock every action of one person, thus making it possible to search his or her past without limitation.[49] If technological hurdles, such as the poor quality of data, seem to hamper the bringing together of new and existing data-sources,[50] it appears that democratic oversight has trouble keeping pace with technological

43 D. Bigo, R. B. J. Walker and C. Elise, *supra* note 29, pp. 115–120; M. Gani *et al.*, *supra* note 36, pp. 67–68; J. Waldron, *supra* note 26, pp. 201–204.

44 See also Vermeulen, this volume.

45 S. Gutwirth *et al.*, *supra* note 28, pp. 29–30.

46 D. Lyon, *Surveillance after September 11. Themes for the 21st Century* (Cambridge: Polity Press, 2003) p.4.

47 T. Bunyan, 'The "digital tsunami" and the surveillance state' (2008) *Statewatch Journal* Vol. 18 No. 2, April-Jun.

48 M. L. Wade, *supra* note 27, p.10; S. Gutwirth *et al.*, *supra* note 28, p.47.

49 D. Solove, 'Data Mining and the Security-Liberty Debate' (2008) *The University of Chicago Law Review*, Vol. 75 No. 1, pp. 56–59.

50 M. Levi and D. S. Wall. 'Technologies, Security, and Privacy in the Post-9/11 European Information Society' (2004) *Journal of Law and Society* Vol. 31 No. 2, pp. 217–218.

innovation in this field. The development of cloud-computing is a case in point, as the recent PRISM revelations have made abundantly clear.[51]

A second debate has emerged in parallel and in close connection to the intense academic discussion pertaining to the balancing act between security and liberty. The trade-off calculus underpinning the image of balance equally frames the analysis of the relationship between privacy and surveillance.[52] In the aftermath of 9/11, the claim that reducing privacy protection would enhance the ability of security agencies to prevent and repress terrorism has readily gained currency in policy circles. It was claimed that privacy was creating a comfortable environment where terrorist groups would thrive away from prying eyes. The protection of privacy was therefore disqualified as a hurdle constraining the efforts of the police.[53] More particularly, in Europe, security measures such as the EU Data Retention Directive,[54] which required electronic communication suppliers to retain certain information for up to two years, was justified by reference to similar allegations.[55]

In a broader perspective, one cannot help but notice that the debate on counter-terrorism resonates strongly with a string of issues that have been brought under examination in the field of surveillance studies.[56] The use of CCTV cameras to elucidate terrorist bombings post facto, is a case in point, although this practice arguably offsets the usual justification of those methods of surveillance as a way to prevent *ex ante* risks (either criminal or terrorist) from actualizing.[57] The intimate connection between enhanced surveillance technologies, which are brought in under the claim that they will bolster counter-terrorist efforts, and a loss of privacy is readily grasped. Ultimately, surveillance impacts privacy, which is a cornerstone of the societal values informing democratic life.[58]

---

51 D. Bigo, G. Boulet, C. Bowden, S. Carrera, J. Jeandesbo, and A Scherrer, *Fighting Cyber Crime and Protecting Privacy in the Cloud* (Brussels: European Parliament 2012); D. Bigo, G. Boulet, C. Bowden, S. Carrera, E. Guild, N. Hernanz, P. de Hert, J. Jeandesboz, and A. Scherrer, *Open Season for Data Fishing on the Web The Challenges of the US PRISM Programme for the EU* (CEPS Policy Brief 293. Brussels: Center for European Policy Studies 2013).

52 A. Amicelle *et al.*, *supra* note 23, pp. 38–40; S. Gutwirth *et al.*, *supra* note 28, pp. 29–30; T. Dragu, *supra* note 26, pp. 65–66.

53 T. Dragu, *supra* note 26.

54 Council of the European Union and European Parliament Directive 2006/24/EC of the European Parliament and of the Council of 15 March 2006 on the Retention of Data Generated or Processed in Connection with the Provision of Publicly Available Electronic Communications Services or of Public Communications Networks and Amending Directive 2002/58/EC *(Official Journal of the European Union* 2006).

55 K. De Vries, R. Bellanova and P. De Hert, *Proportionality Overrides Unlimited Surveillance. The German Constitutional Court Judgment on Data Retention* (*CEPS* Liberty and *Security in Europe*, Brussels: Center for European Policy Studies 2010).

56 D. Lyon, *Surveillance as Social Sorting: Privacy, Risk and Digital Discrimination* (London, Routledge, 2003); D. Lyon, *Surveillance after September 11* (Cambridge, Polity Press 2003).

57 M. L. Wade, *supra* note 27, p.10.

58 W. Webster, *supra* note 11, p.13.

The similarities that emerge from the balancing of security and liberty on the one hand, and the trade-off between surveillance and privacy on the other, help to improve understanding of why the criticism leveled against the former shares so many similarities with objections to the latter. It has been argued that talks of trade-offs conceal the continuous erosion of privacy protection.[59] Surveillance trumps privacy because its excesses go unnoticed for it only bears on a minority, because it is justified by a discourse of risk and because judicial oversight has generally failed, even though one notable exception should be highlighted with regards to the European Data Retention Directive. In 2010, the German Constitutional Court censored its application on disproportionality grounds[60] before the Court of Justice of the European Union struck it down altogether for seriously interfering with private life and the protection of personal data.[61] Any curtailment of privacy protection justified by counter-terrorism needs to demonstrate that the contemplated surveillance technology will actually deliver more security than less privacy-invasive measures, which is not necessarily the case.[62] In addition, it also needs to demonstrate that these gains outweigh the costs and that these costs remain fairly distributed across different societal segments.[63]

The arguments overlap to a certain degree. In a sociological perspective, surveillance is not the same as security, and privacy is not the same as liberty. Privacy entails different kinds of protections and practices. Two main strands can be distinguished in the literature. On the one hand, privacy is understood as the ability of one person to control the extent to which information pertaining to his or her personhood is disclosed, disseminated and used. On the other, privacy is construed as the capacity for one social actor to restrict access to someone's personal domain from third parties. The management of privacy and the 'right to be left alone' are distinct from one another: 'there is privacy even if one chooses to disclose all personal information about oneself. In an absolute restricted access theory of privacy, there is only privacy if one lives in solitary confinement without contacts to others'.[64]

Both approaches substantiate the claim that, instead of being at odds with the interest of the community, as proponents of the 'security first' arguments

59 A. Amicelle *et al.*, *supra* note 23, pp. 41–43; D.J. Solove, *Nothing to Hide: The False Tradeoff between Privacy and Security* (New Haven CT: Yale University Press 2011), p. 2.

60 K. De Vries *et al.*, *supra* note 55; Bundesverfassungsgericht. 2010. Gegen die Regelungen zur Vorratsdatenspeicherung im Gesetz zur Neuregelung der Telekommunikationsüberwachung und anderer verdeckter Ermittlungsmaßnahmen sowie zur Umsetzung der Richtlinie 2006/24/EG vom 21. December 2007 (BGBl I S. 3198).

61 Court of Justice for the European Union (2014) Judgment in Joined Cases C-293/12 and C-594/12 *Digital Rights Ireland and Seitlinger and Others.*

62 T. Dragu, *supra* note 26.

63 S. Gutwirth *et al.*, *supra* note 28.

64 A. Amicelle *et al.*, *supra* note 23, p.17.

have argued,[65] privacy plays a central role in the constitution of social orders. Indeed, privacy underpins and conditions a number of related values such as autonomy, liberty, property, anonymity or political participation in the life of the polity.[66] This societal value of privacy thus considerably offsets the balancing argument, framing privacy as a luxury that needs to be given away when political times become stringent. However, it should be remembered that privacy is not uncontroversial. Criticism has been raised on the grounds that it enables patriarchal practices such as domestic violence, that it advances a liberal notion of democracy, that it is Western-centric and that is it socially biased to the detriment of the disenfranchised.[67]

5. Effectiveness as legitimacy

While they change, displace and sometimes unsettle the societal values underpinning European democratic societies, the exceptionalist argument, the balance metaphor and the trade-off simultaneously legitimize counter-terrorism. More specifically, they are brought in under the claim that enhanced security measures will more efficiently fight terrorism. Thus, the effectiveness of anti-terrorism can fruitfully be fathomed as a specific mode of legitimization that is pursued by European security agencies. Therefore, while the previous section teased out the extent to which European core societal values tend to drift as they are put under the influence of claims embedded in counter-terrorist policies, the following section shifts the focus of our investigation towards a more sociologically informed argument.

We will first contextualize European policies to bring out the particular social setting in which they are designed, negotiated and implemented. Illiberal practices are brought in under the claim that terrorist deeds yield such dreadful consequences that they jeopardize the survival of the collective. According to this point of view, terrorists must therefore be prevented from carrying out their plans. An array of difficult questions follows from this imperative. How to deal with an unknown yet potentially catastrophic future? How to thwart a terrorist who has not yet been identified? How to detect terrorist plots amongst the myriad of digital traces left behind by the majority of law-abiding citizens? How to 'connect the dots' before the unthinkable happens? By and large, the risk prevention rationale that is built into counter-terrorist practices aims at suppressing the unease triggered by these questions.[68]

---

65 A. Etzioni, *Security First: For a Muscular, Moral Foreign Policy* (New Haven, CT: Yale University Press, 2007).

66 S. Gutwirth *et al., supra* note 28, p.24.

67 A. Amicelle *et al., supra* note 23, pp. 19–20.

68 O. Kessler, 'Is Risk Changing the Politics of Legal Argumentation?' (2008) *Leiden Journal of International Law* Vol. 21 No. 4; J. McCulloch and S. Pickering, 'Pre-Crime and Counter-Terrorism Imagining Future Crime in the "War on Terror"' (2009) *British Journal of Criminology* Vol. 49 No. 5; L. Amoore, 'Data Derivatives on the Emergence of a Security Risk Calculus for Our Times' (2011) *Theory, Culture & Society* Vol. 28 No. 6.

As mentioned above, risk prevention has been one of the key counter-terrorist strategies, and it has reached centre stage in the aftermath of 9/11. Counter-measures have been activated *ex ante*, before a terrorist attack occurs. Terrorist plots must be uncovered and suppressed from their early stages, so the imperative goes. Preventing harm through threat anticipation is, indeed, the foremost rationale underpinning current counter-terrorist frameworks. But this turn towards risk assessment entails, within more traditional risk-management methods, a move away from retrospective estimations of harm as they result from events that have already happened on a regular basis, towards an outlook based on lowering the probability of a possible and catastrophic future towards zero.[69]

In a broader perspective, one ought to account for the fact that preventative counter-terrorism is embedded in a larger shift of governmental rationalities towards risk.[70] Counter-terrorist policies partake in a culture of prevention and risk management that has become deeply entrenched in late modern societies. Prior to 9/11, this culture had already taken a firm hold on neighbouring social sectors, such as criminal justice.[71] Repression as a logic of reactivity has been destabilized, challenged and partially replaced by a logic of proactivity where action is taken before a threat becomes a reality.[72] This shift relies heavily on profiling as a detection technique.[73] The elective affinity that risk prevention entertains with counter-terrorism must furthermore be underlined insofar as the label 'terrorist' is inherently a pre-emptive one.[74] As regards counter-terrorism in particular, the specific historicity of this turn towards a preventive rationale is worth bringing to the fore. Current preventative counter-terrorism originates in the criminalization of independence struggles, post-colonial counter-insurgency strategies and the militarization of narcotic prohibition under the heading 'war on drugs'.[75]

---

69 M. De Goede, 'The Politics of Preemption and the War on Terror in Europe' (2008) *European Journal of International Relations* Vol. 14 No. 1, p.164; J. McCulloch and S. Pickering, *supra* note 68, pp. 630–633; G. Mythen and S. Walklate, 'Terrorism, Risk and International Security: The Perils of Asking "What If?"' (2008) *Security Dialogue* Vol. 39 No. 2–3, pp. 231–237; T. Dragu, *supra* note 26, p.65; M. Gani *et al.*, *supra* note 36, pp. 81–83.

70 M. Gani *et al.*, *supra* note 36, p.78.

71 D. Garland, *The Culture of Control: Crime and Social Order in Late Modernity* (Oxford: Clarendon 2001) pp. 167–192.

72 D. Bigo and A. Tsoukala, 'Understanding (in)security' in D. Bigo and A. Tsoukala (Eds.) *Terror, Insecurity and Liberty: Illiberal Practices of Liberal Regimes after 9/11* (London: Routledge 2008), pp. 35–37.

73 D. Bigo, L. Bonelli, D. Chi, and C. Olsson, 'Mapping the Field of the EU Internal Security Agencies' in D. Bigo (Ed.) *The Field of the EU Internal Security Agencies* (Paris: L'Harmattan 2007), pp. 38–39.

74 J. McCulloch and S. Pickering, *supra* note 68, p.630.

75 P. Bonditti, 'L'antiterrorisme aux Etats-Unis (1946–2007): une analyse foucaldienne de la transformation de l'exercice de la souveraineté et de l'art de gouverner' (Anti-Terrorism in the United States (1946–2007): A Foucauldian Analysis of the Transformation of the Exercise of Sovereignty and the Art of Government) Thèse de doctorat, Institut d'études politiques (Paris 2008); J. McCulloch and S. Pickering, *supra* note 68.

Putting such an emphasis on risk prevention may at first glance seem odd in a report dealing with counter-terrorism in Europe since Europe, or at least the European Union, ostensibly stayed cautiously clear of the United States' preventative counter-terrorist practices. Although entrenched in popular imagination, this line of thought does not withstand careful examination. Kessler astutely notices that 'Europe is perhaps more part of the "willing" than it is ready to admit'.[76] One may even consider preventative terrorism as a profoundly European phenomenon. As will become clearer below, agencies embedded in the European field of security professionals have so vigorously appropriated, pursued and developed preventative security practices that they have become part of the European Union as a political entity.[77]

This is all the more true when one takes European databases into consideration.[78] The prevention rationale is indeed underpinned by two closely related imperatives. Only intelligence-led policing can detect unknown terrorists before they act. But intelligence is merely a secondary product, derived from the collection, treatment and processing of a massive amount of information. Enhanced by computational power and bolstered by a powerful belief in the efficiency of information technologies, databases cannot under such circumstances, but become the weapon of choice of the counter-terrorist struggle. Post-9/11 preventative counter-terrorist policies have greatly amplified the importance of data collection, retention and mining. This is why a powerful imperative has taken root, which demands that digital information should remain available for as long as possible. The EU Data Retention Directive (adopted in 2006) typically aimed at enhancing the longevity of this data afterglow.[79] Furthermore, existing databases, such as the Schengen Information System (SIS) or EURODAC have seen their scope and their use widened far beyond their initial remits. The SIS is thus increasingly being turned into an investigative tool. This move is also epitomized by the second generation of this instrument that has been politically endorsed but has not yet come online; it will, for instance, allow for associative researches. A powerful trend is at work, which tends towards the networking and interconnection of still-fragmented databases, thus connecting the layers of the European 'surveillant assemblage'.[80]

These databases are intended to store the greatest amount of digital traces left behind at an increasing pace by average individuals in their most mundane and routine practices. Probabilistic knowledge derived from actuarial, financial and commercial techniques is brought into play in order to detect amongst these data iterative patterns that point out precursory signs of a

76 O. Kessler, *supra* note 68, p.865.
77 M. De Goede, *supra* note 69, p.168.
78 See C. Murphy *et al.*, this volume.
79 Council of the European Union, *supra* note 54.
80 K. D. Haggerty and R. V. Ericson, 'The Surveillant Assemblage' (2000) *The British Journal of Sociology* Vol. 51 No. 4.

possible terrorist plot. Probabilistic association rules, which must carefully be distinguished from causal determination rules, allow for the structured mining of vast datasets. In this way, data derivatives come into being. Most interestingly, these data derivatives do not register any of the primary information as to personal identities, flying habits, means of payment or the like. What they do, on the contrary, is to infer what might become of patterns as revealed by probabilistic association rules. What pattern of social practice whose digital traces were collected is correlated with possible terrorist deeds? This mining of data at a massive scale enhances counter-terrorism insofar it transforms probable associations between people, objects or behaviours into decision-making material.

These administrative routines of massive electronic surveillance aimed at risk suppression enable an array of correlated illiberal practices. Even though a disturbing number of European Member States have willingly collaborated in the US covert renditions program,[81] such hard counter-terrorist practices as targeted assassination and so-called 'enhanced interrogations' have not been a key feature of the EU response to terrorism in the post-9/11 era. The EU has also resorted to blacklisting and asset freezing in order to disrupt terrorist networks.[82] Preventative measures aimed at suspending organizational or individual activities that are suspected to be linked to terrorism, blacklisting or delisting procedures rely on intelligence provided by security agencies. This intelligence usually stems from the above-mentioned electronic data mining as well as transatlantic cooperation. Furthermore, financial institutions are required to contribute actively by reporting financial movements that they deem suspicious, thus playing the role of clearing houses. Blacklisting entails drastic consequences, as the financial assets of blacklisted individuals are instantly frozen. Therefore, although extrajudicial in nature, blacklisting yields stern punitive consequences for targeted individuals and organizations.

6. Effectiveness and impact of counter-terrorism: A reappraisal

The previous sections have provided a cursory examination of the underpinnings and actual practices of counter-terrorism in Europe. Drawing on both,

---

81 D. Marty, *Alleged Secret Detentions and Unlawful Inter-state Transfers Involving Council of Europe Member States. Draft Report – Part II (Explanatory Memorandum)* (Strasbourg: Council of Europe, 2006).

82 Council of the European Union, 'Council Regulation (EU) No. 1286/2009 of 22 December 2009 amending Regulation (EC) No 881/2002 imposing certain specific restrictive measures directed against certain persons and entities associated with Usama bin Laden, the Al-Qaida network and the Taliban'; Council of the European Union, 'Council Implementing Regulation (EU) No. 1285/2009 of 22 December 2009 implementing Article 2(3) of Regulation (EC) No 2580/2001 on specific restrictive measures directed against certain persons and entities with a view to combating terrorism and repealing Regulation (EC) No 501/2009'; Council of the European Union, 'Council Framework Decision 2003/577/JHA of 22 July 2003 on the execution in the European Union of orders freezing property or evidence'; See also C. Murphy *et al.*, this volume.

we are now in a position to hark back to some of the claims that were brought under examination above. We are more precisely able to shape a somewhat clearer understanding of the notions of effectiveness and impact that are, most of the time, implicitly built in the exception argument, the balancing metaphor and the trade-off model.

As regards the last two, both claims rely on a consequentialist assumption according to which, curtailing liberties will effectively and positively bear on security, and that encroaching on privacy will enhance surveillance. In other words, both arguments rest on a built-in requirement for a clear and unequivocal effectiveness evaluation so as to establish their respective legitimacy. In the words of Jeremy Waldron, 'we must insist that those who talk the balancing-talk step up to the plate with some actual predictions about effectiveness'.[83] Indeed, since one suspects that the legitimacy of counter-terrorist measures rests on an implicit trade-off between input (democratic) and output (effective) legitimacy, something must be said on the effectiveness of the purported practices.[84]

In this way, the legitimization of counter-terrorism echoes the issue of proportionality between means and ends. Consequentialist questions about the balancing metaphor and the trade-off model may be raised in a straightforward fashion, although some recall that the practices thus vindicated should be rejected on principled reasons alone.[85] To make matters worse, objections to both modes of legitimization of counter-terrorism may either play out as relatively weak ones, or end up justifying these practices.[86] Be that as it may, one cannot but take into account the logical requirement that follows from this; to assess the legitimacy of counter-terrorism, one needs to determine whether the practices that are brought in under this rubric actually make a difference.

Some studies tend to support the claim that counter-terrorist policies make a positive difference as regards terrorist violence. This difference may be reflected in a variety of heterogeneous indicators such as a decreasing number of terrorist attacks, low casualties resulting from the former, high frequency of arrests related to terrorist offences, high proportion of terrorist-related convictions, fading propaganda or terrorist 'noise' over the Internet or even the mere fact that counter-terrorist measures were adopted in the first place at EU level.[87] Others contend that counter-terrorist policies remain

83 J. Waldron, *supra* note 26, p.210.

84 L. Zedner, *supra* note 38, p.517; J. Goldston, *Ethnic Profiling and Counter-Terrorism Trends, Dangers and Alternatives. Paper Presented to the Anti-Racism and Diversity Intergroup* (Brussels: European Parliament, 2006) p.10; M. L. Wade, *supra* note 27, p.11.

85 B. J. Goold and L. Lazarus, *supra* note 26, p.11; J. Waldron, *supra* note 26, p.194.

86 M. Gani *et al.*, *supra* note 36, p.67.

87 N. Adams, T. Nordhaus and M. Schellenberger, *Counterterrorism since 09/11. Evaluating the Efficacy of Controversial Tactics* (Oakland: Breakthrough Institute 2011); R. Bossong, 'Public Good Theory and the "Added Value" of the EU's Anti-Terrorism Policy' (2012) *European Security*, October; B. Devoic, 'The Post-9/11 European Union Counterterrorism Response: Legal-Institutional Framework' (Monterey, California: Naval Postgraduate School 2012).

largely ineffective. Here again, indicators vary widely. Profiling techniques turn out to be either over- or under-inclusive, so that they yield disproportionate cases of false positives or negatives. Terrorists may be aware of counter-measures and consequently deploy adaptive strategies to circumvent or neutralize them. Instruments crafted at EU level may be marginalized by bilateral and/or informal initiatives. Counter-terrorist policies may have a very low cost-efficiency.[88] Others, still, find that terrorism and counter-terrorism vary rather independently from each other. Reviewing a number of quantitative studies pertaining to the effectiveness of counter-terrorist strategies in Europe and elsewhere, Lum *et al.* find that counter-terrorism does not have any discernible statistical effect on terrorist violence.[89] Finally, counter-terrorist policies may even have negative effectiveness to the extent that they yield counter-productive effects. Controversial counter-terrorist tactics may alienate communities whose support is needed to root out potential terrorist groups. Massive data mining may divert scarce resources from more traditional and effective policing. It may also generate informational noise that makes it difficult to process data into intelligence.[90]

This heterogeneity eclipses a sheer quantitative lack of empirical evaluation. One may bemoan the absence of data pertaining to the effectiveness of dataveillance, profiling and preventative asset freezing. In their oft-cited work, Lum *et al.* underscore that 'of the over 20,000 reports regarding terrorism that we located, only about 1.5% of this massive literature even remotely discussed the idea that an evaluation had been conducted of counter-terrorism strategies'.[91]

The absence of in-depth assessment into the effectiveness of counter-terrorist practices is instrumental in the ability of security agencies to ensure their neat reproduction over time. Amongst the above-mentioned field effect, one can observe that this social space releases a powerful pressure towards an unchecked expansion of the security activities that it hosts. The neutralization of 'reality checks', so to speak, entailed in effectiveness evaluation actively conditions the possibility of such functional growth.[92] A series of anonymous and unintended social processes come into play at this point. Impact assessments, dealing with the effects that a specific measure yields

---

88 J. Goldston, *supra* note 84.

89 C. Lum, L. W. Kennedy and A. J. Sherley, 'The Effectiveness of Counter-Terrorism Strategies' (2006) *Campbell Systematic Reviews* Fairfax County, VA, George Mason University: The Campbell Collaboration.

90 S. Leonard, 'The Use and Effectiveness of Migration Controls as a Counter-Terrorism Instrument in the European Union' (2010) *Central European Journal of International and Security Studies* Vol. 4 No. 1, pp. 46–47.

91 C. Lum *et al.*, *supra* note 89, p.13.

92 A. Spencer, 'The Problems of Evaluating Counter-Terrorism' (2006) *UNISCI Discussion Paper 12.* Madrid: UNISCI, p.180; S. Leonard, *supra* note 90, p.46; M. Brzoska, 'The Role of Effectiveness and Efficiency in the European Union's Counterterrorism Policy: The Case of Terrorist Financing' (2011) *Economics of Security Working Paper Series.* Berlin: European Commission, p. 1.

over a particular audience or phenomenon, are replaced by outcome or output evaluations, which are designed to tackle instead the institutional products delivered by the policy instrument at play. (There is more on the distinctions between impact, outcome and output below.)[93]

Most importantly, the European field of security professionals efficiently insulates itself from demands originating from other social settings. The risk narratives informing the doxa of the field are indeed readily imposed over the understanding of the average person. The media and the professionals of politics lose credibility when their security claims are not backed up by one or more of the agencies of the field. Most of all, actors and institutions embedded in this social space usually succeed in imposing their outputs as the basic material from which any endeavour to look into their effectiveness has to be conducted. A recent doctoral thesis dealing with counter-terrorism in Europe that we have quoted above epitomizes this difficulty to this extent that the effectiveness of these measures are gauged against the EU Terrorism Situation and Trend Report, which is published by Europol – that is one of the institutions whose effectiveness is brought under examination.[94] Indeed, the European field of security professionals successfully monopolizes claims over threats as well as claims over their management, including specific statements pertaining to effectiveness.[95]

The lack of empirical data on this issue casts doubt on the nature of counter-terrorist policies. To what extent do they partake in a kind of 'symbolic use of politics'[96] aimed at conveying the sense that something is getting done, irrespective of what difference this 'something' actually makes at the end of the day?[97] This hypothesis is further backed up by the importance of legitimacy struggles entailed in the relationship between terrorism and counter-terrorism. Many counter-terrorist measures rely heavily on representational strategies aimed at delegitimizing terrorist networks while, sometimes but not often, politicizing their demands.[98]

Building an empirically informed understanding of the effectiveness of counter-terrorist measures, an understanding that does not depend on the knowledge that security actors produce in the first place, therefore amounts to a tremendous challenge. Many epistemological hurdles stand in the way of the different methodological strands that one can single out in the available academic literature. Available studies tend to put the main emphasis

---

93 M. Brzoska, *supra* note 92, p.14.

94 B. Devoic, *supra* note 87, p.98.

95 D. Bigo, 'La mondialisation de l'(in)sécurité?' *Cultures & Conflits* (2005) no. 58 (June), p.68; D. Bigo *et al.*, *supra* note 29, p.111.

96 M. J. Edelman, *The Symbolic Uses of Politics* (Illini books ed. Urbana: University of Illinois Press 1985).

97 J. Waldron, *supra* note 26, p.209.

98 A. Chowdhury and R. R. Krebs, 'Talking about Terror: Counterterrorist Campaigns and the Logic of Representation' (2010) *European Journal of International Relations* Vol. 16 No. 1.

on quantitative approaches aimed at deciphering the influence that counter-terrorist policies yield over terrorist activity. Such approaches usually endeavor to establish statistical correlations between a range of interventions that are implemented at a clearly identified point in the timeline, and variations of terrorist attacks, bombings, hijackings or hostage-takings in the subsequent temporal segment.[99] Comparatively, qualitative data relying on the survey of relevant audiences by the means of interview, opinion polls, targeted surveys or focus groups, are less frequent.[100]

However, let us point out that this methodology has been put forth in British criminology to assess the robustness of the 'suspect community' thesis in the post-9/11 era. In particular, interviews with individuals from the British Muslim community were conducted in order to tease out their subjective perceptions of profiling practices to which they are exposed.[101]

Besides this rather traditional qualitative/quantitative dichotomy, a promising path for further research seems to lie with the above-mentioned output-outcome-impact trichotomy of effectiveness. Output-effectiveness investigates the features characteristic of a given counter-terrorist framework. For instance, the adoption of the Directive pertaining to the freezing of financial assets would, in its own right, be considered as evidence of output-effectiveness in the struggle against terrorist financing. Outcome-effectiveness brings under examination the compatibility of that which is delivered by the policy framework with the provisions that are built into its design. In our example, the quantity of assets effectively frozen under the adopted regulation would meet the standards of proof adjudication. Finally, impact-effectiveness tackles this issue pertaining to the behaviour of the targeted audience. To what extent does asset freezing lower terrorist occurrences?[102]

Qualitative as well as quantitative approaches, whether they look into output-, outcome- or impact-effectiveness, run into the following hurdles.

99 C. Lum *et al.*, *supra* note 89; T. Van Dongen, 'Break It Down: An Alternative Approach to Measuring Effectiveness in Counterterrorism' (*Economics of Security Working Paper* Series 23, DIW Berlin, German Institute for Economic Research 2009).

100 A. Spencer, *supra* note 92; A. Ellis, A. Cleary, M. Innes and M. Zeuthen, 'Monitoring and Evaluation Tools for Counterterrorism Program Effectiveness' (2011) *Policy Brief*, Washington D.C., Center on Global Counterterrorism Cooperation.

101 C. Pantazis and S. Pemberton, *supra* note 12; C. Pantazis and S. Pemberton, 'From the "Old" to the "New" Suspect Community Examining the Impacts of Recent UK Counter-Terrorist Legislation' (2009) *British Journal of Criminology* Vol. 49 No. 5; T. Choudhury and H. Fenwick, 'The Impact of Counter-Terrorism Measures on Muslim Communities' (2011) Research report 72. Equality and Human Rights Commission Research Report Series. Durham University: Equality and Human Rights Commission. For a methodological criticism see S. Greer, 'Human Rights and the Struggle against Terrorism in the United Kingdom' *European Human Rights Law Review* (2008) No. 2; S. Greer, 'Anti-Terrorist Laws and the United Kingdom's "Suspect Muslim Community": A Reply to Pantazis and Pemberton' (2010) *British Journal of Criminology* Vol. 50 No. 6.

102 M. Brzoska, *supra* note 92; E. Van Um and D. Pisoiu, 'Effective Counterterrorism: What Have We Learned so Far?' (2011) *Economics of Security Working Paper* Series 55. DIW Berlin, German Institute for Economic Research.

They tend to assume that terrorist actors behave according to an instrumental rationality, thus reacting to ecological incentives.[103] They all treat the absence of a major attack as a definitive indicator of success, while such a peaceful period may very well correspond to the planning of a future attack.[104] More generally, they use indicators whose reliability and validity depend closely on the type of effectiveness that is being investigated. While those measuring outcome and output dimensions are seemingly unproblematic, the indicators pertaining to impact remain broadly elusive.[105]

Harking back to what we have mentioned above, we cannot but strongly emphasize that indicators of output- and outcome-effectiveness are only unproblematic to the extent that they are controlled by those very actors whose organizational, institutional and professional interests are at stake in such assessments. In other words, the access to independent, precise, reliable information remains one of the core hurdles of this kind of investigation.[106] Finally, these studies run into problems pertaining to the attribution of causality; effects that are teased out by means of statistical methods only remain probabilistic artifacts, while that which is measured by more qualitative methods may turn out to be of anecdotal value.[107]

7. Conclusion

A societal approach to the legitimacy of counter-terrorism underscores, first and foremost, the process-based and contingent nature of legitimization that security actors carry out. The legitimization of counter-terrorism draws intensively on the core values that constitute the European political order as a liberal and democratic polity. But, by so doing, values such as the rule of law, liberty and privacy are reframed and displaced.

Claims to greater effectiveness of security measures are readily built into the rationale that justifies them. Building an empirically informed understanding of the effectiveness of counter-terrorist measures, an understanding that does not depend on the knowledge produced by security actors in the first place, therefore amounts to a tremendous challenge. Most of the methodological hurdles that previous studies into effectiveness or impact of counter-terrorist practices have run into, such as the availability of data, seem to stem from this core epistemological obstacle. However, a distinction between impact-, output- and outcome-effectiveness may be able to offer some critical purchase in this matter.

---

103 A. Spencer, *supra* note 92, p.183.

104 M. Brzoska, *supra* note 92, p.2.

105 E. Van Um and D. Pisoiu, *supra* note 102, pp. 7–10.

106 S. Leonard, *supra* note 90, pp. 40–41; M. Brzoska, *supra* note 92, p.10; E. Van Um and D. Pisoiu, *supra* note 102, p.11; T. Dragu, *supra* note 26, p.75.

107 J. Waldron, *supra* note 26, p.209; E. Van Um and D. Pisoiu, *supra* note 102, pp. 12–17.

Simply put, output-effectiveness gauges the ability of policy-makers to take action in response to a specific development. Outcome-effectiveness brings the design of the adopted policy under examination. It ought to be carefully underlined that output- and outcome-effectiveness have the potential to be readily instrumentalized by security actors as part of the legitimization strategies that they develop within the European field of security professionals.

Impact-effectiveness entails the consequence, both intended and unintended, that a specific measure has actually yielded on its primary audience, as well as on its secondary audience (those who are impacted although they were not meant to be impacted in the first place). Regarding, for instance, the struggle against terrorist financing, one may wonder how many plots or organizations were disrupted by the drying out of their funding due to these specific measures. But most importantly, one may also investigate what happens to those organizations that have nothing to do with transnational political violence but which were disrupted all the same by those very same mechanisms.

6 Democratic legitimacy, effectiveness and impact of EU counter-terrorism measures

*Yulia Chistyakova**

Democracy has multiple meanings and there is no one single measure of the legitimacy of counter-terrorism measures from a democratic theory perspective. This chapter focuses on several aspects of the democratic legitimacy of EU counter-terrorism (CT) measures that are prioritized in contemporary policy and academic debate. These include input, output and rights legitimacy. 'Input' legitimacy is concerned with the capacity of citizens to decide and to have an informed opinion of CT measures, through representation (the role of parliaments), transparency (who decides on what issues and availability of information), accountability (decision-makers account for their decisions to citizens) and participation (citizen involvement in the making of decisions). The effectiveness of counter-terrorism measures (the extent to which they can be said to achieve their intended aims of preventing, or reducing the risk of, terrorism) is seen as a measure of their 'output' legitimacy. Finally, a liberal view of democratic legitimacy prioritizes the impact of these measures on equality and fundamental liberties and rights. The chapter starts by offering an analytical framework for the democratic legitimacy of CT measures, which is then used to assess the democratic legitimacy, effectiveness and impact of EU CT measures.

1. How can the legitimacy, effectiveness and impact of counter-terrorism be understood from democratic theory perspectives?

This chapter will draw upon three democratic theory perspectives on legitimate political authority. First, a state-centred perspective that originates from Hobbesian understandings of legitimacy as derived from the ability of a centralized political authority to guarantee individual and collective security. From that perspective, sometimes referred to as an 'output legitimacy' perspective, CT measures of a political authority are legitimate as long as they are effective in protecting citizens from terrorism: 'government for the people'

* School of Applied Social Sciences, Durham University.

(see Table 1). It does not matter from this perspective how the decisions were made, as long as they achieved their objective of citizen protection. Furthermore, the achievement of security may require and can justify certain infringements of people's rights and freedoms.

In contrast, the second, 'input legitimacy' perspective puts emphasis on the expression of popular will and can be traced back to the classical political theory ideas of the consent of the governed and democratic public participation. The 'popular will' (or input legitimacy) perspective prioritizes various ways in which people can express their will and/or be able to authorize the decisions made on their behalf and hold decision-makers to account, in particular through representation (majority voting and parliaments),[1] participation in decision-making and deliberation, and communicative processes involved in elections and other forms of discursive interactions with the public and civil society.[2] The key questions here are of the transparency of decisions; whether it is clear who decides and on what issues and whether openness and access to information allow citizens to make an informed opinion.[3] From the popular will perspective, CT measures are legitimate if they (a) can be traced back to the authorization given by citizens, (b) the decision-makers can be held effectively accountable for these decisions.

Third, liberal perspectives emphasize the mechanisms of equality, minority protections, and the protection of individual freedoms and human rights (for example, through an independent judiciary, judicial review, liberal laws and checks and balances). From these perspectives, equal treatment of citizens and the protection of fundamental rights and liberties is more important than the achievement of total security. This principle would guide the assessment of security policies in terms of their impact on fundamental rights and civil liberties and respect for minority rights.[4] CT decisions are legitimate

---

1 B. Kohler-Koch and B. Rittberger, 'Charting Crowded Territory: Debating the Democratic Legitimacy of the European Union' in B. Kohler-Koch and B. Rittberger (Eds), *Debating the Democratic Legitimacy of the European Union* (Lanham: Rowman and Littlefield, 2007), p.12; V. Schmidt, 'Democracy and Legitimacy in the European Union Revisited: Input, Output and "Throughput"' (2013) *Political Studies* Vol. 61, pp. 2–22.

2 S. Lucarelli, F. Cerutti and V. A. Schmidt (Eds), *Debating Political Identity and Legitimacy in the European Union* (London: Routledge, 2011); T. Risse, *A Community of Europeans?* (Ithaca NY: Cornell University Press, 2010) pp. 127–57; J. Steffek, 'The Legitimation of International Governance' (2003) *European Journal of International Relations* Vol. 9 No. 2, pp. 249–75; M. Zürn, 'Democratic Governance beyond the Nation-State' (2000) *European Journal of International Relations* Vol. 6 No. 2, pp. 183–221; V. Schmidt, 'Democracy and Legitimacy in the European Union Revisited: Input, Output and "Throughput"', (2013) *Political Studies* Vol. 61, p.5; B. Kohler-Koch and B. Rittberger, 'Charting Crowded Territory: Debating the Democratic Legitimacy of the European Union' in B. Kohler-Koch and B. Rittberger (Eds), *Debating the Democratic Legitimacy of the European Union*, (Lanham: Rowman and Littlefield, 2007) p.12.

3 H. Sjursen 'Not so Intergovernmental after All? On Democracy and Integration in European Foreign and Security Policy' (2011) *Journal of European Public Policy*, Vol. 18, No. 8, pp. 1078–95.

4 C. Kantner and A. Liberatore, 'Security and Democracy in the European Union: An Introductory Framework' (2006) *European Security* Vol. 15 No. 4, pp. 363–83, p.365.

Table 1 A summary of democratic perspectives on legitimacy of counter-terrorism measures

Perspective	*Criteria of legitimacy*	*Mechanisms/principles of governance*	*Measures*
Output (effectiveness)	Effective protection of citizens from terrorism	Expert deliberation, intelligence information sharing and decision-making	Are the measures effective in protecting citizens from terrorism?
Input (popular will)	Decisions can be traced back to the authorization given by citizens and decision-makers can be held to account	Majoritarian institutions and representation through vote/ elections (parliaments) Participation (consultation, citizens' initiative) Accountability mechanisms	Who makes decisions and on what issues? Are decision-making processes transparent? Can public access information and develop informed opinion? Can citizens hold decision-makers to account?
Liberal (equality, rights and freedoms)	Effective safeguards to ensure equality and protection of freedoms and rights	Independent judiciary, judicial review, checks and balances	Are effective safeguards in place to protect the rights of the accused? What is the broader impact of decisions on civil liberties and human rights?

from the liberal perspective if there are effective legal, procedural and institutional safeguards in place to ensure equality and protection of freedoms and rights of citizens.

These three perspectives and corresponding criteria, principles of governance and measures of legitimacy of counter-terrorism measures are summarized in Table 1.

'Democratic legitimacy' can thus be understood as a broad notion comprising output (effectiveness of the measures), input (expression of popular will) and liberal safeguards from abuses of power. The *effectiveness* of counter-terrorism measures is understood as a type of democratic legitimacy that prioritizes outputs of decisions, while the *impact* of counter-terrorism measures can be measured in relation to the various aspects of democratic legitimacy, including: (a) the rights and freedoms that these decisions are likely to affect, (b) the democratic system (the institutions and processes of decision-making in column three), and (c) the values of democracy (for example, greater emphasis on output/effectiveness at the expense of input [popular will], or at the expense of rights and freedoms, or vice versa).

Achieving a proper balance between the three modes of legitimacy is the core issue in achieving democratically legitimate policies. Which aspects of legitimacy should be given more attention in the EU is subject to ongoing debate. The tension between 'output' and 'input' legitimacy is often seen as a trade-off between 'democratic values' and 'effectiveness of policy-making',[5] and while some warn against trading democratic values for effectiveness of policies, others have argued that it is the EU's performance (output legitimacy) that is more of a problem than its input legitimacy.[6]

This analytical framework will be used to make judgements about the legitimacy, effectiveness and impact of EU CT measures. This chapter will review academic debates about EU CT measures and will outline some of the key concerns with regards to legitimacy, effectiveness and impact identified above. Before moving on to this analysis, however, the applicability of the democratic perspectives on legitimacy, effectiveness and impact to the EU polity will be considered.

2. The EU and democracy

The application of the concepts of democratic legitimacy, effectiveness and impact to the EU polity involves questions about the nature of the EU and its relationship with nation-states. The key question is whether the EU represents a realm of intergovernmentalism, which means that the power of decision-making remains in the hands of nation-states, or whether it is a supranational polity to which nation states transfer some of their sovereignty. While some scholars maintain that the EU remains essentially a regulatory tool in the hands of nation-states, others have argued that the EU has made an effort to move beyond intergovernmentalism and 'to define European interests, as well as European values'.[7] In the former case, the criteria of legitimacy, effectiveness and impact of EU CT measures would apply to each Member State rather than to the EU as a whole, as states remain the legitimate decision-makers, providers of security and guarantors of rights. However, if the EU is more than an area of intergovernmentalism, these legitimacy notions may no longer be applicable to the nation-states, and it is the EU as a political authority that must be assessed in terms of the legitimacy, effectiveness and impact of its decisions.

But can one apply a state-centred understanding of democracy to the EU polity? On the one hand, political declarations made on behalf of the EU suggest that there is a perception of the EU as a polity based on a set of democratic principles and values. The Treaty of Lisbon states that the three core principles of democratic governance in Europe are democratic equality (the

5 G. Peters and J. Pierre in B. Kohler-Koch and B. Rittberger, *supra* note 1, p.9.

6 T. Padoa-Schioppa, 'Conclusion' in R. Matarazzo (Ed.) *Democracy in the EU after the Lisbon Treaty* (Rome: Istituto Affari Internazionali, 2011).

7 H. Sjursen, *supra* note 3, p.1088.

European institutions must give equal attention to all citizens), representative democracy (a greater role for the European Parliament [EP] and greater involvement for national parliaments), and participatory democracy (new forms of interaction between citizens and the European institutions, like the citizens' initiative).[8] In addition, 'human dignity, freedom, democracy, equality, the rule of law and the respect for human rights . . . are the core values of the EU which are set out at the beginning of the Treaty of Lisbon'.[9]

On the other hand, it has often been argued that, while the EU is more than an area of interaction between sovereign states, it is not the same as a nation-state. For example, von Bogdandy argues that 'it is beyond question that the principle of democracy requires a specific concretization for the European Union and . . . any analogy to nation-state institutions must be carefully argued'.[10] This raises a number of questions, such as to what extent states collectively share sovereignty over aspects of security decision-making, and how EU security decisions can be legitimate and effective and respect the fundamental rights and freedoms of EU citizens.

One answer to these questions is that that the EU is a regulatory, not a political, body and its decisions should only be judged in terms of *output legitimacy*. According to this position, EU decisions are always positive-sum and the only possible outcomes are those that leave everyone better off or at least not worse off than before.[11] This means that the effectiveness of EU decisions is what really matters and the legitimacy of EU policy-making is based on policy outcomes, not democratic input.[12] Reflecting

8 Europa (n.d.) 'A More Democratic and Transparent Europe' in *Europa, Treaty of Lisbon, Taking Europe into the 21st Century*. Available online at http://europa.eu/lisbon_treaty/glance/democracy/ (accessed 22 September 2013).

9 Ibid.

10 A. von Bogdandy, 'Remarks on European Democracy as a Legal Principle' in B. Kohler-Koch and B. Rittberger (Eds), *Debating the Democratic Legitimacy of the European Union* (Lanham: Rowman and Littlefield, 2007), p.35.

11 G. Marks, L. Hooghe and K. Blank, 'European Integration from the 1980s: State-centric v. Multi-level Governance' (1996) *Journal of Common Market Studies* Vol. 34 No. 3, pp. 341–78; C. Joerges and J. Neyer, 'Transforming Strategic Interaction into Deliberative Problem-solving: European Comitology in the Foodstuffs Sector' (1997) *Journal of European Public Policy* Vol. 4 No. 4, pp. 609–25; C. Joerges and J. Neyer, 'From Intergovernmental Bargaining to Deliberative Political Processes: the Constitutionalisation of Comitology' (1997) *European Law Journal* Vol. 3 No. 3, pp. 273–99; C. Joerges and E. Vos (Eds), *EU Committees. Social Regulation, Law and Politics* (Oxford: Hart, 1999); J. Neyer, 'Discourse and Order in the EU' (2003) *Journal of Common Market Studies* Vol. 41 No. 4, pp. 687–706 cited in E. Eriksen, 'Governance Between Expertise and Democracy: the Case of European Security' (2011) *Journal of European Public Policy* Vol. 18, No. 8, pp. 1169–89, p.1179.

12 G. Majone, 'Europe's "Democratic Deficit": The Question of Standards' (1998) *European Law Journal* Vol. 4 No. 1, pp. 5–28; G. Majone, 'The Credibility Crisis of Community Regulation' (2000) *Journal of Common Market Studies* Vol. 38 No. 2, pp. 273–302; G. Majone, 'The European Commission: The Limits of Centralization and the Perils of Parliamentarization'(2002) *Governance* Vol. 15 No. 3, pp. 375–92; G. Majone, 'Delegation of Regulatory Powers in a Mixed Polity' (2002) *European Law Journal* Vol. 8 No. 3, pp. 319–39 in A. Follesdal and S. Hix 'Why There is a Democratic Deficit in the EU: a Response to Majone and Moravcsik' (2006) *Journal of Common Market Studies* Vol. 44 No 3, pp. 533–62, p.538.

on the future of European integration, Majone anticipates the possibility of the emergence of a number of 'clubs' of European states forming around different 'club goods', collective security being one of such collective goods.[13]

In contrast to the above view, others see the EU as a political body that should be judged in terms of its *input legitimacy.* Some of those who see the input legitimacy of EU decisions as important argue that robust democratic control mechanisms are in place in the EU.[14] These controls include constitutional checks and balances, the European Parliament and indirect control via national governments. It is argued that taken together, these mechanisms ensure that EU policy-making is nearly always transparent, accountable and effective.[15]

Others, while agreeing that the input legitimacy of EU decisions is important, argue that the Union suffers from a 'democratic deficit' – the lack of some of the aspects of political authority that sovereign states possess. One of these aspects is a common citizenry and political identity (or EU demos), which, it is argued, are absent at the EU level because of the lack of common memories, experience and communication.[16] The lack of common citizenry means that democratic debate at the EU level is absent.[17] Furthermore, there are no truly 'European' elections and the EU is "too distant" from voters'.[18] This view is supported by the Spring 2013 Euro-Barometer survey in which over two-thirds of Europeans felt that their voice did not count in the EU (67 per cent), an upward trend from 53 per cent in the spring of 2009.[19] Based on these findings, it could be argued that policy areas which require high levels of solidarity or a common identity (such as CT) should either remain fully within the nation states, or be subject to intergovernmental, rather than supranational, decision-making.

Another democratic deficit argument is that democratic processes do not work properly at the EU level because of the complexity of its institutional architecture and/or overlapping or unbalanced responsibilities of its

---

13 G. Majone, *Dilemmas of European Integration: The Ambiguities and Pitfalls of Integration by Stealth* (Oxford University Press, 2005); in G. Majone 'Rethinking European Integration after the Debt Crisis' (the European Institute, 2012), p.24. Available online at http://www.ucl.ac.uk/european-institute/analysis-publications/publications/WP3.pdf (accessed 23 August 2013).

14 A. Moravcsik, 'In Defence of the "Democratic Deficit": Reassessing Legitimacy in the European Union' (2002) *Journal of Common Market Studies* Vol. 40 No. 4, pp. 603–24.

15 Ibid., p.605.

16 P. Kielmansegg in B. Kohler-Koch and B. Rittberger *supra* note 1, pp. 6–7; M. Jolly, *The European Union and the People* (Oxford University Press, 2007), p.61.

17 See Doody and van der Hilst, this volume.

18 A. Follesdal and S. Hix, *supra* note 12, p.5.

19 Euro-Barometer (2013) 'Public Opinion in the European Union, First Results', in European Commission, *Standard Eurobarometer* 79. Available online at http://ec.europa.eu/public_opinion/archives/eb/eb79/eb79_first_en.pdf (accessed 22 September 2013).

decision-making bodies. One of the issues is the absence of a vertical separation of powers – for example, the Commission combines executive, legislative and bureaucratic functions.[20] Another issue is an imbalance within the dual system of legitimacy (the Council and the EP), with the relatively weak position of the EP.[21] Third, it is argued that the multiple levels of the EU decision-making system and the shift from hierarchy to networking and informality undermine political equality and control. The latter means that there is a combination of horizontal and vertical types of governance, that 'expertocracy' is playing an increasingly influential role and that new governance sites bypass traditional channels of representation and accountability.[22] The combination of different modes and styles of governance makes some suggest that the EU combines supranational, intergovernmental and federal traits,[23] and that it is a new kind of political entity altogether, variously characterized as a 'post-modern' or 'non-state' political entity, or as a 'sui generis system of multilayered and polycentric governance'.[24]A key challenge within this political system is 'who decides' and who should be held accountable for EU decisions.

Some scholars have argued that, while there is a problem of democratic deficit, the democratic potential of the EU can be realized via institutional reforms and societal practice.[25] The Lisbon Treaty, for example, is seen as having the potential to reinforce representative and participatory dimensions of democracy, giving citizens greater control over EU decision-making.[26] Even those who see the EU as a non-political 'club' believe that it would benefit from greater transparency in decision-making, *ex post facto* review by courts and ombudsmen, greater professionalism and technical expertise, rules that protect the rights of minority interests, and better scrutiny by private actors, the media, and parliamentarians at both the EU and national

20 R. Del Sarto, 'Security and Democracy: A Reprise' (2006) *European Security*, Vol. 15 No. 4, pp. 507–18, p.512.

21 B. Kohler-Koch and B. Rittberger, *supra* note 1, p.7; S.S. Andersen and T. Burns (1996) 'The European Union and the Erosion of Parliamentary Democracy: A Study of Post-parliamentary Governance' in S.S. Anderson and K.A. Eliassen (Eds), *The European Union: How Democratic Is It?* (London: Sage, 1996); T. Raunio, 'Always One Step Behind? National Legislatures and the European Union' (1999) *Government and Opposition* Vol. 34 No. 2, pp. 180–202 in A. Follesdal and S. Hix *supra* note 12, p.534.

22 B. Kohler-Koch and B. Rittberger, *supra* note 1, p.10.

23 R. Del Sarto, *supra* note 20; H. Sjursen, *supra* note 3.

24 R. Del Sarto, *supra* note 20, p.512.

25 A. Follesdal and S. Hix, *supra* note 12.

26 J. Mayoral, 'Democratic Improvements in the European Union Under the Lisbon Treaty. Institutional Changes Regarding Democratic Government in the EU' (2011) *Robert Schuman Centre for Advanced Studies*, p.1. Available online at http://www.eui.eu/Projects/EUDO-Institutions/Documents/EUDOreport922011.pdf (accessed 23 August 2013).

levels.[27] Others are more sceptical of the attempts to strengthen democracy at the EU level as they believe these processes may weaken democracy at national levels; some scholars, for example, are concerned about the impact of the Lisbon Treaty on national constitutions and on the role of the Member States in the protection of citizens.[28]

The debate outlined above shows the importance of input (popular will) and output (effectiveness) legitimacy questions at the EU level. The nature of the EU as an area of intergovernmentalism and a regulatory body is increasingly questioned, and concerns are raised about the extent to which decisions made at the EU level are subject to democratic control. The key questions in terms of input legitimacy are 'who decides' and 'who should be held accountable'. At the same time, one cannot underestimate the issue of 'output legitimacy', or the effectiveness of EU decisions. If decisions at the EU level produce 'collective goods', the key question is of the extent to which they benefit (or not) EU citizens collectively. The importance of these questions is clear when it comes to CT measures that promise to enhance collective security in the EU. A comprehensive assessment of the legitimacy of EU CT decisions requires, therefore, the use of both input and output legitimacy criteria.

A further question concerns the extent to which EU decisions should take account of the protections of equality, fundamental rights and freedoms of EU citizens (the liberal conception of democracy in Table 1), as well as the extent to which the EU is able to provide such guarantees. Should the protection of rights and freedoms be left to nation-states, or should it be, to one extent or another, delegated to the EU level? The answer depends on whether the EU is seen as a realm of 'intergovernmentalism' or a political body in its own right, and whether one adopts a cosmopolitan 'global citizen' perspective,[29] or a nationalist perspective on rights.[30] A global perspective

27 G. Majone, 'Europe's "Democratic Deficit": The Question of Standards' (1998) *European Law Journal* Vol. 4 No. 1, pp. 5–28; G. Majone, 'The Credibility Crisis of Community Regulation' (2000) *Journal of Common Market Studies* Vol. 38 No. 2, pp. 273–302; G. Majone, 'The European Commission: The Limits of Centralization and the Perils of Parliamentarization' (2002) *Governance* Vol. 15 No. 3, pp. 375–92; G. Majone, 'Delegation of Regulatory Powers in a Mixed Polity' (2002) *European Law Journal* Vol. 8 No. 3, pp. 319–39; R. Dehousse, 'Constitutional Reform in the European Community: Are There Alternatives to the Majoritarian Avenue?' in J. Hayward (Ed.), *The Crisis of Representation in Europe* (London: Frank Cass, 1995) cited in A. Follesdal and S. Hix, *supra* note 12, p.538.

28 K. Kruma, 'Constitutional Courts and the Lisbon Treaty the Future Based on Mutual Trust' (2010) in *The Area of Freedom, Security and Justice, Ten Years On* (CEPS, 2010) available online at http://www.isn.ethz.ch/Digital-Library/Publications/Detail/?ots591=0c54e3b3–1e9c-be1e-2c24a6a8c7060233&lng=en&id=117517 (accessed 23 August 2013).

29 B. Hudson, 'Justice in a Time of Terror' (2009) *British Journal of Criminology* Vol. 49, pp. 702–17.

30 B. Van Riezen and K. Roex, 'Counter-Terrorism in the Netherlands and the United Kingdom: a Comparative Literature Review Study' (2011) *Social Cosmos, URN:NBN:NL:UI:10-1-112469*, p.100. Available online at http://socialcosmos.library.uu.nl/index.php/sc/article/viewFile/52/47 (accessed 23 August 2013).

would imply that 'the subject of rights moved from the citizen to the human being'.[31] However, the relationship between global or supranational rights and democracy is not straightforward.[32] And if rights only apply to EU citizens, one must ask what happens to the rights and liberties of non-citizens travelling to or residing in the EU (and who are likely to be affected by EU CT measures), as well as of those living outside the EU.

To explore the three dimensions of the democratic legitimacy of EU CT measures further, the next section will identify and outline several key concerns that arise in this respect.

3. Concerns about the democratic legitimacy of EU counter-terrorism measures

European Union security policies reveal most clearly the urgency of the democratic deficit and legitimacy questions. The last two decades saw the EU emerging on the global stage as a security player with a distinct identity, shifting its focus from economic, social and environmental to security issues.[33] This includes the development of the Common Foreign and Security Policy (CFSP), the Justice and Home Affairs 'pillar' and later, the area of freedom, security and justice (AFSJ), the adoption of the European security strategy[34] and the Stockholm programme,[35] and particularly the adoption of the whole raft of counter-terrorism legislation since 9/11.[36] This arguably means that EU security policies no longer belong to the realm of national policies and relationships among sovereign states.[37] The apparent loss of national sovereignty in this area and the alleged democratic deficit of the EU have raised concerns about the risks of undermining democratic principles, values and fundamental rights and freedoms, together with concerns about the effectiveness of these policies.[38]

---

31 D. Bigo, S. Carrera and E. Guild, 'The Changing Landscape of European Liberty and Security: Mid-Term Report on the Results of the Challenge Project' (2006) *CEPS, Justice and Home Affairs, Challenge Papers*, p.23. Available online at http://www.ceps.be/book/changing-landscape-european-liberty-and-security-mid-term-report-results-challenge-project (accessed 23 August 2013).

32 H. Sjursen, 'The EU's Common Foreign and Security Policy: the Quest for Democracy' (2011b) *Journal of European Public Policy* Vol. 18 No. 8, pp. 1069–77.

33 C. Kantner and A. Liberatore, *supra* note 4. pp. 372–3; H. Sjursen, *supra* note 3, p.1088.

34 Council of the European Union, *European Security Strategy, A Secure Europe in a Better World* (2009). Available online at http://www.consilium.europa.eu/uedocs/cms_data/librairie/PDF/QC7809568ENC.pdf (accessed 30 August 2014).

35 European Council, *The Stockholm Programme – an Open and Secure Europe Serving and Protecting Citizens* (2010). Available online at http://europa.eu/legislation_summaries/human_rights/fundamental_rights_within_european_union/jl0034_en.htm (accessed 30 August 2014).

36 See B. Hayes and C. Jones, this volume.

37 C. Kantner and A. Liberatore, *supra* note 4.

38 C. Kantner and A. Liberatore, *supra* note 4, p.374; M. Den Boer, C. Hillebrand and A Nölke, 'Legitimacy under Pressure: The European Web of Counter-Terrorism Networks' (2008) *Journal of Common Market Studies*,Vol.46 No. 1, pp. 101–24.

Several key areas of concern regarding the democratic legitimacy of EU CT measures can be identified. The first one is the expansion of the security governance area, which arguably leads to the weakening of democratic control. Initially, CT policies were developed within Justice and Home Affairs, but later expanded to a more intergovernmental area of policy-making where democratic controls are considerably weaker.[39] This policy area also expands beyond existing democratic controls via networks of experts characterized by variable patterns of information sharing.[40]

The second matter of concern is the lack of transparency and accountability in horizontal governance networks.[41] Horizontal CT networks involve various agencies and create informal communication forums between them in addition to the formal ones. They also involve third parties. For example, in the CFSP area, decisions are taken by the foreign ministers of all the Member States in the Foreign Affairs Committee (FAC), or by the heads of state and government in the European Council. However, NGOs and private corporations also influence decisions, and most importantly, the permanent intergovernmental institutions in Brussels are involved. These include the Political and Security Committee, various working groups such as the EU Military Committee, the Committee for Civilian Aspects of Crisis Management, the High Representative and the European External Action Service. The international nature of the CT networks, their loose structure and the variety of actors involved fragments accountability and limits the effectiveness of parliamentary and judicial scrutiny of decisions.[42] Decisions are made by 'experts' in secrecy and 'behind closed doors'.[43] The use of flexible mechanisms and the employment of urgency procedures create further challenges in terms of holding decision-makers to account.[44] CT policing is an area that lacks parliamentary and judicial scrutiny, even though the Lisbon Treaty extended the European Parliament's powers of oversight and co-decision in this area.[45] The key issue appears to be the difficulty of identifying

---

39 E. Guild, 'The Uses and Abuses of Counter-Terrorism Policies in Europe: The Case of the "Terrorist Lists", (2008) *Journal of Common Market Studies*, Vol. 46 No 1, pp. 173–93, p.174; S. Carrera and E. Guild, 'Does the Stockholm Programme Matter? The Struggles over Ownership of AFSJ Multiannual Programming' (2012) *CEPS, Justice and Home Affairs, Liberty and Security in Europe Papers*, p. 200. Available online at http://www.ceps.eu/book/does-stockholm-programme-matter-struggles-over-ownership-afsj-multiannual-programming (accessed 23 August 2013). See also J. Doody, this volume.

40 D. Bigo, 'Liberty, Whose Liberty? The Hague Programme and the Conception of Freedom' in T. Balzacq and S. Carrera (Eds), *Security v Freedom? A Challenge for Europe's Future* (Aldershot: Ashgate, 2006) cited in E. Guild, *supra* note 39, p.174.

41 M. Den Boer et al, *supra* note 38.

42 C. Hillebrand, *Counter-Terrorism Networks in the European Union: Maintaining Democratic Legitimacy after 9/11* (Oxford: Oxford University Press, 2012).

43 E. Eriksen, *supra* note 11, p. 1175–6.

44 G. Bono, 'Challenges of Democratic Oversight of EU Security Policies' (2006) *European Security* Vol. 15 No. 4, pp. 431–49, p.432.

45 C. Hillebrand, *supra* note 42.

those responsible for particular decisions and holding them to account. Other challenges include the problems of representation in the EU and the lack of clear separation between law-making and executive functions, the ambiguous nature of laws and norms that govern the security domain and the lack of international oversight. All of which suggests that EU CT measures lack input legitimacy and tend to undermine democratic oversight and civil liberties.[46]

The Lisbon Treaty has introduced a number of changes to the EU's AFSJ policy landscape with potentially significant implications for the democratic legitimacy of CT measures. Of particular relevance are the increased powers of the EP (the co-decision power)[47] and the jurisdiction of the Court of Justice of the European Union to review and interpret AFSJ law and actions.[48] The voting down in February 2010 of the so-called SWIFT agreement between the EU and the US can arguably be seen as an example of the new role of the EP.[49] The agreement on banking data transfers to the USA via the SWIFT network was voted down on the grounds of poor protection of fundamental rights, such as the right to privacy, and concerns about potential misuse of data. A number of concessions were gained, even though, when the agreement was eventually adopted, concerns about privacy remained.[50] An example of the role of the Court of Justice in interpreting decisions affecting the fundamental rights of EU citizens is the recent striking down of the Data Retention Directive by the Court.[51] The Directive was introduced in 2006, after the London and Madrid bombings, requiring telecoms firms to retain citizens' communication data for up to two years and allowing the

---

46 T. Delpech, 'International Terrorism and Europe' (2002) *EU-ISS Chaillot Paper No.56*; D. Keohane, 'The EU and Counter-Terrorism' (2005) *London: CER Working Paper*; E. Guild, *Security and European Human Rights: Protecting Individual Rights in Times of Exception and Military Action* (Nijmwegen: Wolf, 2007); D. Bigo, 'Liberty, Whose Liberty? The Hague Programme and the Conception of Freedom' in T. Balzacq and S. Carrera (Eds) *Security v Freedom? A Challenge for Europe's Future* (Aldershot: Ashgate, 2006); I. Loader, 'Policing, Securitization and Democratization in Europe' (2002) *Criminal Justice* No. 2, pp. 125–53 cited in G. Edwards and C. Meyer, 'Introduction: Charting a Contested Transformation' (2008) *Journal of Common Market Studies* Vol. 46 No. 1, pp. 1–25, p.15.

47 European Union, *Treaty of Lisbon Amending the Treaty on European Union and the Treaty Establishing the European Community*, 13 December 2007, 2007/C 306/01, article 294. Available online at: http://www.refworld.org/docid/476258d32.html (accessed 30 August 2014).

48 Ibid., articles 251–81.

49 S. Carrera and E. Guild, *supra* note 39, p.20.

50 Digital Civil Rights Europe (2010) 'SWIFT Agreement Adopted by the European Parliament', in EDRi-gram – Number 8.14, 14 July, *Digital Civil Rights in Europe*. Available online at http://www.edri.org/edrigram/number8.14/swift-20-adopted-european-parliament (accessed 4 October 2013).

51 Court of Justice of the European Union (2014) *The Court of Justice Declares the Data Retention Directive to Be Invalid*, Press release No 54/14, Judgment in Joined Cases C-293/12 and C-594/12 Digital Rights Ireland and Seitlinger and Others, Luxembourg, 8 April 2014. Available online at http://curia.europa.eu/jcms/upload/docs/application/pdf/2014–04/cp140054en.pdf (accessed 5 September 2014).

competent national authorities to access the data.[52] In April 2014, the ECJ declared the Directive invalid on the basis that it violated the fundamental rights to respect for private life and to the protection of personal data. This, however, does not stop individual Member States adopting their own laws enabling retention and access to communications data (as the UK government did with the Data Retention and Investigatory Powers Act 2014).

While the Lisbon Treaty enhanced democratic control in some areas, other areas remain outside normal democratic processes; for example, operational police cooperation is not subject to the co-decision powers of the EP and remains 'subject to the unanimity in the Council and where the EP has only to be consulted'.[53] Furthermore, the Lisbon Treaty provides new tools to enhance police and judicial cooperation. The executive remains the most powerful player in this field, while citizens have only limited capacity to influence this area of policy-making.[54] It is also important to note that the vast majority of the currently legally binding CT measures were adopted before the Lisbon Treaty and thus were not subject to co-decision.[55]

Furthermore, the Commission retains unilateral legislative decision-making powers in respect of secondary legislation and the Council of the EU with regard to many security, military and foreign policy matters.[56] Parliamentary control remains limited in the area of CFSP as the EP does not have a formal role in this area. There is also an overlap between the competences of AFSJ and CFSP that create a potential for inter-institutional conflicts, particularly in relation to CT law.[57] An example of this was the conflict that emerged in the process of adoption of the amendments to Regulation 881/2002/EC imposing restrictive measures against certain persons and entities associated with Al-Qaida, the Taliban and Osama Bin Laden. The Council had adopted this Regulation on the basis of (CFSP) Article 215(2) TFEU under which a unanimously adopted CFSP decision is implemented by qualified majority in the Council on a joint proposal from the High Representative and the Commission. The EP only has to be informed about

52 See also B. Hayes and C. Jones, *The EU Data Retention Directive: a Case Study in the Legitimacy and Effectiveness of EU Counter-terrorism Policy* (SECILE Consortium, 2013). Available at http://secile.eu/wp-content/uploads/2013/11/Data-Retention-Directive-in-Europe-A-Case-Study.pdf (accessed 5 September 2014).

53 General Secretariat of the Council of the EU (2009) in C. Hillebrand, 'Guarding EU-wide Counter-terrorism Policing: The Struggle for Sound Parliamentary Scrutiny of Europol' (2011) *Journal of Contemporary European Research* Vol. 7 No. 4, pp. 500–19, p.506.

54 C. Hillebrand, *supra* note 53.

55 B. Hayes and C. Jones, 'Report on the Transposition of EU Counterterrorism Measures' (SECILE Consortium, 2013).

56 B. Hayes and C. Jones, *supra* note 55.

57 J. Monar, 'The External Dimension of the EU's Area of Freedom, Security and Justice Progress, Potential and Limitations after the Treaty of Lisbon' (2012) *Swedish Institute for European Policy Studies* pp. 28–9. Available online at http://www.sieps.se/sites/default/files/Rapport%202012_1_A5.pdf (accessed 23 August 2013).

the adopted measures. In contrast, under (AFSJ) Article 75 TFEU, the Council and the EP act in accordance with the ordinary legislative procedure, and without a prior CFSP decision. The Committee on Legal Affairs of the EP contested this decision, which resulted in an action of annulment before the European Court of Justice (as it then was).[58] Monar comments that Article 75 'provides an explicit legal base for the adoption of administrative measures aimed at freezing terrorist assets but the Council had preferred – no doubt primarily in order to avoid co-decision by the European Parliament under the "ordinary legislative procedure" . . . to use the much wider legal basis provided by Article 215(2) TFEU for imposing economic and financial sanctions in the CFSP context'.[59]

The third area of concern is the lack of clarity and consensus as to what it is that EU CT measures are meant to target: '"counter-terrorism"' is not yet a clearly defined area in its broadest and fullest sense' argues Oldrich Bures.[60] Similarly, Cian Murphy argues that states and international organizations 'have failed to agree a definition of that which they seek to combat'.[61] Even though, since 2002, the EU possesses a common definition of terrorism,[62] it has been criticized by many scholars for breadth and lack of precision.[63] The definition has been described as complex and uncertain and as leaving room for contrasting interpretations.[64] If there is no clarity of definition, then it becomes difficult to assess both the effectiveness of the measures (output legitimacy) and their impact.

The fourth area of concern is unevenness in Member States' perceptions of and responses to terrorism and the speed and extent to which they implement the Framework Decision.[65] Edwards and Meyer[66] argue that perceptions and conceptions of threat are very different in different Member

58 InfoCuria – Case-law of the Court of Justice (2012), Case C-130/10 European Parliament v. Council of the European Union. Available online at http://curia.europa.eu/juris/document/document.jsf?text=&docid=118841&pageIndex=0&doclang=EN&mode=lst&dir=&occ=first&part=1&cid=417783 (accessed 5 September 2014).

59 J. Monar, *supra* note 57, pp. 28–9.

60 O. Bures, *EU Counterterrorism Policy: a Paper Tiger?* (Farnham: Ashgate, 2011), p.1.

61 C. Murphy, *EU Counter-Terrorism Law* (Oxford and Portland: OR, 2012), p.5.

62 European Union: Council of the European Union, *Council Framework Decision 2002/584 on the European Arrest Warrant and the Surrender Procedures between Member States*, 13 June 2002, -002/584/JOHAN. Available online at: http://www.refworld.org/docid/3ddcfc495.html (accessed 5 September 2014).

63 O. Bures, *supra* note 60, pp. 2–3; E. Symeonidou-Kastanidou, 'Defining Terrorism' (2004) *European Journal of Crime, Criminal Law and Criminal Justice* Vol. 12 No. 1, pp. 14–35, p.28; J. Lang, 'EU Counter-Terrorism: Security, Justice, Democracy and Opportunity for All?' (2011) *E-International Relations*, p.4. Available online at http://www.e-ir.info/2011/08/14/eu-counter-terrorism-security-justice-democracy-and-opportunity-for-all/ (accessed 14 October 2013).

64 D. Casale, 'EU Institutional and Legal Counter-terrorism Framework' (2008) *Defence Against Terrorism Review* Vol. 1 No. 1, pp. 49–78, p.62.

65 Ibid.

66 G. Edwards and C. Meyer, *supra* note 46, pp. 5–7.

States. For example, there are stark differences between Scandinavian countries and many Eastern European countries on the one hand, and the UK, France and the Netherlands on the other, where the radicalization of European Muslims is seen as a concern and international terrorism is perceived as being linked to a wide range of other threats. The priority given to terrorism also varies significantly across countries. The majority of terrorist acts reported by the Member States are embedded in local and national contexts and only national and local authorities have full access to them.[67] Others note the lack of full and timely implementation at the national level of the key legal EU CT instruments, including the common definition of terrorism.[68] Similarly, Hayes and Jones[69] report uneven and slow transposition of EU CT measures. Casale[70] notes that 'whereas some Member States have not diverged significantly from their own national terrorism legislation, those who lacked such a basis in the first place have basically transposed the Framework Decision exactly into their national legislation – "failing to remedy the problem of vague definition"'. The main obstacle to harmonization of the legal framework is that Member States continue to perceive terrorist threats as national ones and prefer to develop national responses rather than to subject themselves to supranational rules, institutions and decision making.[71] The uneven, inconsistent and slow transposition of EU CT law is also related to the differences in state structure and policy processes.[72] The variation in national responses means that some states tend to overreact to the threat of terrorist violence.[73] Anti-terrorism objectives agreed upon by the Member States in the Council can then lead to more restrictive measures at the national level.[74] As noted by Hayes and Jones,[75] this has led to accusations of 'policy laundering' (states trying to pursue unpopular national CT objectives through EU fora). They also note that this is an area outside the normal parliamentary process as Member States use delegated powers to transpose the EU law. Democratic legitimacy is a problem because of the complexity of the connection between EU legislative procedure and domestic transposition,[76] meaning that it is difficult to identify who is responsible and for what issues (Table 1, input legitimacy)

67 S. Carrera and E. Guild, *supra* note 39.

68 O. Bures, *supra* note 60, pp. 1–2; J. Monar, 'Common Threat and Common Response? The European Union's Counter-Terrorism Strategy and its Problems' (2007) *Government and Opposition*, Vol. 42 No. 3, pp. 292–313, p.310.

69 B. Hayes and C. Jones, *supra* note 55.

70 D. Casale, 'EU Institutional and Legal Counter-terrorism Framework' (2008) *Defence Against Terrorism Review* Vol. 1 No. 1, pp. 49–78 in J. Lang, *supra* note 63, p.4.

71 J. Monar, *supra* note 68, p.309.

72 B. Hayes and C. Jones, *supra* note 55.

73 C. Murphy, *supra* note 61, pp. 6–7.

74 J. Monar, *supra* note 68, p.311.

75 B. Hayes and C. Jones, *supra* note 55.

76 Ibid.

and also because of a significant negative impact of the measures on civil liberties and human rights (see Table 1, the liberal conception of democratic legitimacy). This also raises questions concerning the effectiveness, appropriateness and proportionality of these measures;[77] research conducted by Hayes and Jones[78] shows that the rate of failure to implement CT-related directives is high, although the causes of this are not entirely clear. What this does make clear is that the effectiveness of the measures (output legitimacy, Table 1) is also in question.

A further, fifth, area of concern is the lack of provisions for evaluation of the legitimacy, effectiveness and impact of the measures on fundamental rights (*ex ante* consultation, *ex post facto* review and substantive reviews) and the lack of public access to this information, as well as the lack of meaningful consideration of independent expert reports.[79] All of this suggests that there is currently a severe lack of input legitimacy of EU CT measures (lack of access to information impairing the ability of citizens to have an informed opinion) and of their legitimacy in terms of impact on rights (Table 1).

4. Are counter-terrorism measures effective?

This section will look more closely at whether EU counter-terrorism measures are legitimate in the first sense outlined in Table 1, in terms of 'output legitimacy'.

Robust evaluation of the effectiveness of counter-terrorism measures is impeded by the lack of provisions for review, lack of information from Member States, and the difficulty of locating some of the relevant information or even knowing if it exists. Unsurprisingly, a number of commentators offer negative assessments of the output legitimacy of EU counter-terrorism. Bossong,[80] for example, argues that the EU is unlikely to acquire the necessary competences to prevent terrorism, which will undermine the output legitimacy of its counter-terrorism effort. Bossong's analysis of the EU's capacity to achieve the (pursue, protect, respond and prevent) objectives set out in the EU's counter-terrorism strategy shows that the effectiveness of these policies will continue to be restricted, on the one hand, by the lack of intelligence, information sharing and cultural and institutional obstacles to more police and criminal justice cooperation under an EU framework which 'can only be overcome very slowly',[81] and on the other hand, by judicial and political criticism of the policies. Bossong goes on to argue that

77 O. Bures, *supra* note 60, pp. 1–2.

78 B. Hayes and C. Jones, *supra* note 55.

79 B. Hayes and C. Jones, 'Report on How the EU Assesses the Impact, Legitimacy and Effectiveness of its Counter-terrorism Laws' (SECILE Consortium, 2013).

80 R. Bossong, 'The Action Plan on Combating Terrorism: A Flawed Instrument of EU Security Governance' (2008) *Journal of Common Market Studies* Vol. 46 No. 1, pp. 27–48.

81 Ibid., p.13.

the EU has almost no competences in matters of integration, education and social policy and thus cannot effectively counteract processes of radicalization and recruitment to terrorism and that 'there is only sporadic evidence that the EU is an effective "normative power" for global justice and democracy'.[82] He concludes that the inability of the EU to do much in terms of preventing terrorism seriously limits its output legitimacy.[83] Another issue noted in academic literature is that, when it comes to implementation, the EU still has to struggle with twenty-seven different systems with their own priorities and procedures,[84] and that national CT agencies continue to prefer bilateral and/or non-EU multilateral arrangements, while the capacity of EU CT agencies remains low.[85] In large part, the weakness of EU agencies stems from the lack of information. For example, Europol's main problem is arguably the imperfect flow of information from national intelligence services,[86] which are reluctant to share intelligence with it. Eurojust experiences similar problems.

However, there are some more optimistic assessments of the effectiveness of EU CT measures. For example, the Spokesman of the European People's Party European Parliament group (EPP-ED), Panayiotis Demetriou,[87] argues that 'The European Arrest Warrant has proved to be one of the most effective instruments in the field of police cooperation in the fight against organized crime, especially as compared to the traditional extradition proceedings. Some reforms are however necessary to improve on its effectiveness'. In terms of the expediency of extradition, EAW seems to be able to claim success, as it is broadly acknowledged that it has been successful in terms of reducing delays in extradition within the EU.[88] Some others also provide positive assessments of CT policy and particularly the EAW; for example, Bures argues that 'at least in some aspects and areas, the EU counter-terrorism policy is, albeit slowly and inconsistently, becoming a real tiger'.[89] The main achievement in his view was the adoption of a common definition of terrorism in 2002, allowing for the introduction of such instruments as the

82 Ibid., pp. 18–20.

83 Ibid., pp. 22–3.

84 J. Monar, *supra* note 68, p.310.

85 O. Bures, *supra* note 60, pp. 1–2.

86 D. Casale, *supra* note 64, p.57; G. Edwards and C. Meyer, *supra* note 46, p.9.

87 P. Demetriou, 'European Arrest Warrant – An Effective Instrument Against Organised Crime' (2006) *EPP Group in the European Parliament,* Press Release, par. 1. Available online at http://arc.eppgroup.eu/press/showpr.asp?prcontroldoctypeid=1&prcontrolid=4636&prcontentid=8396&prcontentlg=en (accessed 23 August 2013).

88 Euromove, 'The European Arrest Warrant'. Available online at http://www.euromove.org.uk/index.php?id=14973 (accessed 23 August 2013); Europa (n.d.) 'A More Democratic and Transparent Europe' *Europa, Treaty of Lisbon, Taking Europe into the 21st Century.* Available online at http://europa.eu/lisbon_treaty/glance/democracy/ (accessed 22 September 2013); See also Murphy et al, this volume, for an outline of this positive view of EAW from the case studies.

89 O. Bures, *supra* note 60, pp. 2–3.

European Arrest Warrant. Bures also argues that Europol and Eurojust are also increasingly recognized as doing a good job in the area of counter-terrorism.

With regards to asset freezing, the European Commission (2012) in its roadmap for 'the Framework for administrative measures for the freezing of funds, financial assets and economic gains of persons and entities suspected of terrorist activities inside the EU'[90] lists several advantages of the measures, such as the widening of the scope of control (measures are no longer limited to respective Member States), the ease with which financial institutions working in various Member States can control whether funds are linked to listed persons/entities, the possibility for all Member States to contribute to the identification of persons/entities concerned and take advantage of other Member States' experience and knowledge regarding persons and entities linked to terrorism, and potentially better compliance by Member States with the global Financial Action Task Force standards.

The effectiveness of EU CT measures can be assessed, not only in terms of the achievement of their objectives, but also in terms of alternative use of resources used to implement them, or costs associated with them. Schneider and colleagues argue that the 'second order effects' of CT measures are often overlooked.[91] For example, CT efforts might divert public spending away from potentially more effective projects towards security. An example of measures that may have undesirable costs and effects, while not having any positive impact, are security measures at borders, ports and airports that produce transportation costs that may distort economic activity, while not being a particularly effective security means at the same time. A change in foreign policy is also a second-order effect of CT in Europe; it may bring short-term benefits, but support of non-democratic regimes may contribute to the production of more grievances and thus transnational terrorism. Schneider and colleagues also argue that CT efforts may lead to transference and substitution effects such as transference of terrorist activity to more vulnerable countries in other parts of the world or changes in the tactics of terrorists (for example, making attacks on trains or buses instead of airports).

And yet, attempts to evaluate the capacity of CT measures to reduce the risk of terrorism are rare. An evaluation by Lum and colleagues concludes that 'not only did we discover an almost complete absence of evaluation

---

90 European Commission (2012) Roadmap, Framework for administrative measures for the freezing of funds, financial assets and economic gains of persons and entities suspected of terrorist activities inside the EU (Article 75 TFEU). Available online at http://ec.europa.eu/smart-regulation/impact/planned_ia/docs/2011_home_002_asset_freezing_en.pdf (accessed 5 September 2014).

91 F. Schneider, T. Brück and D. Meierrieks, 'The Economics of Terrorism and Counter-Terrorism: A Survey (Part II)' (2010) *Social Science Research Network* pp. 45–6. Available online at http://papers.ssrn.com/sol3/papers.cfm?abstract_id=1590148 (accessed 23 August 2013).

research on counter-terrorism interventions, but from those evaluations that we could find, it appears that some interventions either did not achieve the outcomes sought or sometimes increased the likelihood of terrorism occurring'.[92]

If effectiveness is understood as 'output legitimacy', the question then is whether there is a trade-off between the output and input legitimacy of CT measures such that it can justify an input legitimacy deficit (or, if greater output legitimacy, can justify the lack of input legitimacy). In the view of Den Boer et al, we need a systematic evaluation of CT initiatives in order to establish 'whether an (assumed) superior output legitimacy is able to compensate for the shortcomings in terms of input legitimacy'.[93] Lister and Jarvis in turn argue that '. . . clearly whether counter-terrorism powers are effective is a key concern, perhaps even a central one, to their assessment. But this rather narrow criterion cannot be the only concern meriting the revision of such powers'.[94] A major issue that needs to be considered, they argue, is the impact of these measures on communities and civil liberties.[95]

5. The impact of counter-terrorism measures on civil liberties and human rights

This section considers the impact of counter-terrorism measures in the third, liberal meaning outlined in Table 1, in terms of their impact on equality and citizens' rights and liberties. The main concern here is with the rights of those suspected of involvement in terrorism, although it must be recognized that CT measures also have broader eroding impact on the rights and freedoms of EU citizens.[96]

In that respect, scholars have noted some negative effects of CT measures, such as the uneven distribution of the restrictions of freedoms and the creation of suspect communities.[97] It has also been argued that CT has a

92 C. Lum, L. Kennedy and A. Sherley, 'Are Counter-terrorism Strategies Effective? The Results of the Campbell Systematic Review on Counter-terrorism Evaluation Research' (2006) *Journal of Experimental Criminology* Vol. 2, pp. 489–516, p.489.

93 M. Den Boer, C. Hillebrand and A. Nölke, *supra* note 38, p.120.

94 M. Lister and L. Jarvis, 'The Counter-Terrorism Review: Trading Liberty for Security' (2011) *Our Kingdom, Power and Liberty in Britain*, p.1. Available online at http://www.opendemocracy.net/ourkingdom/dr-michael-lister-dr-lee-jarvis/counter-terrorism-review-trading-liberty-for-security (accessed 23 August 2013).

95 Ibid., p.1. See also F. de Londras, this volume, on the need for evaluation.

96 See also M. Vermeulen, this volume.

97 G. Mythen, S. Walklate and F. Khan, '"I'm a Muslim, But I'm Not a Terrorist": Victimization, Risky Identities and the Performance of Safety' (2009) *British Journal of Criminology* Vol. 49 No. 6, pp. 736–54; C. Pantazis and S. Pemberton, 'Reconfiguring Security and Liberty: Political Discourses and Public Opinion in the New Century' (2012) *British Journal of Criminology* Vol. 52, pp. 651–67.

'criminalizing' impact on civil society organizations.[98] It is far from clear whether such restrictions and erosions of civil liberties are always justified.

In 2010, the Venice Commission identified several areas of criminal justice that were 'especially exposed to the risk that fundamental human rights be sacrificed most in the fight against terrorism: they are, above all, the principle of legality in defining terrorist offences, the right of defence, personal liberty of the accused and the presumption of innocence, inhuman and degrading treatment over the lengthy periods of preventive detention'.[99] The Commission also noted that persons who have been arrested and detained were particularly vulnerable, especially if they were suspects of terrorist crimes. The Commission called for a careful review of any counter-terrorist legislation adopted since 2001 'for its necessity and effectivity, and where necessary, modified to ensure it is human rights compatible'. The Commission also argued that this legislation must be assessed against the international tests of legality, necessity, proportionality and non-discrimination.[100]

CT measures tend to categorize and govern certain people in certain ways 'because of their constructed incompatibility with determined values, such as democracy, the rule of law, freedom or security, among others'.[101] The 2002 Framework Decision on combating terrorism has been criticized for its focus, not on the actual acts, but on the control of individuals who are perceived to be a threat.[102] Mitsilegas argues that 'the shift to prevention in the new offences is evident, as is the attempt to extend the criminal law sphere to certain profiles of individuals and subjective elements whose link with the actual commission of terrorist offences is more and more tenuous'.[103] He also notes that the 2008 amendment of the 2002 decision (Framework Decision 2008/919/JOHAN) introduces three new offences: public provocation to commit a terrorist offence, recruitment for terrorism, and training for terrorism. He points out that 'for any of these acts to be punishable it is not necessary that a terrorist offence is actually committed'.[104] The law thus has a net-widening effect, expanding the list of punishable acts that are seen to be linked to terrorism.

98 N. Quigley and B. Pratten, 'Security and Civil Society, The Impact of Counter-Terrorism Measures on Civil Society Organisations' (2007) *NCVO*. Available online at http://www.ncvo-vol.org.uk/uploadedFiles/NCVO/Policy/Civil_Society_and_Participation/2007%2001%2024%20Security%20and%20Civil%20Society-A%20report%20from%20NCVO.pdf (accessed 22 September 2013).

99 The Venice Commission, 2010, Report on Counter-Terrorism Measures and Human Rights, Strasbourg, p.20, available at http://www.venice.coe.int/webforms/documents/?pdf=CDL-AD(2010)022-e.

100 Ibid., p.21.

101 I. Barbero, 'Orientalising Citizenship: the Legitimation of Immigration Regimes in the European Union' (2012) *Citizenship Studies* Vol. 16 No. 5–6, pp. 751–68, p.764.

102 M. Kaiafa-Gbandi, 'The Prevention of Terrorism and the Criminal Law of Pre-Preventive Enforcement: New Criminal Acts for the Fight against Terrorism in the European Union' (in Greek) (2009) *Poinika Chronika* 385 cited in V. Mitsilegas, 'The Third Wave of Third Pillar Law: Which Direction for EU Criminal Justice?' (2009) *European Law Review* Vol. 34 No. 4, pp. 523–60, p.526.

103 V. Mitsilegas, *supra* note 102, p.526.

104 Ibid., p.525.

Finally, concerns have been expressed about the wider impact of CT measures on civil liberties. Freedom of expression and the right to privacy are arguably the two freedoms most likely to be affected.[105] It has been observed that national governments can use EU fora to pursue and push through more invasive measures at the domestic level, even when the need for these measures is far from clear.[106] Surveillance programmes are clearly among the measures that are likely to have such an impact. Christine Wicht worries that the plans to join up databases and increase capacities to control the World Wide Web with regard to 'terrorist activities' within the EU will be used to pave the way for comprehensive censorship of the Internet.[107]

Will the Lisbon Treaty strengthen human rights guarantees? Its full implications and effects are probably too early to assess, not least because, argues Šlosarcík, it 'provides a very complicated system of human rights guarantees in the European Union'.[108] However, there are certainly grounds for cautious optimism regarding the potential of the Treaty to enhance rights guarantees. The recent invalidation of the Data Retention Directive mentioned earlier in this chapter provides clear evidence of this capacity.

6. Conclusions: the implications of counter-terrorism measures for democracy in Europe

This chapter has provided an assessment of the implications of EU counter-terrorism measures for democracy. Three perspectives on democratic legitimacy were used to provide the assessment: first, output legitimacy, or the effectiveness of CT measures in protecting EU citizens from terrorism; second, input legitimacy, or the capacity of citizens to have a say in the making of CT measures; and third, rights legitimacy, or the compatibility of the measures with the principles of equality and protections of fundamental rights and freedoms.

It has been shown that all three aspects of democratic legitimacy of EU CT measures suffer from democratic deficit. In terms of input legitimacy, several areas of concern were identified, which include (a) the limited role of parliaments; (b) the limited transparency of measures and lack of citizen access to information; (c) the lack of accountability of decision-makers; and (d) the inequality of participation in decision-making. In terms of output legitimacy, there is currently a lack of evidence of the effectiveness of CT

105 C. Murphy, *supra* note 61.

106 J. Monar, *supra* note 68, p.311.

107 C. Wicht, 'More Security at Any Price, The Stockholm Programme of the European Union' (2010) *Eurozine.com*. Available online at http://www.eurozine.com/articles/2010–03–24-wicht-en.html (accessed 23 August 2013).

108 I. Šlosarcík, 'EU 's Area of Freedom, Security and Justice: From Post-Lisbon Tactics to EU Citizen-Oriented Strategy' (2011) *CEPS, Freedom, Security and Justice*, p.208. Available online at http://www.notre-europe.eu/media/tgae20114dslosarcik.pdf?pdf=ok (accessed 23 August 2013).

measures. And in terms of impact on equality and fundamental rights, many CT measures were found to lack effective safeguards to ensure equality of treatment and protection of the freedoms and rights of citizens.

It has been observed that the three measures of democratic legitimacy are interdependent. Sometimes this interdependency is understood as a trade-off (between input and output legitimacy or between security and freedoms). However, as the review of literature and analysis of evidence in this chapter shows, there is not enough evidence to say that restrictions on liberties or on citizen input are compensated by effective protection from the terrorist threat. It is, therefore, at least questionable whether it is an issue of a trade-off, or whether EU CT policies lead to an erosion of input democracy and rights with no gains in security. There is clearly a need for more evidence of output effectiveness, but also a need to rethink the ways in which input legitimacy, output legitimacy and impact on rights are interrelated. For example, how can the use of expert competences and knowledge be combined with proper input legitimacy that ensures the inclusion of everyone in decisions and democratic accountability? What evidence is there, or could be provided, to link certain restrictions of rights or liberties to certain gains in protection and/or reduction in risks?

In principle, there is no reason why the arguments of urgency and secrecy should exempt EU CT measures from democratic control. For example, Bono argues that the use of specialized parliamentary committees is one of the mechanisms that can 'simultaneously . . . protect state secrets and allow parliaments, the courts and affected citizens to be involved'.[109] Eriksen similarly argues that 'as long as the principles and guidelines for secrecy are publicly debated and regulated, actors may operate, within given parameters, in secrecy without violating democratic norms'.[110] Some authors see the solution to the lack of accountability of experts and the executive in the return to the principle of intergovernmentalism, while others argue that it is necessary to develop more democratically accountable and transparent institutions at the EU level, and to make executive decision-making and lines of authority and power more transparent and accessible to citizens.[111] For example, an inter-parliamentary forum is proposed as a way to strengthen the democratic accountability of CT policies at the EU level.[112]

It is also clear that any CT measures and any claims that such measures are required must be based on precise definitions and robust methods of evaluation in terms of input, output and rights legitimacy. Lack of systematic, timely and comprehensive evaluation is a key problem; there also remains, in the words of Edwards and Meyer 'a blind-spot in the scholarly analysis of the policies of counter-terrorism, which stems both from the inadequacy

109 G. Bono, *supra* note 44, p.443.
110 E. Eriksen, *supra* note 11, p.1174.
111 H. Sjursen, *supra* note 3.
112 C. Hillebrand, *supra* note 53.

of the traditional research methods as well as the increasing institutional and judicial restrictions imposed on alternative methods of academic inquiry'.[113] This means that EU CT measures are often based on ill-informed assumptions or unverified claims and that questions about their democratic legitimacy are not being asked.

113 G. Edwards and C. Meyer, *supra* note 46, p.17.

7 Social appropriateness in EU counter-terrorism law and policy

Bruno Oliveira Martins

1. Introduction

The quick emergence of an autonomous European Union (EU) counter-terrorism policy in the aftermath of the terrorist attacks of 9/11 brought new challenges to some of the foundations of the Union. As early as 2008, Geoffrey Edwards and Christoph O. Meyer argued that the EU's response to international terrorism had changed the governance of the Union.[1] Some of these changes were verified in areas beyond security or counter-terrorism, where dynamics such as cross-pillarization, the growth of horizontal governing networks, cooperation outside the treaty framework and the impact of third countries gained new impetus. If counter-terrorism policy-making can be considered the driving force for these changes in EU governance, what have been the foundations for the formulation of this policy? This chapter argues that the constitutional foundations of the EU play a decisive role in the definition and implementation of its counter-terrorism policy. Most importantly, they perform the fundamental function of granting legitimacy to EU counter-terrorism law and policy and ensuring its recognition as socially acceptable.

This chapter opens with a discussion on the merits of theorizing EU counter-terrorism policy, highlighting the reasons why it is important to approach this policy field from theoretically informed viewpoints. This exercise opens the ground for a subsequent section on the politics of law. Here, some contributions from policy-orientated traditions of legal theory are engaged with, exploring the ways they can bring original insights to the understanding of EU counter-terrorism policy. The third and fourth sections of this chapter address the fundamental sociological concept of social appropriateness, i.e., 'a perspective that sees human action as driven by rules of appropriate or exemplary behavior, organized into institutions', in a definition put forward by James G. March and Johan P. Olsen.[2] According to this logic, rules are followed because

1 G. Edwards and C. O. Meyer 'Introduction: Charting a Contested Transformation' (2008) vol. 46 *Journal of Common Market Studies*, p.1.

2 J. G. March and J. P. Olsen, 'The Logic of Appropriateness' (2009) ARENA Working Papers WP 04/09.

they are interpreted as natural, rightful, expected and legitimate within particular institutions. By capturing these additional insights from sociology, this contribution therefore pleads for multidisciplinary approaches to study complex political objects such as EU counter-terrorism policy. This approach is then applied through a sociological institutionalist analysis of EU counter-terrorism policy and by a systematization of the way the constitutional foundations of the EU impact on the formulation, implementation and supervision of policies adopted within the realm of counter-terrorism. The chapter closes with a concluding section where its main arguments are systematized and the concepts of constitutionalism and social appropriateness are seen as mutually constitutive in the sphere of EU counter-terrorism.

2. Why theorize EU counter-terrorism?

From a European studies perspective, there are five particularly interesting features of EU counter-terrorism that challenge common theoretical conceptions about the EU or bring new elements for assessing specific theoretical problems.

First, decision-making and governing structures in countering terrorism within the EU are spread across a vast array of actors, encompassing all the major EU institutions—European Commission, Council of the European Union, European Parliament, European Council, the European External Action Service (EEAS), the Court of Justice of the European Union (CJEU)), several agencies (Europol, Eurojust, Frontex, the European Union Situation Centre (SitCen)—and other coordination and negotiation bodies such as the Council's Committee on Terrorism (COTER) or the EU Counter-Terrorism Coordinator. At the same time, the vast majority of the counter-terrorism efforts in Europe remains within the realm of the Member States, which conduct their policies in coordination with Brussels while developing parallel networks with other Member States or external partners. From a theoretical point of view, the coexistence of several layers of decision-making makes EU counter-terrorism a particularly interesting case for assessing multi-level governance within the Union.[3] These dynamics are verified mostly at the internal level but their effects can also be explored in international counter-terrorism cooperation. For example, Newman argues that EU-US disputes on counter-terrorism matters are often rooted in internal multi-level governance processes within Europe.[4] These dynamics present different

3 For a thorough exploration of the concept of multi-level governance, see for example, I. Bache and M. Flinders, (Eds), *Multi-level Governance* (Oxford: Oxford University Press, 2004); I. Bache, *The Politics of EU Regional Policy: Multi-level Governance or Flexible Gatekeeping?* (Sheffield: Sheffield Academic Press, 1998); G. Marks and L. Hooghe, *Multi-level Governance and European Integration* (Lanham, MD: Rowman & Littlefield Publishers 2001).

4 A. Newman, 'Transatlantic Flight Fights: Multi-level Governance, Actor Entrepreneurship and International Anti-terrorism Cooperation' (2011) vol. 18 *Review of International Political Economy* p.481.

structures of opportunity for actors to influence international debates and eventually spill over to the external dimension. These actors, especially the security professionals within EU agencies, constitute, in the words of Didier Bigo *et al.*, 'a field of confrontation where the same sense of the "social game" being played, and of what is at stake in it, merely fuels struggles between the institutions, their bureaucracies and, ultimately, between individual actors'.[5] In this way, the levels of governance of EU counter-terrorism policy are deconstructed in consecutive sub-levels and constitute a dense network whose dynamics are theoretically difficult to grasp.

Second, EU counter-terrorism is theoretically relevant because it mitigates the internal/external divide in EU policy-making. In other words, the characteristics of the threat posed by terrorism and the elements and tools employed by the EU to address it represent a thorough example of the current blurring of boundaries between the *internal* and the *external* in policy-making, especially in the field of security. This trend is rooted in the intertwined policies and politics of a globalized world and does not apply to the EU exclusively. Nevertheless, it has received particular attention within the EU, where the external dimension of former EU internal policies has been explored by the literature in areas such as asylum and migration, social policy, or the area of Freedom, Security and Justice in general.[6] The dual nature of contemporary international terrorism (at once both home-grown and external) highlights new aspects of those internal/external dynamics and enables new explorations of the field.

Third, EU counter-terrorism crosses several areas of EU intervention. From security policy to legal cooperation, from financial tools to police investigation, from integration policies to external development aid, EU action in counter-terrorism spans the three former pillars of the EU structure. This action receives inputs from the Member States in several ways and, in a second stage, influences the way those same Member States address the terrorist threat in their own territory. The comprehensiveness of EU counter-terrorism and the dynamics of mutual influence between Brussels and the

5 D. Bigo, L. Bonelli, D. Chi, and C. Olsson, 'Mapping the Field of the EU Internal Security Agencies' in Didier Bigo (Ed), *The Field of the EU Internal Security Agencies* (Paris: L'Harmattan 2007), p.30.

6 See, for example, C. Kaunert and S. Leonard, 'The External Dimension of the EU Asylum and Border Management Policy' in C. Kaunert, *European Internal Security: Towards Supranational Governance in the Area of Freedom, Security and Justice* (Manchester: Manchester University Press 2010), p.150; W. Eichhorst, M.J. Kandzia, J.B. Knudsen and D. Wahl-Brink, *The External Dimension of EU Social Policy*, IZA Research Report 26, Policy Department (Brussels: European Parliament 2010); M. Cremona, J. Mönar and S. Poli (Eds), *The External Dimension of the European Union's Area of Freedom, Security and Justice* (Brussels: Peter Lang 2011); T. Balzacq (Ed), *The External Dimension of EU Justice and Home Affairs: Governance, Neighbours, Security*, (Basingstoke: Palgrave 2009); S. Wolff, N. Wichmann and G. Mounier (Eds), *The External Dimension of Justice and Home Affairs: A Different Security Agenda for the European Union* (London: Routledge 2009).

Member States provides fertile ground for exploring the dynamics of Europeanization, both top-down and bottom-up.[7]

Fourth, counter-terrorism provides a particularly apt lens through which to explore the concept of EU actorness, i.e., the EU's *persona* in the international scene. Studies such as the ones of Beyer,[8] Brandão,[9] and Brattberg and Rhinard[10] have developed the categories and elements of *actorness* presented by Bretherton and Vogler,[11] applying them to the case of EU external counter-terrorism and reaching different conclusions. The external dimension of EU counter-terrorism encompasses EU relations with several states, international organizations and non-state actors (such as NGOs and private actors) as well as the use of different instruments, and therefore enables different approaches to the same object. Exploring the external dimension of EU counter-terrorism brings new elements for the assessment of the main vectors of EU external actorness and to the understanding of EU foreign policy more broadly.[12]

Finally, by having a primary focus on the usage of legal instruments to fight terrorism, EU counter-terrorism enables advances in the study of the legal dimension of EU integration as well as the importance of law and the EU's constitutional foundation in the definition of EU policies. This issue has not received enough attention from the political science literature, which has mainly focused on the characteristics of EU counter-terrorism that are related either to the nature of the EU as a polity, or to the nature of terrorism as a threat. In the field of EU counter-terrorism, as in many other

---

7 See, for example, J. P. Olsen, 'The Many Faces of Europeanization' (2002) vol. 40 *Journal of Common Market Studies* p.921; J. Caporaso, 'The Three Worlds of Regional Integration Theory' in P. Graziano and M. Vink (Eds), *Europeanization: New Research Agendas* (Basingstoke: Palgrave 2007); T. Risse, M. G. Cowles and J. Caporaso, 'Europeanization and Domestic Change: Introduction' in M. Cowles, J. Caporaso and T. Riise (Eds), *Transforming Europe: Europeanization and Domestic Change* (Ithaca, NY: Cornell University Press 2001); and T. Börzel and T. Risse, 'Europeanization: The Domestic Impact of European Union Politics' in Knud-Erik Jørgensen, M. Pollack and B. Rosamond (Eds), *Handbook of European Union Politics* (London: Sage 2006).

8 C. Beyer, 'The European Union as a Security Policy Actor: The Case of Counterterrorism'(2008) vol. 13 *European Foreign Affairs Review* p.293.

9 A. P. Brandão, 'A *security actorness* da União Europeia e o terrorismo transnacional' (The European Union's external actorness and transnational terrorism) in Ana Paula Brandão (Ed), *A União Europeia e o Terrorismo Transnacional (The European Union and Transnational Terrorism)* (Coimbra: Almedina, 2010).

10 E. Brattberg and Mark Rhinard, 'The EU as a Global Counter-terrorism Actor in the Making' (2012) vol. 21 *European Security*, p.557.

11 C. Bretherton and J. Vogler, *The European Union as a Global Actor* (New York: Routledge, 2006).

12 See, for example, L. Ferreira-Pereira and B. Oliveira Martins (Eds), *The EU's Fight Against Terrorism: The CFSP and Beyond* (Abingdon: Routledge, 2014); C. Kaunert, 'The External Dimension of EU Counter-Terrorism Relations: Competences, Interests, and Institutions' (2009) vol. 22 *Terrorism and Political Violence*, p.41; A. MacKenzie, 'The European Union's Increasing Role in Foreign Policy Counter-terrorism' (2012) vol. 6 *Journal of Contemporary European Research*, p.147.

EU policy areas, political and legal scholarships mostly speak to different audiences – a tendency that this volume tries to counter. It can be argued that the importance of the constitutional vector in the definition of EU policy-making in counter-terrorism has not been explored sufficiently and that this prevents a full understanding of the reasons explaining EU counter-terrorism. This chapter aims to fill this gap and therefore to contribute to a broader understanding of this policy field.

3. Law is policy: politicizing the law

EU counter-terrorism law, like any other body of legal prescriptions, can be analysed as an outcome, i.e. as an end product. But it can also be analysed as a process, i.e. as a dynamic sequence of events where norms, actors and procedures contribute to the formulation of legislation. This approach enables a refocus of the legal analyses to highlight particular aspects that have an impact on the final legal outcomes. According to this line of reasoning, then, law should not be seen as a body of rules, but rather as a process of community decision. In any given field of law, the legislative process operates a projection of social preferences, exposing dynamics where the legal, political and social arenas intersect.

Understanding law as a process is one of the main contributions of the New Haven School, an influential school of legal thought developed after World War II at Yale Law School through the works of Myres S. McDougal and Harold D. Lasswell. By framing itself as a policy-orientated jurisprudence, it suggests a delimitation of the focus of inquiry to locate authoritative decisions in the largest community process which it affects and is affected by.[13] Therefore, law cannot be understood outside the social context it is embedded in. According to Oona Hathaway, the New Haven School has three central features that today are deeply embedded in contemporary international law: a resistance to the realism that once dominated the discipline of international relations, an interdisciplinary approach to law, and a special focus on policy and policy-making.[14] Of these three elements, the latter is here used as a stepping stone to understand less-explored facets of EU counter-terrorism law and policy. What are the principles guiding the process of elaborating EU counter-terrorism law and policy? Where do the foundations of EU counter-terrorism policy lie? In this chapter, I argue that the security of the EU's citizens and infrastructures, and the respect for the constitutional foundations of the EU, are the main guiding principles of EU action. Yet, given that the security of the EU's citizens still remains mostly within the realm of their state of origin (Member States are still the

13 M. S. McDougal, 'Jurisprudence for a Free Society' (1966) vol.1 *Georgia Law Review*, p.14.

14 O. A. Hathaway, 'Commentary: The Continuing Influence of the New Haven School' (2007) vol. 32 *Yale Journal of International Law*, p.565.

main security providers to their citizens), the EU's main task is one of policy coordination, ensuring the observance of respect for fundamental rights while countering terrorism. Only when this is observed is the EU seen as a legitimate actor in the field of counter-terrorism in Europe. This last point is particularly well explained by sociological institutionalist theory and this approach reveals the added value of analysing legal phenomena in a social context, as prescribed by the New Haven School.

4. EU counter-terrorism policy: an institution

If law should be seen as a process of community decision, as argued above, what are the norms and principles to which the community adheres? In the case of the EU, what are the sources of legitimacy for action? In other words, if EU law (like any other legal system) is understood as emanating from a community in which it is embedded, what are the definitional traces of that community that will eventually be transformed into law?

Starting from the common-sense assumption that institutions matter in political action, political scientists mainly use three different forms of new institutionalism to study political objects. Rational choice institutionalism, historical institutionalism and sociological institutionalism constitute what has been called 'new institutionalism'[15] since the 1980s and present different notions of 'institution' when addressing political objects from different approaches.[16]

The 'new institutionalisms'

The label 'new institutionalism' was introduced by March and Olsen in 1984 to signal the recent concern with institutions that had been manifested by political studies in the preceding years. For these authors, despite the differences between these new institutionalist studies, they shared an emphasis on the 'relative autonomy of political institutions, possibilities for inefficiency in history, and the importance of symbolic action to an understanding of politics'.[17]

According to Hall and Taylor, rational choice institutionalism, historical institutionalism, and sociological institutionalism are approaches 'developed

15 J. G. March and J. P. Olsen 'The New Institutionalism: Organizational Factors in Political Life' (1984) vol. 78 *American Political Science* Review, p.734.

16 Due to its less relevant contribution to the analysis conducted in this research, some versions of new institutionalism theory will not be covered. This applies to rational choice as well as to historical institutionalism. It is important to note that in recent years the literature has provided new assessments of institutionalism, highlighting different aspects of the theory. Among these are discursive institutionalism, normative institutionalism and constructivist institutionalism.

17 J. G. March and J. P. Olsen 'The New Institutionalism: Organizational Factors in Political Life' (1984) vol. 78 *American Political Science Review*, p.734.

Table 1 Features of sociological institutionalism that distinguish it from historical institutionalism and rational choice institutionalism according to Hall and Taylor (1996)

Definition of 'institution'	*Individual-institution relationship*	*Explanation for origin and change in institutional practices*
• Broad definition • Includes not only formal rules, procedures and norms, but also symbol systems, cognitive scripts and moral templates • Challenges the common distinction between 'institutional explanations' based on organizational structures and 'cultural explanations' based on understanding of culture as shared attitudes or values	• 'Cultural approach' to the relationship between the individual and the institution • Highly interactive and mutually-constitutive • 'Normative dimension' of institutional impact on individuals: institutions affect behaviour because individuals socialized into particular institutional roles internalize the norms associated with these roles • Self-images and identity of the actors are constituted from the institutional forms, images and signs provided by the social life	• Enhancement of the social legitimacy of the organization or its participants • Organizations embrace specific institutional forms or practices because these are widely valued within a broader cultural environment
Fundamental question: What confers 'legitimacy' or 'social appropriateness' to some institutional arrangements but not to others?		

in reaction to the behavioural perspectives that were influential during the 1960s and 1970s and all seek to elucidate the role that institutions play in the determination of social and political outcomes'.[18] These three versions of institutionalism became established in the literature as the 'new institutionalisms' of political science. Among these, sociological institutionalism seeks explanations for 'why organizations take on specific sets of institutional forms, procedures or symbols; and it emphasizes how such practices are diffused through organizational fields or across nations'.[19] They distinguish themselves from rational choice or historical institutionalism studies in terms of the definition of institution, the relations between the individuals and the institution, and the explanations for the origin of institutional practices and changes in those practices. Table 1 refers to the vectors within each of these categories that are particular to sociological institutionalism.

18 P.A. Hall and R. Taylor, 'Political Science and the Three New Institutionalisms' (1996) vol. 44 *Political Studies*, p.936.

19 P.A. Hall and R. Taylor, 'Political Science and the Three New Institutionalisms' (1996) vol. 44 *Political Studies*, p.947.

Table 2 Fundamental questions in sociological institutionalism as presented by Peters

Definition	*Individual and institutional relation*	*Institutional change*	*The good institution*
• More concerned with the creation of values and cognitive frames within an institution than with the end state	• Processes of institutionalization evolve in three stages: habituation; objectification; sedimentation	• Occurs through institutionalization or deinstitutionalization • Institutions will attempt to mould their environments to meet their own needs rather than passively responding to those environments	• Longevity (population ecology approach) • Capacity to adapt to external pressures for isomorphism (isomorphism approach) • Capacity to inculcate its values (normative approach) • Capacity to control behaviour of individuals (regulative approach) • Capacity to process information

Other accounts of sociological institutionalism have highlighted additional distinguishable characteristics of this theoretical approach. Guy Peters, for example, explores the vectors of definition, individuals and institutional relations, institutional change and the characteristics of 'a good institution'[20] in the terms explained in Table 2.

These vectors are particularly important in the collection of elements for addressing the importance of the EU's constitutional foundations in the practice of EU counter-terrorism. For the purpose of this contribution, though, the two most important characteristics of sociological institutionalism are: (1) the fact that organizations embrace specific institutional forms or practices because these are widely valued within a broader cultural environment, and (2) the search for legitimacy and social appropriateness in an institution.

Departing from Hall and Taylor's definition of institution as encompassing 'the formal and informal procedures, routines, norms and conventions embedded in the organizational structure of the polity or political economy',[21]

---

20 G. Peters, *Institutional Theory in Political Science: The 'New Institutionalism'* (London: Continuum, 1999) p.105–109.

21 P.A. Hall and R. Taylor, 'Political Science and the Three New Institutionalisms' (1996) vol. 44 *Political Studies*, p.938.

EU counter-terrorism can be seen as an institution that has emerged in the aftermath of the terrorist attacks of 9/11. This sociological approach to institutional theory argues that institutions evolve through mechanisms of path dependency but they do not change through critical junctures only; ideas, norms and other rules can also generate change. The use of this approach brings structure to the analysis and enlightens the fact that policy-making in this field follows a logic where the relationship between the individuals (i.e., the policy-makers), the organizations (i.e., EU institutions) and the institution (EU counter-terrorism policy) is highly interactive and mutually-constitutive. This idea goes hand in hand with the process-orientated approach to understanding and analysing law as advocated above. It is understood that institutions affect behaviour because individuals socialized into particular institutional roles internalize the norms associated with these roles. This normative vector is also present in the sociological institutionalist idea that the self-images and identity (of the actors and organizations) are constituted from the institutional forms, images and signs provided by social life.

Such a dynamic understanding of EU counter-terrorism as an institution fits well with the multitude of actors that intervene in this policy field. Member States, EU institutions, EU agencies and foreign actors (third countries and international organizations) play important roles.[22] But they do not shape the whole picture. One of the first and most decisive effects in Europe of the September 2001 attacks in the US was the change in threat perception within the EU. Fear of terrorism became familiar to EU citizens and politicians alike, and it was that important societal change that led to policy action. The emergence of a cascade of political declarations and adoption of legal instruments was enabled by a change in threat perception. Therefore, in order to understand more fully the EU counter-terrorism legal structure, one needs to take into account the social environment from which it derived. From this, it follows that it was the social environment that provided EU policy and legal entrepreneurs with legitimacy and a mandate to address the issue of international terrorism. In other words, EU counter-terrorism policy is a policy response to a social phenomenon: the perception of the threat posed by international terrorism.

This circumstance is particularly well perceived considering the tradition that several EU Member States had in dealing with terrorism. Despite decades of national counter-terrorism in Europe, the EU did not develop an autonomous, pan-European counter-terrorism policy before September 2001. It is true that other structural factors contributed to this outcome, namely the fact that in the 1970s and 1980s, the EU had not developed institutions and practices that facilitated the adoption of a common policy on such an ambitious issue. Yet, the promptness and the comprehensiveness of the EU's

22 See further Doody, this volume, and Hayes and Jones, this volume.

counter-terrorism policy action in the months following the terrorist attacks in New York and Washington indicate that something fundamental had changed beyond the mere existence of institutions and practices. Indeed, many of today's counter-terrorism institutions, agencies and practices in Europe were either created or expanded since 2001. In addition, as authors such as Argomaniz have demonstrated, several EU legal instruments that today are used in counter-terrorism existed before 2001 but were not used to fight international terrorism.[23]

A good institution?

While theorizing about sociological institutionalism, Guy Peters introduced the idea of a 'good institution' exposed in Table 2. For sociological institutionalist theory, there are five main characteristics that different studies use to characterize a good institution: longevity, capacity to adapt to external pressures for isomorphism, capacity to inculcate its values, capacity to control the behaviour of individuals, and capacity to process information. The EU's counter-terrorism policy presents these five characteristics, albeit to different degrees. It has been created and expanded bearing a long-term perspective (criterion of longevity) and reveals the capacity to process information and adapt to the requirements of the external and internal environments (criterion of information-processing capacity).

Regarding longevity, the EU counter-terrorism policy was not created with a time frame in sight. Its instruments and policies were made part of the EU's security portfolio and will certainly be active into the foreseeable future. In addition, the importance of the observance of the EU's constitutional foundations will increase if the costs of terrorism and also counter-terrorism continue to rise. As for its capacity to adapt to external pressures for isomorphism (isomorphism approach), the EU has exhibited a certain resistance to external pressures. This was observed in the *Kadi* case,[24] in which the Court of Justice invoked the autonomy of EU law from international law emanating from the UN,[25] but also in cases where pressure from the United States faced resilience from the EU, of which the Passenger Name Record and the SWIFT agreements are the most paradigmatic examples. To be certain, there are also abundant examples of an opposite trend in which the EU is

23 J. Argomaniz, 'Post 9/11 Institutionalisation of European Union Counter-terrorism: Emergence, Acceleration and Inertia' (2009) vol. 18 *European Security*, p.151.

24 Joined cases C-402/05 P and C-415/05 P *Yassin Abdullah Kadi and Al Barakaat International Foundation v Council of the European Union and Commission of the European Communities.*

25 The Court's decision in this particular issue was based on Advocate General Maduro's opinion. Opinion of Mr Advocate General Poiares Maduro delivered on 16 January 2008, in *Yassin Abdullah Kadi and Al Barakaat International Foundation v Council of the European Union and Commission of the European Communities,* Joined cases C-402/05 P and C-415/05 P. European Court reports, 2008, page I-006351.

the 'norm taker',[26] giving in to pressures from the outside; but its capacity to resist in some cases makes it theoretically relevant and important in the context of the present analysis.

Finally, both the capacity to inculcate its values (normative approach) and the capacity to control the behaviour of individuals (regulative approach) can also be observed on a regular basis. As will be explained further below, this is performed through a system of parliamentary and judicial supervision where the European Parliament and the CJEU exert ulterior supervision of the implementation of EU counter-terrorism measures. For these dynamics to be fully understood, it is necessary to develop the idea that the EU is an artificial legal construction. This is a fundamental step for understanding that the source of the EU's *difference* in countering terrorism does not lie in the superiority of its values when compared to other Western liberal democracies, but rather in its nature as a peculiar constitutional polity.

5. The EU as an (artificial) legal construction

The EU is, first and foremost, a legal construction. Lacking a *demos* and a *pouvoir constituant* (i.e. an original constituent power), the EU is an artificial construction of which the law is one of its main supporting pillars, if not the most decisive one. The EU was created *ex lege*, and law, norms and rules increasingly regulate expanding facets of the political, economic and social lives within the Union. In the words of Fossum and Menéndez, the EU establishes much of the basic regulatory framework of social interaction.[27]

The EU is a polity ruled by a system with a constitutional nature, composed by the Treaties, the case-law of the CJEU, the constitutional traditions and practices of the Member States, and general principles of law. EU constitutionalism, therefore, regulates the political function of the EU by distributing competences, supervising the compatibility of the political behaviour of the actors with that same constitutional space, solving conflicts, and setting the guidelines for political action. Moreover, it constitutes an upper level when compared with the national legal orders. EU law has primacy over the legal orders of the Member States and the CJEU acts as the last instance of disputes related to EU law and politics, performing the role of a *de facto* EU constitutional court. Most importantly, the EU sees itself as founded on a set of principles that justify its existence. This idea is clearly stated in Art. 2 of the Treaty on European Union (TEU), according to which, 'the Union is founded on the values of respect for human dignity,

26 J. Argomaniz, 'When the EU is the "Norm-taker": The Passenger Name Records Agreement and the EU's Internalization of US Border Security Norms' (2009) vol. 31 *Journal of European Integration*, p.119.

27 J. E. Fossum and A. J. Menéndez, *The Constitution's Gift: A Constitutional Theory for a Democratic European Union* (Lanham, MD: Rowman & Littlefield Publishers 2011), p.2.

freedom, democracy, equality, the rule of law and respect for human rights, including the rights of persons belonging to minorities.'

Thinking about the EU in constitutional terms entails a specific understanding of the sources of EU law. The primary source of EU law is the Treaties, the secondary is made up of Decisions and Directives emanating from EU institutions, and the tertiary source comprises CJEU case-law and general principles of law. This approach looks into this legal order and interprets it as having a constitutional nature. This also requires that primary law, i.e. the law emanating from the Treaties, is seen as having a constitutional nature. This has been explicitly recognized already by the CJEU in the landmark decision on the case *Les Verts* where it held that the European Community was a 'Community based on the rule of law, inasmuch as neither its Member States nor its institutions can avoid a review of the question whether the measures adopted by them are in conformity with the basic constitutional charter, the Treaty'.[28] The literature has also contributed to expanding and refining this claim, providing more concrete justifications for treating EU primary law as constitutional in its essence. In the words of Bogdandy,

> The primary law justifies the exercise of public power, it legitimizes acts of the EU, it creates a citizenship, it grants fundamental rights, and it regulates the relationship between legal orders, between public power and the economy, and between law and politics. Numerous common elements of EU common primary law and national constitutions emerge in a functional comparison. Yet, not only the functions but also the 'semantics' support a constitutional law approach: the Treaty of Amsterdam provides in Article 6(1) TEU the key concepts of constitutional discourse: freedom, democracy, rule of law, protection of fundamental rights. Correspondingly, the constitutional *semantics* of the ECJ have just taken a big step with the introduction of the terms 'constitutional principle' and 'constitutional guarantee'.[29]

It derives from this that the constitutional nature of the EU impacts decisively on its workings. In the particular case of the fight against terrorism, it is argued here that the constitutional foundations of the EU contribute to the characteristics presented by EU counter-terrorism, namely what can be called the criminalization approach. The latter can be defined as an approach employing legal instruments to fight terrorism and treating terrorism as a crime, i.e. as a law-enforcement issue. The argument goes beyond the notion that constitutionalism limits and sets the boundaries for political action, because this is true for all constitutional democracies in the world. In the particular case of the EU, the argument also means that the fact that the EU

28 Case 294/83 *Parti Ecologiste Les Verts v European Parliament* [1986] ECR 1339, at paragraph 23.

29 A. Bogdandy, 'Founding Principles of EU Law: A Theoretical and Doctrinal Sketch' (2010) vol. 16 *European Law Journal*, p.96.

was artificially created and expanded via treaty reform and case-law of the CJEU makes derogation from constitutional principles more difficult than in constitutional polities with other sources of legitimacy such as a *demos* and a *pouvoir constituant*. In the case of sensitive policies, such as counter-terrorism, the legitimacy and social appropriateness that enable their existence derive from the constitutional nature of the EU and from the constitutional principles, norms and rules that sustain the EU as a political entity.

This kind of theoretical reasoning has bridges with other streams of intellectual thought that use the EU as a laboratory. It enables a close relationship with literature on cosmopolitanism, EU *ethos*, the EU's *raison d'être* and *finalité* in a theoretical journey that goes back to Kantian conceptions of perpetual peace. At the same time, this reasoning extends to important theoretical concepts such as 'normative power Europe',[30] a notion that, building on works by Galtung,[31] Duchêne[32] and Rosecrance,[33] argues that the EU, more than a civilian or military power, is a promoter of norms in the international scene. For Manners, the EU's comparative difference as an international actor has three main roots: its historical context, its hybrid polity and its political-legal constitution.[34]

The EU legal community was developed and progressively enhanced and expanded by the action of the CJEU and successive stages of treaty reform; this factor, together with the constitutional traditions of the Member States, led to the adoption of the rule of law, democracy, the separation of powers and the protection of human rights as fundamental principles. Although they were already part of the material EU constitution, they were explicitly mentioned in Art. 2 TEU, as adopted by the Treaty of Lisbon. As mentioned above, Article 2 provides that

> The Union is founded on the values of respect for human dignity, freedom, democracy, equality, the rule of law and respect for human rights, including the rights of persons belonging to minorities. These values are common to the Member States in a society in which pluralism, non-discrimination, tolerance, justice, solidarity and equality between women and men prevail.

---

30 I. Manners, 'Normative Power Europe: a Contradiction in Terms?' (2002) vol. 40 *Journal of Common Market Studies*, p.235; I. Manners, 'Normative Power Europe Reconsidered: Beyond the Crossroads' (2006) vol. 13 *Journal of European Public Policy*, p.182; I. Manners, 'European Union "Normative Power" and the Security Challenge' (2006) vol. 15 *European Security*, p.405; A. Hyde-Price, '"Normative" Power Europe: A Realist Critique' (2006) vol. 13 *Journal of European Public Policy*, p.217.

31 J. Galtung, *The European Community: A Superpower in the Making* (London: Allen & Unwin 1973).

32 F. Duchêne, 'Europe's Role in World Peace' in R. Mayne (Ed), *Europe Tomorrow: Sixteen Europeans Look Ahead* (London: Fontana 1972), p.32.

33 R. Rosecrance, 'The European Union: A New Type of International Actor' in J. Zielonka (Ed) *Paradoxes of European Foreign Policy* (London: Kluwer Law International 1998), p.15.

34 I. Manners, 'Normative Power Europe: a Contradiction in Terms?' (2002) vol. 40 *Journal of Common Market Studies*, p.240.

These are the elements that are seen by the members of the EU counter-terrorism institution (i.e. all EU citizens, agencies and institutions) as granting legitimacy to this same institution. EU disputes with the UN, with the US and within the EU itself (as in the case of *Commission vs Parliament*[35] in front of the CJEU in the Passenger Name Record affairs, for example) show that when the EU's constitutional principles are not observed, the EU normally reacts to enforce them. But how do the constitutional foundations of the EU impact on its counter-terrorism policy? How can this influence be theorized?

6. Explaining the impact of the constitutional foundations of the EU on its counter-terrorism policy

I argue here that there are three constitutionalism-defined moments in the practice of EU counter-terrorism. The impact of the EU's constitutional foundations is observed in three separate phases during policy-making and implementation in counter-terrorism: aprioristic presence, legislative and executive presence, and ulterior supervision. Although consecutively observable in the adoption and implementation of each legal instrument or political document, these three moments will be analysed individually.

Aprioristic presence

The first moment when the presence of EU constitutional foundations can be observed in counter-terrorism policy-making happens before the EU actually acts. In all strategic documents, action plans and programmes introducing guidelines for action, the need to ensure the protection of EU citizens and infrastructures from the terrorist threat comes accompanied by a reference to the necessity of protection of fundamental rights and the observance of the rule of law. This means that, even before EU institutions and agencies adopt legislative and executive acts, the constitutional principles upon which the EU is based present a clear guideline and a strict limitation to their agency, which is regularly screened *ex ante* by the European Commission in its impact assessments. Irrespective of the contending issues at stake, EU action cannot overrule those constitutional principles.

Empirical evidence of this first moment can be collected in the Hague Programme, for example, which has the objective of improving the common capability of the EU and Member States to guarantee fundamental rights, minimum procedural safeguards and access to justice, among others, and to provide protection to security threats such as terrorism.[36] From the

35 Joined cases C-317/04 and 318/04, *Parliament vs Council of the European Union and Commission of the European Communities*.

36 Council of the European Union, 'The Hague Programme: Strengthening Freedom, Security and Justice in The European Union', Council of the European Union, *Official Journal* C 53/01 of 3.3.2005.

equivalence of level at which these objectives are placed, one can understand that the pursuit of one objective – protection from terrorism – cannot derogate another – fundamental rights and procedural safeguards, for example. Similar logic applies to the Stockholm Programme[37] that replaced The Hague Programme.

Symptomatically, the same assurances are given even in the strategic documents that address the particular case of counter-terrorism. The first and main objective of the EU Counter-Terrorism Strategy,[38] as well as its strategic commitment, is 'to combat terrorism globally while respecting human rights'. The EU strategy for combating radicalization and recruitment to terrorism,[39] on the other hand, mentions in its Point 6 that '. . . we will ensure that we do not undermine respect for fundamental rights'. All important strategic documents reveal similar patterns. For the European Security Strategy, for example, 'spreading good governance, supporting social and political reform, dealing with corruption and abuse of power, establishing the rule of law and protecting human rights are the best means of strengthening the international order'.[40] As for the European Internal Security Strategy, it refers in its introduction to the fact that Europe 'must consolidate a security model, based on the principles and values of the Union: respect for human rights and fundamental freedoms, the rule of law, democracy, dialogue, tolerance, transparency and solidarity'.[41]

This last aspect is particularly important. From a conceptual point of view, the EU sees respect for fundamental rights and fundamental freedoms as part of its security model. It can be inferred from this that EU security policies can neither contradict fundamental rights nor fundamental freedoms: that would go against the EU's own security model.

Legislative and executive presence

Critical views of the EU would agree that these principles are mentioned and declared but would claim that they are not always actually implemented or observed when the EU moves from the declaratory sphere to real policy-making and implementation. Without wishing to argue that the EU always takes correct decisions and opts for solutions that protect fundamental rights, I argue here that the constitutional foundations are *normally* observed when

37 Council of the European Union, 'The Stockholm Programme: An Open and Secure Europe Serving and Protecting Citizens', Council of the European Union, *Official Journal* C 115 of 4.5.2010.

38 Council of the European Union, *The EU Counter-Terrorism Strategy*, Council of the European Union, 14469/4/05 REV 4, 30 Nov. 2005.

39 Council of the European Union, *The European Union Strategy for Combating Radicalisation and Recruitment to Terrorism*, Ref. 14781/1/05 REV 1, 24 Nov. 2005.

40 Council of the European Union, *European Security Strategy*, 15895/03, 16 Dec. 10.

41 Council of the European Union, *Draft Internal Security Strategy for the European Union: 'Towards a European Security Model*, Ref. 5842/2/10 REV 2 JAI 90, 8 Mar. 2010.

the EU acts on counter-terrorism. EU counter-terrorism is a relevant case to assess the impact of norms on policies not only because of the strength of those constitutional foundations, but also because they are part of the very definition of the counter-terrorism policies. In other words, respecting fundamental rights and observing the rule of law is part of the strategy to combat terrorism. Fighting terrorism within the EU with legal instruments is cause and consequence of the EU's peculiarity. These are two sides of the above-explained criminalization approach adopted by the EU to fight terrorism.

Concern with the observance of these principles can be assessed both within the EU but also in the framework of the broader external dimension of EU counter-terrorism policy. For instance, the EEAS has supported the UN in internal projects to encourage the countries of Central Asia to implement the UN global counter-terrorism strategy, including its human rights aspects. In parallel, the issue of fundamental rights and freedoms is an element conducting the pace of external cooperation with the UN and the US, often leading to tensions. The extent of external cooperation goes as far as the measures adopted are compatible with EU's constitutional features.

Ulterior supervision

The last moment where EU constitutional foundations can be observed in the practice of counter-terrorism happens *a posterior*, i.e. after the adoption of a given legal document, after the adoption of an international agreement, or as a result of the implementation of a counter-terrorism measure. This function is executed by the Parliament and also by the EU courts and constitutes a real parliamentary and judicial review of EU counter-terrorism. This third moment is fundamental in the construction of the argument according to which constitutionalism impacts decisively on the practice of counter-terrorism. And it is so because the nature of terrorism, its securitization as a fundamental threat, the existence of external influences and the phenomenon of inter-institutional bargaining, make counter-terrorism a typical case where fundamental rights are regularly breached.

The terminology of the 'war on terror' and the social construction of several terrorism myths emphasized the terrorist threat and *normalized* many security-related measures that used to be unacceptable or, at best, highly exceptional. The post-9/11 world introduced and/or expanded the usage of torture, indefinite detentions, warrantless wiretapping, extraordinary renditions, targeted killings, and extra-judicial detentions, all in the name of the fight against terrorism. In this wave of extra-securitization and over-reaction, the EU was caught several times breaching some of its constitutional principles. In the majority of these occasions, the Parliament and the EU courts stepped in to bring legality back in and to assure the compliance of the EU polity with its constitutional foundations. Examples of this dynamic were verified in the *Kadi* case as well as the European Arrest Warrant, the list of items banned from air passengers' hand luggage and the Data Retention Directive case, for example.[42]

The supervision of counter-terrorism action in the EU is not an exclusive competence of the judiciary. Inter-institutional rivalry and bargaining plays a fundamental role in ensuring the compliance of the practice of EU counter-terrorism with the EU's constitutional foundations. The main institution in these dynamics is the European Parliament. With an array of competences expanded by the Treaty of Lisbon and vested by direct democratic legitimacy, the Parliament has been revealing important entrepreneurship in the protection of the fundamental rights of EU citizens affected by the implementation of EU counter-terrorism measures. The culmination of this process and the functioning of these mechanisms grant EU counter-terrorism the legitimacy and social appropriateness from which it benefits.

7. A proposed causal mechanism

Against this background, I propose a mechanism establishing causal links between EU constitutional foundations and the practice of counter-terrorism. In this setting, the influence of the former on the latter happens in four stages: in stage 1, the legal principles and social norms are internalized by the EU counter-terrorism actors (EU institutions, agencies and non-state actors). In stage 2, these principles are reaffirmed in strategic guidelines, action plans and legal documents that frame EU action on counter-terrorism. Stage 1 and stage 2 take place in the *aprioristic presence* phase, i.e., they are observed *before* the EU actually performs counter-terrorism actions.

In stage 3, actors behave according to the principles and norms internalized. As previously mentioned, this does not always happen, but it can be observed in the majority of cases. This stage corresponds to the *legislative and executive presence* phase. Finally, in cases where actors do not act in accordance with those EU constitutional foundations, stage 4 takes place via the supervision of institutions that exert control over policy-making and implementation of counter-terrorism measures. This corresponds to the third chronological phase, here called *ulterior supervision*. Table 3 illustrates these dynamics.

This table advances a causal mechanism with four different stages distributed along the three chronological phases described above. In line with the sociological institutionalist analysis of the EU counter-terrorism policy introduced earlier, it suggests that these mechanisms confer the legitimacy and

42 For a deeper analysis of these cases, see X. Barros-Garcia, 'The External Dimension of EU Counter-terrorism: The Challenges of the European Parliament in Front of the European Court of Justice' (2012) vol. 21 *European Security*, p.518.

Table 3 Phases and stages of the causal mechanism.*

X	*Causal mechanism (EU constitutional foundations)* →				Y
EU constitutional foundations	Legal principles and social norms are internalized by the actors	Strategic guidelines, action plans and legal documents reaffirm EU constitutional foundations	Actors behave according to the principles and norms internalized	Supervision institutions exert control over policy-making and implementation	Practice of EU counter-terrorism

* Model inspired by Beach, D. and Pedersen, R. B. (2013: 103) *Process Tracing Methods: Foundations and Guidelines*, Ann Arbor: Michigan University Press.

social appropriateness that the EU counter-terrorism policy requires in order to be socially accepted.

8. Conclusion: constitutionalism as social appropriateness

When theorizing about how and why the logic of appropriateness impacts on the workings of an institution, March and Olsen suggest that

> . . . institutions create elements of order and predictability. They fashion, enable, and constrain political actors as they act within a logic of appropriate action. Institutions are carriers of identities and roles and they are markers of a polity's character, history, and visions. They provide bonds that tie citizens together in spite of the many things that divide them.[43]

In the EU's counter-terrorism policy, the elements of order and predictability referred to by March and Olsen are the constitutional foundations of the EU. In the process of policy and legal formulation in counter-terrorism, the EU always employs the jargon of its constitutional foundations, namely the respect for fundamental rights and the rule of law. This can be seen in the political declarations, preambles of resolutions and framework decisions, strategic documents, and case-law of the CJEU. These are the norms that make EU policy-making socially appropriate on such a sensitive issue. This claim mirrors Hall and Taylor's argument that one of the distinctive vectors of sociological institutionalist analyses is investigating *why*

43 J. G. March and J. P. Olsen, Elaborating the 'New Institutionalism' (2005) ARENA Working Papers, Working Paper 11, pp. 5–6.

organizations take on specific sets of institutional forms, procedures or symbols instead of others. In its fight against terrorism, the EU uses mostly legal instruments and treats terrorism predominantly as a crime, partially because of its constitutional foundations. In other words, only by incorporating the constitutional foundations of the EU into the analysis, can one explain why the EU fights terrorism the way it does.

This chapter argued for the added value of approaching and understanding law as a process, and not necessarily as an outcome. It revealed that an incorporation of sociological elements in the analysis of complex legal phenomena highlights new facets and expands our understanding of them. In the particular case of the EU's counter-terrorism policy, the sociological institutionalist analysis carried out here illuminated the importance of the constitutional foundations of the EU in granting legitimacy to this policy. This is more important when considering the challenges arising in an artificial polity, such as the EU, by acting on such a sensitive topic. In the EU, issues such as the security versus justice equation, privacy and data protection, and broader respect for fundamental rights when countering terrorism are framed by the Union's constitutional foundation. Only when respect for these principles is observed, is the policy understood as socially accepted and the EU seen as a legitimate actor. To borrow the words of March and Olsen, EU counter-terrorism policy needs to carry the identities and roles of the EU, and its constitutional foundations are the markers of its character, history and visions. Its absence affects EU counter-terrorism policy and prevents it from having the support of the EU citizens; without it, its legitimacy is lost.

Part III

Practical perspectives on EU counter-terrorism

8 The perspectives of counter-terrorism operatives on EU counter-terrorism law and policy

*Cian C. Murphy, Aldo Zammit Borda and Lucy Hoyte**

1. Introduction

Although counter-terrorism law and policy have been the subject of a rich literature since the attacks in the United States on 11 September 2001 there had been, until recently, little work undertaken to afford a comprehensive understanding of EU counter-terrorism law and policy. Recent years have seen a number of works emerge that address this gap in the literature.[1] However, there remains little examination of how the law and policy operate in practice. Although some EU counter-terrorism measures, such as the European Arrest Warrant (EAW), have been the subject of scrutiny by civil society and the academy, others have not. In counter-terrorist finance, for example, the pre-eminence of writings in the legal literature address the question of due process for those under suspicion of financing terrorism.[2] Some of those working in the field of criminology have taken a broader view – but there remains little empirical study of the law in action.[3]

This chapter presents the principal findings from the research conducted by the King's College London research team on the Securing Europe through Counter-terrorism: Impact, Legitimacy and Effectiveness project (SECILE). The work sought to address the limitations in our knowledge of EU counter-terrorism law and policy. The fieldwork undertaken by King's involved three case studies using focus groups on the EAW, counter-terrorist finance (CTF)

* Cian C. Murphy is Senior Lecturer in Law at The Dickson Poon School of Law at King's College London and Academic Co-Director of the Center for Transnational Legal Studies. Aldo Zammit Borda is Senior Lecturer in Law at Anglia Ruskin University and previously Research Associate at The Dickson Poon School of Law. Lucy Hoyte was Research Assistant on the SECILE project at The Dickson Poon School of Law. We are grateful to the editors for their comments, to colleagues at King's for their support, and to Consortium colleagues for their cooperation.

1 See, for example, C.C. Murphy, *EU Counter-terrorism Law: Pre-emption and the Rule of Law* (Oxford: Hart Publishing, 2012); for a different disciplinary perspective, R. Bossong, *The Evolution of EU Counter-Terrorism: EU Security Policy after 9/11* (Abingdon: Routledge Publishing 2012).

2 See, for the leading text, C. Eckes, *EU Counter-terrorist Policies and Due Process: The Case of Individual Sanctions* (Oxford: Oxford University Press, 2009).

3 M. Levi, 'Combating the Financing of Terrorism: A History and Assessment of the Control of "Threat Finance"' (2010) 50(4) *British Journal of Criminology* 650.

and EU border control databases (BOR) to report on the perspectives of operational actors on the impact, legitimacy and effectiveness of EU counter-terrorism law and policy. Each of the focus groups comprised participants from a variety of EU Member States. Although the research team sent invitations to participants from all Member States for each focus group, not all invitees were able and willing to participate. The total participant number was twenty-six with the breakdown as follows. The EAW focus group involved eight participants, consisting of prosecutors, judicial officers, governmental officials and one 'national expert'.[4] The CTF focus group involved eleven participants, each of whom was a current or former official from a financial intelligence unit (FIU) or a civil servant with experience in the field.[5] The BOR focus group involved seven participants – all were current or former law enforcement officers – six of whom were from civil law enforcement and one from the military. The BOR participants had a variety of professional experience, in particular with the Schengen information system.[6] The focus groups took place in London on 10–12 December, 2013.[7]

There are clear limitations on the generalizability of the claims made by the research participants owing to the small sample size, the process of participant selection, and as a result the limited extent to which the participants can be said to be representative of counter-terrorism operatives as a whole. If there is a single conclusion from this research as a whole it is that this is a field in which more empirical research with operational actors is necessary to obtain a more complete picture of the workings of counter-terrorism law and policy. The work we present here may be part of the beginning of a turn towards empiricism in EU counter-terrorism law and policy research – it is by no means the end.

The project as a whole took as its focus the impact, legitimacy and effectiveness of counter-terrorism measures.[8] These terms were taken because of

4 Participant A (Estonia); Participant B (Ireland); Participant C (Italy); Participant D (Romania); Participant E (United Kingdom [Scotland]); Participant F (Sweden); Participant G (Netherlands); and Participant H (Netherlands).

5 Participant A (United Kingdom); Participant B (Ireland); Participant C (Malta); Participant D (Belgium); Participant E (Bulgaria); Participant F (Latvia); Participant G (Latvia); Participant H (Portugal); Participant I (Romania); Participant J (Poland); and Participant K (United Kingdom).

6 Participant A (Spain); Participant B (Ireland); Participant C (Spain); Participant D (Latvia); Participant E (Greece); Participant F (Greece) and Participant G (Spain).

7 For a full account of the methodology of the project see C.C. Murphy, A. Zammit Borda & L. Hoyte, *Law Enforcement Officers Perspective on Impact, Legitimacy & Effectiveness of EU Border Control Databases* (SECILE, 2014); C.C. Murphy, A. Zammit Borda & L. Hoyte, *Counter Terrorism Finance Operatives Perspectives on Impact, Legitimacy & Effectiveness of EU Counter-Terrorist Finance Law and Policy* (SECILE, 2014); C.C. Murphy, A. Zammit Borda & L. Hoyte, *Prosecutor and Government Officials Perspectives on Impact, Legitimacy & Effectiveness of the European Arrest Warrant* (SECILE, 2014).

References in this chapter follow the system in those reports – taking the format subject-question-participant.

8 See http://www.secile.eu (accessed 6 September 2014). See further the work of de Londras and Doody in the introduction to this volume.

their frequent use in popular and political debate on the measures. However, in the focus groups undertaken by the King's research team, the question of definition was left to the participants themselves. As the remainder of this chapter makes clear, there were sometimes conflicting, at other times converging, understandings of the concepts.

The participants in all focus group held that the events of 11 September 2001 intensified the urgency of adopting and implementing counter-terrorism measures. For instance, one participant in the EAW focus group set out that, even though the principle of mutual recognition in criminal justice was already in the Tampere European Council Conclusions of 1999, it was the events of 11 September 2001 that increased the sense of urgency to adopt the EAW Framework Decision.[9] Similarly, despite the prior existence of an anti-money laundering framework, the CTF focus group participants keenly felt the effect of the 11 September 2001 attacks. One participant from Belgium said clearly, 'September 2001 occurred. And then everything moved.'[10]

However, while acknowledging the importance of 11 September 2001, the same participant was not sure that the measures adopted in the aftermath were effective today. In particular, he was sceptical as to the appropriateness of merging the anti-money laundering and counter-terrorist finance policy fields.[11] A similar thought was expressed by a participant in the BOR focus group, in relation to the balance between human rights and effectiveness. According to this participant, in '[t]he period after 11 September 2001, I think that there was a great motivation all over the world, in the laws against terrorism and a great motivation against human rights, it was very strong.'[12] The same participant stated: 'I think, as yet, we try to find ways to balance between effectiveness and human rights.'[13] This tension – between effective security policies and respect for constitutional principles and human rights – runs throughout the fieldwork data.

2. The impact of EU counter-terrorism law and policy

In carrying out the focus groups, the King's research team was keen to ascertain not just what the impact of counter-terrorism measures had been, but also what the operational actors' perspectives were on how to identify and understand such an impact. The participants were given broad scope to discuss their perceptions of European security and the contribution, if any, of the measures in question. The frame for the discussion was whether Europe was more secure or less secure as a result of the measures – with the participants left to explore these questions in the light of their experiences.

9 EAW-Q4-H – Netherlands.
10 CTF-Q1-D – Belgium.
11 CTF-Q1-D – Belgium.
12 BOR-Q7-E – Greece.
13 BOR-Q7-E – Greece.

Assessing the impact of counter-terrorism measures

Although the question of how to assess the impact of the respective measures arose in the CTF and BOR focus groups, it did not arise in the EAW focus group. This may be because the impact of the EAW Framework Decision may be more easily assessed in terms of the stated objectives of that measure and also in relation to the operation of the previous extradition arrangements in Europe.[14] Indeed, many of the participants compared and contrasted procedures under the EAW Framework Decision to those that had existed before. However such a benchmark may be more difficult to identify in relation to CTF and BOR. For instance, in the BOR focus group, one participant emphasized the need for quantitative data to assess the impact of the EU border control databases: 'I think, the answer is facts – how many bombs [were] exploded this year, last year?'[15]

In the CTF focus group, the participants' consideration of impact in this policy field brought about a discussion of how difficult it is to determine impact in the absence of 'a global or European-wide risk assessment [for terrorist finance]'.[16] Such a risk assessment would, of course, need to identify what the risks to be addressed are and what the objectives of any system to manage those risks should be. At a more general level, some participants suggested that the overall objectives of these measures included the prevention of terrorism[17] and improving the safety of citizens.[18] Others were less sure. For example, one participant reflected, 'I don't think [counter-terrorism] will ever end crime and terrorism but at least [these measures may serve] to disrupt it as best you can'.[19] In contrast to this actuarial approach, another participant held that the objective may be to collect evidence in order to prosecute suspects of terrorism activities.[20] There was disagreement on this point, with the first participant countering that, while the prosecution of suspects of terrorism may be desirable, 'disrupting them is an end in itself'.[21] This exchange indicates the tension between actuarial justice (going beyond crime control) and criminal justice as a system built around prosecutions through due process – a tension that is salient to counter-terrorist finance.[22]

There was also some disagreement as to the appropriate geographic basis for any risk assessment. One participant's view was that it was the security

---

14 Council Framework Decision of 13 June 2002 on the European Arrest Warrant and the Surrender Procedures between Member States (2002/584/JHA).

15 BOR-Q5-A – Spain.

16 CTF-Q2-A – United Kingdom.

17 CTF-Q3/4-K – United Kingdom.

18 CTF-Q4-B – Ireland.

19 CTF-Q4-B – Ireland.

20 CTF-Q3-A – United Kingdom.

21 CTF-Q4-B – Ireland.

22 See C.C. Murphy, *EU Counter-terrorism Law: Pre-emption and the Rule of Law* (Oxford: Hart Publishing, 2012) Chapter One.

risks facing each Member State that was an appropriate basis rather than the risk to the EU as a whole. He held that, in spite of the EU's global position in the area of CTF, particularly in the area of restrictive measures (financial sanctions), it was 'difficult to give a picture of Europe as a whole'.[23] This was because the threat of terrorism was best understood at the level of the Member States: 'there are different EU Member States which are more or less secure . . . this is not about the EU as a whole'.[24] Thus, according to this participant, the impact of CTF measures could differ amongst EU Member States: 'does the Polish citizen feel safe in Poland? Yes, he does. And I don't know about other states, the answer might be totally different'.[25] These concerns echo those made by civil society representatives and EU policy-makers in other aspects of the SECILE consortium's work.[26]

Impact on European security

While acknowledging the challenges of any assessment of impact, the participants did express a view as to the measures' contribution to European security. The responses to the question of whether participants thought the measures in question (EAW, CTF, or BOR measures) made the EU more secure were mixed. In general, the EAW focus group participants agreed that the impact of the EAW has been positive and that it has contributed to improving EU security. Thus, in response to the question 'Do you think the European Arrest Warrant makes the EU more secure?', all participants replied in the affirmative. Moreover, in response to the converse question, 'Do you think the European Arrest Warrant makes the EU less secure?', participants generally agreed that they did not consider the EAW system makes the EU less secure. With the exception of improbable scenarios wherein the operation of the system might preclude the otherwise appropriate surrender of a suspect or convict, the participants could not imagine how the EAW might render Europe less secure.[27]

In contrast, when the CTF focus group participants were asked the same question in respect of counter-terrorism measures in their field, they considered that, although this is an important question, it is difficult to answer.[28] Nevertheless, one participant answered in the affirmative and noted that the development of common measures in this area across EU Member States is, to some extent, a necessary corollary of the development of the common market in the EU. For this participant, CTF measures represent an important step in matching the potential for abuse of the common market by

23 CTF-Q2-J – Poland.
24 CTF-Q2-J – Poland.
25 CTF-Q2-J – Poland.
26 See Chapter 9, this volume.
27 EAW-Q3-E – United Kingdom (Scotland).
28 CTF-Q1-J – Poland.

criminals.[29] However, not all participants agreed. One participant gave two reasons for answering in the negative to this question.[30] First, he pointed out that when CTF measures were adopted in the aftermath of 11 September 2001, they were modelled on anti-money laundering law and policy, which may not have been appropriate and may have potentially undermined the effectiveness of existing strategies. Second, he contended that the European system did not acknowledge that FIUs (those offices or agencies that give effect to CTF measures in the Member States) operate as a 'sort of secret financial service,'[31] dealing with 'future possible crime.'[32] This limited the positive impact that CTF measures could have on EU security.

There was a similar divergence of views with respect to the above question in the BOR focus group. In response to the question 'Do you think that EU databases or systems of information exchange make Europe more secure?', a participant from Spain replied '[a]bsolutely, yes'.[33] Furthermore, in response to the converse question, namely 'Do you think that EU databases and systems of information control make Europe less secure?', the same participant answered 'I think this is just the contrary.'[34] Another participant agreed that '[f]rom a maritime perspective it definitely is working.'[35] However, there was scepticism as to the role of border controls and databases in particular. One participant set out that although databases helped law enforcement officers to do their job more efficiently, it would be a mistake to overstate their importance or to base European security on databases alone.[36] Thus, while agreeing that databases could play a useful role in improving security, a participant from Greece set out that 'we need databases but [we] don't need *only* databases.'[37] The same participant also held that it would be wrong to think that the use of such databases could reduce the threat of terrorism. According to this participant 'the threat remains the same, the threat from outside.'[38] When asked to explain what he considered to be the 'outside', his reply was 'everywhere . . . everywhere.'[39]

Broader impact: to displace insecurity?

The discussion of security risks was not limited to Europe. Participants in all three focus groups, to varying degrees, made reference to the potential

29 CTF-Q1-B – Ireland.
30 CTF-Q1-D – Belgium.
31 CTF-Q1-D – Belgium.
32 CTF-Q1-D – Belgium.
33 BOR-Q1-A – Spain.
34 BOR-Q2-A – Spain.
35 BOR-Q5-B – Ireland.
36 BOR-Q1-F – Greece.
37 BOR-Q1-E – Greece.
38 BOR-Q6-F – Greece.
39 BOR-Q6-F – Greece.

for EU action to displace activity by suspects of terrorism to jurisdictions outside Europe. For example, one participant observed that, perhaps as an unintended consequence of the operation of the EAW, criminals may move to third countries where they know extradition is more difficult than in the EU. While this may become a problem, with respect to the operation of the EAW within the EU itself, in the words of this participant, there 'is no safe haven anymore.'[40]

A participant in the CTF focus group also made this point with conviction. He considered that, as a result of CTF laws and policies adopted within the EU, certain industries may move away from the EU to avoid the European regulatory framework.[41] He referred to the diamond industry as an example. While the departure of some businesses in this sector to the Middle East may be indicative that the European system may disrupt terrorist financing within the EU, he was concerned that some businesses in 'these countries might help . . . movements which might be involved in terrorist action', and thereby create security problems for Europe.[42] A participant in the BOR focus group also referred to the possibility of suspects of terrorism moving to third countries. He reflected that, owing to globalization, those who wish to commit acts of terrorism may move from state to state, and therefore information exchange amongst law enforcement officials was 'very important.'[43]

The definition of terrorism and the classification of measures

In the EAW and BOR focus groups, participants agreed that the respective measures were not primarily regarded as counter-terrorism measures and had far wider application. In the EAW focus group, participants considered that, even though the EAW Framework Decision had been adopted in the aftermath of the 11 September 2001 terrorist attacks, the EAW is an instrument that has a much broader application than counter-terrorism. One participant said:

> [I] would not necessarily see the EAW as . . . an instrument which has a specific or unique value in terms of counter terrorism. Yes, it has a value [in respect of counter-terrorism] but it obviously has a far wider application.[44]

Although counter-terrorist finance measures are, by definition, about counter-terrorism, some participants in the CTF focus group sought to

40 EAW-Q2-D – Romania.
41 CTF-Q1-D – Belgium.
42 CTF-Q1-D – Belgium.
43 BOR-Q3-G – Spain.
44 EAW–Q4–B – Ireland.

highlight the links between terrorism and other crimes. For instance, one participant posited that, in the context of terrorism, 'the discussion always falls on organised crime [and] drug trafficking because this is the source, the income for . . . eventual terrorist action'.[45] This participant made note of the close links between crimes because 'when we talk about controls on organised crime in Europe, definitely, this affects the ability of terrorist strands or groups to . . . deploy their . . . terrorist resources'.[46] Another participant also drew out this link between terrorism and organized crime:

> There is demonstrable and inextricable links between organised crime and terrorism . . . and actions that are taken to counter money laundering . . . can be very effective in disrupting organised crime.[47]

The participant from Belgium went on to note that it is 'quite difficult to find a distinction between terrorist financing and money laundering.'[48] The use of databases is prevalent in both border controls and counter-terrorist finance. However, in general, participants considered that databases were more effective in fighting organized crime than terrorism. Indeed, a participant in the BOR focus group noted that 'the object of the criminals in general is money . . . but . . . terrorists fight against other things or targets [which] could be more important for this society.'[49]

A recurring problem for the participants in the EAW and BOR focus groups, which may influence any assessment of the impact (as well as effectiveness) of such measures, was the absence of a common definition of terrorism across EU Member States. Thus, for instance, in the EAW focus group, while participants agreed that terrorism-related uses of the EAW represented a very small percentage of overall EAW uses, one participant reflected that these numbers might be influenced by the absence of a definition of terrorism in the EAW Framework Decision.[50] In the BOR focus group, some participants also raised the question of the definition of terrorism. One participant set out that before databases can be used in counter-terrorism 'we have to agree on our definition of terrorism.'[51] Another participant agreed, stating that 'to help prevention [of] terrorism we have to define exactly what we mean by terrorism.'[52]

---

45 CTF-Q1-C – Malta.
46 CTF-Q1-C – Malta.
47 CTF-Q4-B – Ireland.
48 CTF-Q2-D – Belgium.
49 BOR-Q3-C – Spain.
50 EAW-Q4-E – United Kingdom (Scotland).
51 BOR-Q3-C – Spain.
52 BOR-Q3-E – Greece.

3. The effectiveness of EU counter-terrorism law and policy

The line between participants' views on the impact of counter-terrorism law and policy and the effectiveness of those measures is not an easy one to draw. The King's research team, drawing on the data from the three focus groups, took the view that effectiveness was most often understood by the participants as relating to the details of a measure's operational efficacy rather than the extent to which it achieved broader objectives relating to European security. However, this line was a blurry one and the division between impact and effectiveness owes as much to the need for presentational coherence as it does to categorical definition. The aspects of effectiveness that arose across the focus groups include mutual trust, cooperation and information exchange across Member States, cooperation within Member States (between agencies and with the private sector), the challenges of differences in legal systems and limitations on the effectiveness of any single measure to alter the security landscape.

Mutual trust, cooperation and information exchange

The theme that emerged most often across the three focus groups in respect of effectiveness is the central role of mutual trust, cooperation and information exchange between Member States in the operation of such measures. However, the degree to which participants considered that such mutual trust exists, and the level of cooperation and information exchange that occurs, was different across the three focus groups. The EAW Framework Decision, as a legal measure, is based on the principle of mutual recognition: that Member State authorities will recognize and give effect to legal decisions of other Member State authorities.[53] In this regard, one participant in the EAW focus group observed that the high percentage of successful surrenders in his country is, in large part, 'because of mutual respect and mutual recognition'.[54] Another participant emphasized:

> It is absolutely central to this area of work for practitioners . . . It has reinforced not only the judicial culture, but also brought prosecutors closer together, I think, to work together, on the basis that they know . . . that the decision . . . will be recognised abroad.[55]

Participants thought that a further achievement of the EAW is that it facilitates direct contact between judicial authorities. Some participants

53 See, for a general assessment V. Mitsilegas, 'The Limits of Mutual Trust in Europe's Area of Freedom, Security and Justice: From Automatic Inter-state Cooperation to the Slow Emergence of the Individual' (2012) *Yearbook of European Law*, p. 319.

54 EAW-Q3-B – Ireland.

55 EAW-Q2-E – United Kingdom (Scotland).

agreed that direct contact is one of the features of the EAW system that makes it better than the previous extradition system. One participant noted that 'it really makes it possible to speak with each other . . . maybe to look for an alternative or if we don't understand each other'.[56] The participant compared the EAW system with the previous extradition system, which fell under the remit of the Ministry of Justice in his Member State and was a slower process.[57] On this point, another participant said that:

> One of the very valuable things that we find, which is a huge difference, is the fact that if we have a problem with a particular warrant which has been issued by a Member State, we simply contact the judge directly. Or we can go through the European Judicial Network. Very rarely, unless it's a particularly complex case, will we approach Eurojust.[58]

However, the same participant indicated that there is scope to improve direct contact. For instance, he held that the relevant authorities should seek to engage with each other earlier in the criminal justice process in order for prosecutors to agree on jurisdiction and then to deal with evidence, which is a difficult subject. He emphasized that the EAW is best issued after such direct contact has taken place.[59]

This cooperation may lead to a convergence in legal cultures in national criminal justice systems. One participant made reference to potential changes in the Polish legal system in relation to the proportionate use of the EAW. The participant suggested that Polish authorities are taking steps towards changing the law as a result of dialogue in the operation of the EAW.[60] He held that 'cooperation or pressure between judicial authorities' might therefore provide a better approach to balancing national systems than changing legal frameworks.[61]

However, some participants also drew out problems in relation to mutual trust in this field. They considered that perhaps one of the greatest challenges to the effectiveness of the EAW was the use of human rights arguments as a ground for refusal to execute an EAW. These participants emphasized that all EU Member States were signatories to the European Convention on Human Rights (ECHR).[62] Nevertheless, the participant from the United Kingdom (Scotland) made clear that human rights arguments in the UK had been raised on various grounds, such as on Article 3 (prison conditions); Article 5 (length of pre-trial detention), and Article 8 (separation of parents

56 EAW-Q2-A – Estonia.
57 EAW-Q2-A – Estonia.
58 EAW-Q2-E – United Kingdom (Scotland).
59 EAW-Q5/6-E – United Kingdom (Scotland).
60 EAW-Q3-H – Netherlands.
61 EAW-Q3-H – Netherlands.
62 EAW-Q2-E – United Kingdom (Scotland).

from children) of the ECHR.[63] Although participants generally agreed that only a minority of EAW requests were unsuccessful on account of human rights challenges, one participant observed that it 'goes against the principle of recognition and trust that, even within the Member States, they still take account of human rights arguments'.[64] Another participant reflected that, in cases where suspects or convicts have successfully argued on human rights grounds, it appeared to be 'a contradiction of the underpinning of the [EAW Framework Decision] by mutual respect and mutual recognition which is obviously predicated on every Member State signing up to common human rights standards'.[65] Yet another participant expressed the concern that 'mutual recognition [and] human rights are growing apart from one another'.[66]

In the CTF focus group, participants were far more sceptical about the level of mutual trust amongst Member States and about the willingness of national agencies to cooperate and exchange information on counter-terrorism matters. One participant, for instance, expressed significant scepticism about the willingness to cooperate beyond existing bilateral agreements:

> Are we – all Member States – really interested in exchanging intelligence and information? Honestly – are we? Or we are not? Or, we are really interested when you have something to give and I will give you something . . . this is the first point I want to stress. . . The second is trust: domestic trust and external trust. If we want to exchange information we have together to have the information from our financial entities. . . And do they trust on us? Do they give us all the information, all the intelligence, we want and we need or not? In my opinion it's not a question of being a law enforcement type of FIU or administrative type of FIU – it's a question of respect and trust. If they trust us they will send us information.[67]

Another participant drew attention to the reluctance amongst some Member States to facilitate cooperation in this field, prompting him to suggest that such Member States might ask 'are we in or are we out?'[68] In this context, some participants wondered whether EU structures, working on a multilateral basis, could achieve as much as bilateral cooperation. For example, the participant from the United Kingdom deliberated: 'effective intelligence procedures – intelligence is still shown bilaterally at times and is shared between trusted partners and I think in some ways the EU lacks that credible intelligence to turn what the intelligence produces into effective

63 EAW-Q2-E – United Kingdom (Scotland).
64 EAW-Q2-E – United Kingdom (Scotland).
65 EAW-Q2-B – Ireland.
66 EAW-Q2-G – Netherlands.
67 CTF-Q1-H – Portugal.
68 CTF-Q2-D – Belgium.

measures'.[69] The participant from Ireland also held information sharing to be an important but difficult area of operation:

> [We need] to find ways around that for the intelligence sharing community that allows them to be more effective in perhaps the bilateral interactions in the European Union. Some Member States find it easier than others to manage those relationships – they may have a unitary system of policing and intelligence. Other Member States have various organisations that are engaged in various aspects and there may be internal coordination problems that arise, first of all, before there's any external coordination problem within the EU or indeed external coordination in further countries.'[70]

The centrality of mutual trust, cooperation and information exchange was also apparent in the BOR focus group. In particular, information exchange was said to be necessary for the protection of both land and sea borders. For instance, with respect to land borders, a participant emphasized the need for such exchange between Spanish and French police to monitor members of the Basque separatist group ETA who might move from Spain to France. With respect to sea borders, another participant observed that 'information sharing is paramount for military security at sea'.[71] For this reason, there is a project in development to facilitate an information-sharing environment for maritime surveillance.[72]

However, while acknowledging the importance of information exchange, several participants in the BOR focus group thought that the issue of mutual trust impacted the degree to which information was shared through databases, or even whether it was shared at all. One participant observed that 'the states or the organisations in the state don't trust the others, don't trust the users and don't share the . . . important information in database[s].'[73] This participant elaborated:

> Many states . . . use bilateral exchanges and don't use the databases, especially in terrorism matters. They prefer it, because they don't trust it to put their data in the databases of international organisations – or in [the] EU organisation.[74]

Other participants also sought to stress the challenges of information exchange. One participant, for instance, considered that the need-to-know

---

69 CTF-Q1-A – United Kingdom.

70 CTF-Q1-B – Ireland.

71 BOR-Q1-B – Ireland.

72 BOR-Q1-B – Ireland. See further F. de Londras, J. Doody and E. Dowling, *Report on Operational Perspectives on Impact, Legitimacy and Effectiveness in Counter-terrorism* (SECILE, 2013).

73 BOR-Q3-F – Greece.

74 BOR-Q4-F – Greece.

principle was 'too restraining [and . . .] the intelligence made for one country is not shared with all.'[75] This participant considered that the sharing of information on the basis of this principle was not sufficiently effective.[76] Others made the suggestion that Member States may input 'irrelevant details' into databases, which could hinder the effectiveness of these databases.[77]

Cooperation within Member States and information exchange

The CTF and BOR focus groups also drew attention to the importance of cooperation and information exchange between agencies within each Member State – as well as the need for cooperation with the private sector. As one participant in the CTF focus group pointed out, sometimes agencies within a Member State do not share relevant information in a timely manner. He noted that:

> [I]n Latvia we have different institutions that are involved in decisions about fighting counter terrorism and sometimes this information doesn't go from one national service to another national service. So just like in your country if people don't know what's going on or what next door is doing so . . . it's also a big problem.[78]

In this context, some participants in the CTF focus group asked whether FIUs should be understood as a form of secret service:

> What we are collecting is sometimes important information, sensitive intelligence, which are not going to be used in the process of prosecuting somebody but which may be used in the process of preventing terrorist acts to be committed . . . FIUs are [a] sort of secret financial service . . .[79]

This point found support from some, but not all, of the other participants. For example, another participant observed that:

> Financial Intelligence Units could be aligned – could be considered as intelligence structure in terms of secret service . . . but as providers of intelligence products for the law enforcement or for any other interested parties in the national system for combating terrorist financing.[80]

75 BOR-Q4-A – Spain.
76 BOR-Q4-A – Spain.
77 BOR-Q3-F – Greece.
78 CTF-Q1-G – Latvia.
79 CTF-Q1-D – Belgium.
80 CTF-Q5-I – Romania.

The status of FIUs (whether they are administrative units, part of the criminal justice system, or intelligence agencies) may influence their powers to request and exchange information. Participants also discussed the need for cooperation and information exchange between the public and private sectors, distinguishing between those who regulate and those who are subject to regulation. The participants considered various entities that, depending on one's perspective, could be regarded as the regulator or the regulatee in counter-terrorist finance. For instance, the regulator could be an entity devising and applying certain controls, such as the government and FIUs, whereas the regulatee could be an entity subject to such controls, such as financial service providers.[81] However, regulators could also be private actors involved in counter-terrorist finance, such as financial service providers, while regulatees could be consumers of financial services. Thus, for the participants, there is a 'circularity running right the way through [the system]'.[82]

Some participants also referred to the 'inequality of interests' between regulators and regulatees,[83] and took the view that 'aligning the interests'[84] of all sides was a 'key point'.[85] However, the lack of a risk assessment as to threats in this field could make it harder to agree on common goals. As one participant put it, 'you have no way of measuring what your risk is, you don't know how far you're getting short or beyond . . . the goal'.[86] There was strong agreement, particularly between the participants from Ireland and the United Kingdom, on this topic. They agreed on the importance of 'narrowing the gap between the interests on both sides'[87] because otherwise 'you're building a dichotomy into your system'.[88] The participant from Ireland said that 'buy-in' was needed from financial service providers and that this had to be based on self-interest:

> It is buying them [financial service providers] in as an arm of the state in effect but it's buying them in on a basis of self-interest in that you're improving the system of financial regulation generally, and it's a protection for these institutions themselves.[89]

The participant from the United Kingdom asserted that, in order to minimize potential discord in the system, it was necessary to 'get everybody willing to stop terrorism'.[90] This might in part be achieved through privatizing

81 CTF-Q3/4-K – United Kingdom.
82 CTF-Q3/4-K – United Kingdom.
83 CTF-Q3/4-B – Ireland.
84 CTF-Q2-K – United Kingdom.
85 CTF-Q3/4-B – Ireland.
86 CTF-Q2-K – United Kingdom.
87 CTF-Q3-B – Ireland.
88 CTF-Q2-K – United Kingdom.
89 CTF-Q3-B – Ireland.
90 CTF-Q3/4-K – United Kingdom.

controls for terrorism, establishing a sort of 'shareholders relationship with the [financial service providers] rather than a command-control, master-servant relationship'.[91] In addition, the participant from Ireland held that it is important to incorporate terrorist financing into 'not just anti-money laundering but into financial regulation generally'.[92] This may be one way to narrow the intelligence-sharing gap between governments and FIUs on the one hand and financial service providers on the other.[93]

In the BOR focus group, participants also referred to the wide array of databases, from both the public and private sectors, which may be useful in counter-terrorism operations. However, in contrast with the CTF focus group, the need for cooperation and information exchange with the private sector did not give rise to significant debate in the BOR focus group. In addition to the official databases, one participant held that there were many 'databases in the private sector, the databases that the banks have, that healthcare has, other kinds.'[94] In another intervention, this participant also made reference to the databases of telecommunications service providers, noting that these can be made available to law enforcement under relevant national legislation.[95]

Another participant said that the police might collect information from various different databases.[96] In addition to public (EU-level and Member State-level) databases, and the databases of private enterprises such as banks, the healthcare system and telecommunication enterprises, one participant also referred to 'big data coming from Facebook, Twitter.'[97] Another participant agreed that 'there is the possibility for the police to . . . learn . . . a lot of things from private sector databases'.[98] However, he hastened to add that such databases should only be used with appropriate permission.[99]

Legal system diversity and effectiveness

The diversity of legal systems across the EU Member States and potential incompatibilities between them may, according to the EAW focus group participants, undermine the effectiveness of counter-terrorism. Many participants in the EAW focus group referred to the strain arising from differences between civil and common law systems that could hamper the effectiveness of the EAW system. One participant noted:

91 CTF-Q3/4-K – United Kingdom.
92 CTF-Q3/4-B – Ireland.
93 CTF-Q3-B – Ireland.
94 BOR-Q6-E – Greece.
95 BOR-Q4-E – Greece.
96 BOR-Q6-A – Spain.
97 BOR-Q6-A – Spain.
98 BOR-Q6-E – Greece.
99 BOR-Q6-E – Greece.

> Perhaps the EAW is coming under a little strain in relation to trying to marry the two systems [common law and civil law]. It is, in many ways, an instrument that is predicated on a civil law system.[100]

For instance, he noted that, in Ireland, which has a common law system, authorities from other Member States have no way of engaging directly with an Irish judge responsible for an EAW; 'everything goes through various intermediaries' and this may be a cause for frustration and complaint.[101] Another participant agreed that the different models of central authority could, in their own way, affect the operation of the system.[102] One participant made the claim that, perhaps as a result of these tensions, 'some persons that should serve their imprisonment in Estonia have found a perfect hide-out in the UK'.[103] However, another participant, while acknowledging that different legal traditions can cause problems, observed that cooperation is evolving and is better than it was before the EAW system. She was 'positive that it will improve'.[104] The question of the coherence of counter-terrorism measures also arose in relation to counter-terrorist finance, where a participant made the point that incoherent policy action may undermine the legitimacy of that action.[105]

A further point in this vein, emerging from the CTF and BOR focus groups, was that the growing complexity of counter-terrorism measures could undermine the effectiveness of those measures. Thus, one participant in the CTF focus group argued that Europe may be less secure, not only because of the actual threat of terrorism, but also because European CTF law and policy action was unduly complex.[106] In the midst of such complexity, one participant observed that one might lose sight of the ultimate ends of CTF measures, and that the system would become self-perpetuating or an end in itself, which, in turn, could threaten the rule of law.[107] In this context, the same participant said:

> What you're doing is ending up with a means as an end to itself, which all looks nice and tidy, but in effect what you're doing is subverting the existing rules of law in order to achieve an end . . . which doesn't achieve [that] end.[108]

---

100 EAW-Q2-B – Ireland.
101 EAW-Q2-B – Ireland.
102 EAW-Q2-E – United Kingdom (Scotland).
103 EAW-Q2-A – Estonia.
104 EAW-Q2-D – Romania.
105 CTF-Q4-D – Belgium. See further the discussion of legitimacy later in this chapter.
106 CTF-Q1-J – Poland.
107 CTF-Q3/4-A – United Kingdom.
108 CTF-Q3/4-A – United Kingdom.

In the BOR focus group, some participants also expressed concern at the growing size and complexity of border control databases. For instance, in discussing the development of SIS II, one participant commented that 'we are trying to have over 70 million [records] in 5 years – more or less – finger prints, pictures, some kind of biometrics data. . .'[109] Another participant went on to say that this should serve as an important reminder about 'why we have huge databases . . . There's always a new database, more and more data,'[110] and these databases every year tend to be 'more complicated'.[111] In light of these developments, there was a concern that the increasing size of databases could create 'a panoptical system'.[112] Another participant expressed concern that:

> We create a huge number of databases, we store a huge amount of information, and finally, we can't manage with [the] information stored on [the] database. We need specialists to deal with the stored data. It's too difficult to deal with huge databases with millions [of pieces] of information. . .[113]

The same participant went on to observe that, in view of this complexity, it was sometimes difficult to manage the various databases and to find the 'correct answer to my question which I put in [the] database'.[114] In this regard, this participant stressed the importance of 'experience and training'.[115]

A related discussion that arose in the EAW and CTF focus groups was that discrete counter-terrorism measures had to be understood as part of a package of instruments. In this context, in the EAW focus group, one participant suggested that there are several other instruments that can be used instead of the EAW, especially in the trial stage of the case, such as the use of conference calls. She noted that, in Romania, measures had been put in place to train the 'judiciary to use these alternative instruments'.[116] She emphasized that the EAW should be used 'really for those serious offences and . . . as a last resort'.[117] This view resonated with several other participants. For instance, one participant posited that the EAW should come in 'really at the far end of the spectrum'[118] while another participant agreed that it is 'the end piece.'[119]

109 BOR-Q8-A – Spain.
110 BOR-Q8-E – Greece.
111 BOR-Q8-E – Greece.
112 BOR-Q1-E – Greece.
113 BOR-Q8-F – Greece.
114 BOR-Q8-F – Greece.
115 BOR-Q1-F – Greece.
116 EAW-Q9-D – Romania.
117 EAW-Q9-D – Romania.
118 EAW-Q5/6-B – Ireland.
119 EAW-Q5/6-E – United Kingdom (Scotland).

In this context, in the CTF focus group, one participant made the point that policies and measures in this area should not only focus on terrorist financing but should have a broader scope. She observed that 'terrorist organizations do not need only money to survive . . . They need also logistical equipment, they need knowledge, they need exercise, they need proper training, guns and so on . . . '[120] She noted that although EU rules on customer due diligence were strong, there are ways to circumvent these measures, such as through trade.[121] She made the claim that it is possible to use trade to obtain guns or explosive materials – or even food.[122] In this context, any strategy with a sole focus on financial transfers to suspects of terrorism is incomplete.[123]

4. Legitimacy of EU counter-terrorism law and policy

The discussion of the legitimacy of EU counter-terrorism law and policy yielded some of the richest data across the three focus groups. It is clear from the data that for the research participants, legitimacy, as a consideration in counter-terrorism law and policy, can be understood either in terms of lawfulness or in a broader sense. The cultivation of a broader sense of legitimacy involves, for the participants, legal processes to vindicate human rights as well as appropriate scrutiny of governmental action. The discussion of legitimacy also brought the discussion in the focus group back to the Tampere Programme and the development of the EU's area of freedom, security and justice.[124]

Lawfulness as legitimacy

The relationship between lawfulness and legitimacy is a classic locus of debate in constitutional theory and it arose in the discussions in both the EAW and BOR focus groups. A key exchange between two participants in the EAW focus group illustrates clearly the assumption of legitimacy when there is a legal basis for action but also that this assumption is open to question:

Participant H: 'Maybe I don't understand the word "legitimate" but it's in law . . . this is why it's legitimate at least . . .'
Participant A: 'That only makes it legal!'
Participant H: 'Yep. Maybe I don't understand the word "legitimate". . .'[125]

120 CTF-Q1-I – Romania.

121 Directive 2005/60/EC of the European Parliament and of the Council of 26 October 2005 on the prevention of the use of the financial system for the purpose of money laundering and terrorist financing.

122 CTF-Q1-I – Romania.

123 CTF-Q1-I – Romania.

124 For a general introduction on this point see C.C. Murphy and D. Acosta Arcarazo, 'Rethinking Europe's Freedom, Security, and Justice' in D. Acosta Arcarazo and C.C. Murphy, *EU Security and Justice Law: After Lisbon and Stockholm* (Oxford: Hart Publishing, 2014).

125 EAW-Q9-H – Netherlands with interjection from A-Estonia.

Similarly, in the BOR focus group, one participant's straightforward response to the question of the legitimacy of border control databases was: 'Yeah, my opinion is – it's legal'.[126] However, participants in all focus groups went on to discuss the question of legitimacy in a broader sense.

Need for broader legitimization

This need for broader legitimization arose in different ways. In the EAW focus group, one participant said: 'so is it legitimate? Yes because it's the law we've been given to work with. I would say that what lies behind your question is: is it fair?'[127] In a discussion on the proportionate use of criminal justice measures, two participants emphasized that the use of the EAW for seemingly trivial cases may damage the public's view of the EAW system. This indicates that the participants are aware of the social dimension to legitimacy. For instance, one participant asserted that:

> [I]t probably has had some damage in undermining public confidence and public trust in the EAW – when people see families being sundered – people who've been living in that Member State for 10 years, paying taxes, law abiding and being arrested and possibly extradited in relation to an offence, which in the host Member State would be regarded as trivial.[128]

In the CTF focus group, a participant identified the democratic bases of the treaties as another element of legitimacy. This participant explained why, in his opinion, CTF law and policy is legitimate. First, he pointed out that:

> The treaties are very clear and have democratic bases: in the European Union; in the Member States getting together as collective action to create an area of freedom, security and justice . . . which inevitably implies taking actions where it can to improve the safety of citizens.[129]

Despite the reference to democracy, the research participants were unclear on how aware the public are of counter-terrorism measures and their operation. The issue of lack of public awareness did not arise in respect of the EAW – perhaps because the EAW has often been in the public spotlight. Indeed, as set out above, participants thought that over-use, or inappropriate use of the EAW, 'probably has had some damage in undermining public confidence and public trust in the EAW'.[130] In contrast, one participant in the CTF focus group observed that there was a lack of awareness of EU

126 BOR-Q7-A – Spain.
127 EAW-Q9-E – Scotland.
128 EAW-Q3-B – Ireland.
129 CTF-Q4-B – Ireland.
130 EAW-Q3-B – Ireland.

action in the CTF sphere: 'I doubt that very many people, outside . . . a narrow group, are aware of what the EU does in a . . . [counter-]terrorist financing way'.[131] The lack of awareness of databases also arose in the BOR focus group. One participant stated:

> I'm not sure that citizens know what databases exist and which of their personal data are stored in those databases. Every European citizen must know that, and today, our citizen does not know.[132]

There was general agreement with this statement. The importance of democratic and social legitimization of EU counter-terrorism law and policy was therefore clear to the research participants – even if they had significant doubts as to whether the various systems achieve such legitimization at present.

Legal protection, due process and human rights

Across the three focus groups, participants placed emphasis on the role of legal protection, due process and respect for human rights in their discussions on legitimacy. However, there was a marked divergence of views as to whether existing legal protections and accountability mechanisms provide sufficient safeguards for individuals affected by counter-terrorism measures. For instance, as discussed above in respect of the EAW focus group, some participants thought that one of the greatest challenges to the effectiveness of the EAW was the use of human rights arguments as a ground for refusal to surrender a suspect or convict. Given that all EU Member States are members of the ECHR, such challenges were seen as unnecessary and contrary to the principle of mutual recognition.[133]

However, for the participant from Sweden, the existing safeguards were not enough; rather this participant thought it was also necessary to legislate for the rights of those subject to surrender:

> [The EAW] is a significant improvement of the law enforcement agencies' powers and you have to create an instrument, a new directive, procedural rights that balance . . . those powers. And then it is not enough, like the European Union is doing at the moment, to create very slowly, very general directives on procedural rights that are very close to the European Convention.[134]

The participant went on to call for the development of a 'transnational procedure' including, for example, the availability of dual representation for

131 CTF-Q5-K – United Kingdom.
132 BOR-Q7-F – Greece.
133 EAW-Q2-B – Ireland.
134 EAW-Q9-F – Sweden.

suspects and convicts wherein counsel have appropriate access to the prosecution file. If such a balance could be struck then legitimacy would, in the participant's view, be stronger. The participant from the United Kingdom (Scotland) also stated that it is 'unfortunate that . . . it has taken so long within the EU and all of the democracies to eventually agree that you're entitled to translation and interpretation or access to a lawyer'.[135] Other participants were more sceptical on this point, however, because in their view the introduction of additional procedures would run contrary to the aims of a simplified extradition system.[136]

A participant in the CTF focus group also emphasized the need to ensure due process in terrorism-related cases, such as bringing the people involved before a court of law, and ensuring they are not 'shuffled off into some secret court where it's all quiet'.[137] In this light, this participant reflected that 'we can only bring in emergency measures for so long'.[138]

In the BOR focus group, it was suggested that, although the legal protection accorded to individuals might have been adequate in the early years of these databases when the Schengen Information System I (SIS I) was established, due to the growing sophistication of databases, the current law may be inadequate. In this context, one participant said:

> When the SIS I was established, it was simple . . . there was the possibility for one country to see the database of another country. Only that! Nothing more – nothing less! But with SIS II there are a lot of needs, a lot of information to get in . . . it's a motivation I think. Not only that each country has national law . . . it's the need to have other information . . . and to motivate national law against human rights. So when we speak that what we do now is legal, it's legal under the law[s] that are more conservative let's say.[139]

This suggestion, that the increasing sophistication of the SIS II system raises questions as to the quality of the law, was the subject of further discussion. Although the participants in this focus group were clear that they saw the use of EU border control databases as legitimate because of their lawfulness, they also saw the need for accountability through external controls, both formal and informal. Therefore, with respect to formal controls, one participant made reference to 'the judicial system' and the need to 'justify very well' the operation of border control databases.[140] And with respect to informal controls, another participant noted that 'it's a legal tool but I

135 EAW-Q9-E- Scotland.
136 EAW-Q9-G – Netherlands.
137 CTF-Q3/4-A – United Kingdom.
138 CTF-Q3/4-A – United Kingdom.
139 BOR-Q8-E – Greece.
140 BOR-Q4-E – Greece.

think that we need more transparency. We need more external control from organizations like NGOs . . .'[141]

A key form of legal protection in respect of databases in both counter-terrorist finance and border controls is data protection law. While participants in both focus groups agreed that data protection law is necessary, and that it aids legitimation, there was some difference of opinion on whether it struck the right balance between the protection of personal data and the need to provide data to law enforcement. In the CTF focus group, some participants made the claim that data protection law is too restrictive and may hinder FIUs from exchanging information.[142] One participant referred to the tension between the need for FIUS to exchange information relating to counter-terrorist finance and data protection law that sets restrictions on the sharing of personal data.[143]

This participant argued that if such data protection law does not take into account law enforcement's need to exchange information 'then it's going to be a total mess'.[144] Another participant made the point that the law may facilitate access to data by criminals (for example through requirements of transparency and due process), but may prevent access to data for law enforcement agencies.[145] In this context, this participant made reference to a European Commission Framework Programme 7 project that aims to create a hybrid system for combating terrorism and money laundering.[146] However, she said that some FIUs may not be able to use some of the tools developed by this project because of 'European legislation on data protection'.[147]

A participant in the BOR focus group acknowledged that there are, in general, concerns about the uses of personal data by law enforcement agencies and about the adequacy of data protection law. She said:

> I think people get very worried about data protection laws when it comes to information sharing in general, and I think that's across the board, not just when it comes to terrorism, but certainly I think, yes it is legal and once you can justify the access to the information then, you know, most data protection laws, in the EU anyway, will cover you as a crime fighting agency or state [authority].[148]

Nevertheless, another participant held that the data protection law governing the use of EU border control databases is very restrictive: 'we all have

141 BOR-Q7-F – Greece.
142 CTF-Q4-D – Belgium and CTF-Q4-I – Romania.
143 CTF-Q4-D – Belgium.
144 CTF-Q4-D – Belgium.
145 CTF-Q4-I – Romania.
146 The Hybrid Enhanced Money Laundering Intelligence, Investigation, Incrimination and Alerts (HEMOLIA) project.
147 CTF-Q4-I – Romania.
148 BOR-Q7-B – Ireland.

very restrictive laws about the personal information and it's very complicated to ask for . . . access to personal information'.[149] This point of tension did not result in clear resolution in any of the three focus groups.

A corollary of the fundamental freedoms

An overarching theme in the focus groups was that EU counter-terrorism law and policy in general – and these measures more specifically – operate as a legitimate corollary to the free movement of capital, goods and persons that lies at the heart of the common market. One participant in the EAW focus group set out 'it's part of the deal, if you open your borders, people can travel, goods can travel, criminality travels . . . it's in everyone's interest'.[150] Another participant had a similar view – stating that 'it might be legitimate because we are in a system in which . . . in which we have four fundamental freedoms'.[151] Thus, the participants saw the use of the EAW (and the potential for EU citizens to be subject to surrender under an EAW) to be a legitimate corollary of the free movement made possible by the EU.

Similarly, in the CTF focus group, one participant set out that the development of counter-terrorist finance measures by the EU is necessary, owing to the development of the common market. For this participant, counter-terrorist finance measures represent an important step in matching the potential for abuse of the common market by criminals.[152] The point emerged most strikingly in the BOR focus group. Some participants in that focus group observed that the use of databases and systems of information exchange is absolutely essential, owing to the free movement of persons across the EU. A participant from Spain made this point in several of his interventions. For example:

> My point is – we don't have internal borders. That is, if we don't use high technology in order to check external EU borders it would be impossible to [ensure] a safe society. In order to keep the peace, criminal control, we need to . . . use high technology.[153]

This participant made the point that, without internal borders, criminals and terrorists can 'move around Europe without control, without borders'.[154] He referred, for example, to the ability of members of the Basque separatist movement, ETA, to move to France.[155] In this regard, the need for databases and information exchange was seen as vital to ensure European security.

149 BOR-Q4-C – Spain.
150 EAW-Q9-G – Netherlands.
151 EAW-Q9-C – Italy.
152 CTF-Q1-B – Ireland.
153 BOR-Q1-A – Spain.
154 BOR-Q1-A – Spain.
155 BOR-Q1-A – Spain.

5. Conclusions

The three focus groups undertaken by the King's research team can offer only a snapshot of the perspectives of a small sample of counter-terrorism operatives on the law and policy they implement. It would be foolish to attempt to generalize the claims set out in this chapter or to advocate policy changes on this basis alone. However, it is striking that the operatives' views echo many of the debates that exist in the academic literature – and increasingly in political and popular debate. This is a policy field where those responsible for giving effect to law and policy are deeply aware of the tensions involved in delivering on the Tampere programme's promise of an area of freedom, security and justice.

The broad acceptance of EU criminal justice cooperation as a corollary of the free movement made possible by European integration demonstrates that the Tampere narrative has taken root in the minds of counter-terrorism operatives. Those operatives are also very cognizant of the importance of, and limitation of, trust as a necessary foundation for cooperation on the basis of the principle of mutual recognition. The need to consider adaptations in national law and legal culture, to introduce appropriate 'transnational procedures', and to ensure broader public accountability, all speak to aspects of the Stockholm programme and the development of EU justice and home affairs in general.[156]

The operatives' perspectives bear out the idea that although we are now in a post-'war on terror' world, there remain challenges in counter-terrorism law and policy after 11 September 2001 – the day that 'everything moved'. The lack of common threat perceptions and agreed objectives, as well as somewhat clumsy institutional frameworks, mean that Europe's efforts at efficacious – and just – counter-terrorism law and policy remain more aspiration than reality.

156 See the contributions to Acosta Arcarazo and Murphy, in n. 124 above, and in general, S. Peers, *EU Justice and Home Affairs Law* Third Edition (Oxford: Oxford University Press 2011).

9 Civil society and policy-maker perspectives on EU counter-terrorism

*Josephine Doody and Rosemarijn van der Hilst**

1. Introduction

It is often assumed that civil society and policy-makers coexist in a necessary but antagonistic relationship where policy-makers develop counter-terrorism measures and civil society criticizes them. We argue here, however, that this portrayal is an oversimplification of a complex relationship. This chapter explores the concepts of impact, legitimacy and effectiveness of European counter-terrorism measures from the perspective of civil society and policy-makers. It examines how each group defines and measures each concept through the lens of three case studies: the European Arrest Warrant, border control and the disruption of the financing of terrorism. While it might be expected that civil society would be more critical of the measures than policy-makers, our analysis reveals that, on the whole, the two groups share similar concerns, with both groups demonstrating a critical reflexive approach.

2. Methodology

In our attempt to gather data on civil society's perception of the impact, legitimacy and effectiveness of European counter-terrorism measures, we conducted a focus group and a series of semi-structured interviews. The focus group was conducted in December 2013 in London. It was envisaged that it would be composed of eight participants. There are numerous civil society stakeholders, and they can be categorized into many different types, such as NGOs, lobby groups, academics, cultural communities, charities and interest organizations.[1] Seeing that a certain level of

* Josephine Doody was a researcher on the SECILE project at Durham University and is currently employed as an Associate Lecturer at The Open University. She can be contacted at j.doody@open.ac.uk. Rosemarijn van der Hilst was a senior researcher at the Peace Research Institute Oslo and can be contacted at rosemarijn.hilst@prio.org.

1 London School of Economics 'Counter-Terrorism and Civil Society', *National Council for Voluntary Organisations Seminar Report*, NCVO/ESRC NGPA seminar 6 March 2009. Available online at http://www.lse.ac.uk/internationaldevelopment/research/ngpa/publications/counter-terrorism%20and%20civil%20society%20final%20version.pdf (accessed 30 August 2014).

familiarity with the counter-terrorism measures was considered necessary, random selection would not have been useful; nomination seemed a better recruitment method. Despite tremendous efforts to recruit the target number of participants, only seven people participated in the actual focus group. Of these, five were academics and two were related to NGOs/ interest groups/journalism. The participants primarily worked in the UK, Belgium, and Spain. The participants in the focus group are referred to here as CS1–CS7.

In order to supplement the views ascertained in the focus group, a set of semi-structured interviews were undertaken with policy-makers and officials in European institutions whose positions and roles are such that participation in a focus group would not have been appropriate or possible. Ten interviewees were recruited from a variety of key policy-making institutions across Europe, including DG Home, Europol, Eurojust and the Office of the Counter-Terrorism Coordinator to name but a few. The interviewees are referred to here as P1–P10. They were interviewed in January and February 2014. A discussion guide was used in both scenarios. The research was transcribed, amounting to a total of 145 pages, and analysed by reference to the case study areas (the European Arrest Warrant, border control and the disruption of the financing of terrorism), by reference to the key themes of the study, and by reference to framing concerns in EU counter-terrorism. Thus, this chapter presents the results and a discussion based on the analysis of the data gathered from seventeen representatives of European civil society and policy-makers. It does not profess to be a representative view of European civil society or policy-makers on this topic. Rather, it offers an original and multidisciplinary perspective based on new empirical evidence that contributes to the existing civil society understanding of impact, legitimacy and effectiveness.[2]

2 Other attempts to capture civil society's perspective on this topic are, for example: London School of Economics (2009) 'Counter-Terrorism and Civil Society', *National Council for Voluntary Organisations Seminar Report*, NCVO/ESRC NGPA seminar 6 March 2009. Available online at http://www.lse.ac.uk/internationaldevelopment/research/ngpa/publications/counter-terrorism%20and%20civil%20society%20final%20version.pdf (accessed 30 August 2014). This report presents the view of four academics and a representative of the charity sector; The Organization for Security and Co-operation in Europe (OSCE) Office for Democratic Institutions and Human Rights (ODIHR) and the Centro de Investigaciones de Relaciones Internacionales y Desarrollo (2007) 'Informal Working Level Meeting on the Role of Civil Society in Preventing Terrorism', ODIHR.GAL/34/07, 16 May 2007. At this meeting, thirty participants from civil society and NGOs, as well as ODIHR participated; and JUSTICE *European Arrests Warrants, Ensuring an Effective Defence*, JUSTICE report, 2012, ISBN 9780907247548, a report based on a two-year project involving interviews and self-reporting by lawyers on the effectiveness of the European Arrest Warrant. Because of the different methodological approaches of these studies, the references to these studies should not be considered as a thorough comparison of the different views within civil society. These reports are rather used to confirm (or disconfirm) trends in the data gathered through the focus group in order to place some of the statements in context.

3. Impact

The first concept explored here is impact. This study sought to define more clearly how impact is understood and measured according to civil society and policy-makers in relation to three different counter-terrorism measures.

Defining impact

The starting point in defining impact is understanding how the measure works in practice, which then needs to be compared with what the measure set out to do in the first place. Both groups agreed on this, with policy-makers noting 'you first have to set the goal, you have to define what your purpose is and then you measure impact against that said purpose'.[3] P8 described it as 'effects, consequences, positives, negatives and to the extent in which some of those measures – and that happens of course quite frequently – are violating some principles'.[4]

In terms of the specific elements relevant to the definition of impact, clear purpose, a strong problem definition and awareness of perspective were identified as important. There was some criticism that counter-terrorism measures can lack a clear purpose, rendering it difficult to assess and measure impact. One participant noted that while advocates of further measures argue that they are useful, necessary and essential, it is very difficult to define and measure impact with a clear purpose.[5] In addition, an adequate problem definition seemed to be an important factor: 'In order to be able to evaluate something, you need a good diagnosis; you need a good plan, a good problem definition and then a solution'.[6] But problems can be defined in different ways raising the issue of the importance of perspective. Having established the importance of purpose, problem definition and perspective, we began to probe further into the concept of impact. Who and what does it refer to?

The first point to consider is *who* a measure impacts on. A number of interviewees approached impact from the perspective of the individual. Exploring impact in this way entails a consideration of the impact of counter-terrorist measures on the enjoyment of individual human rights and of the extent to which a human right has been infringed. There was, however, a recognition that individuals do not exist in a vacuum but rather come together to form communities and, thus, that impact can be considered at a broader societal level. This entails placing counter-terrorism measures in a wider context going beyond a purely operational perspective and exploring

3 SECILE/IV/7.
4 SECILE/IV/8.
5 SECILE/IV/7.
6 SECILE/CS/3.

how they affect our democratic values, practices, principles and identity. P2 engaged in such a rights-based consideration of impact:

> '[T]o the extent that you would deprive certain categories of people certain rights you undermine this idea of a society as we believe in, and it may also be kind of food for terrorists.'[7]

P6 agreed that a rights-based approach 'is not just something that we want but also something that we have to do' in order to avoid resentment and potential radicalization.[8]

Within the broader societal examination of impact, there were divergent views on whether specific groups within the community were impacted in different ways. There was disagreement over whether counter-terrorist measures originating in the EU have led to alienation of communities, with P6 denying that they had.[9] A distinction was made between EU and national counter-terrorism policies; however, this arguably ignores the fact that citizens are quite often unaware of the origin of a measure and do not know and/or do not care where it comes from. In contrast, academic research conducted in relation to national measures suggests that particular Muslim communities have been impacted in quite negative ways, which has led to alienation.[10] One of the participants revealed clear frustration with the impact of counter-terrorist financing (CTF) measures on NGOs' ability to do their work. According to the participant concerned, this was caused by three things: (1) additional reporting and accounting requirements take up resources that need to be taken away from the resources actually doing the core work; (2) increased financial transparency and regulation leads to donor aversion, leaving NGOs and aid organizations with fewer financial means; and (3) stricter counter-terrorism measures are, by some governments, used as an excuse to clamp down on NGOs that are not to the government's liking.[11]

The second point to consider in any definition of impact is *what* we are measuring. The guidelines for undertaking an *ex ante* impact assessment by the European Commission make reference to economic, social and

7 SECILE/IV/2.

8 SECILE/IV/6.

9 SECILE/IV/6.

10 T. Choudhury and H. Fenwick 'The Impact of Counter-terrorism Measures on Muslim Communities' (2011) *International Review of Law, Computers & Technology* Vol. 25 No. 3. The concern over discrimination with reference particularly to Muslims was also a key point in the observations made by Prof. Jude Howell and Dr. Jeremy Lind in NCVO/ESRC NGPA seminar 6 March 2009 as reported in London School of Economics 'Counter-Terrorism and Civil Society', *National Council for Voluntary Organisations Seminar Report*, p.4.

11 SECILE/CS/5. These sentiments are also reported in the observations of the participants of the OSCE Office for Democratic Institutions and Human Rights and the Centro de Investigaciones de Relaciones Internacionales y Desarrollo (2007) 'Informal Working Level Meeting on the Role of Civil Society in Preventing Terrorism', ODIHR.GAL/34/07, 16 May 2007 pp. 8–9.

environmental impact.[12] A detailed breakdown of potential impacts within each category is provided, but the relative weight given to them is not clear.[13] Ultimately, while the question of relative weighting may be a political matter, four different types of impact were discerned in the interviews: economic impact, operational/practical impact, impact on operational actors and impact on level of security.

For policy-makers, economic impact featured strongly. P1 summarized that 'the cost effectiveness of the measure is to a large extent a matter of economic, trade and financial variables'.[14] Factors that need to be considered and balanced include

> . . . the cost of the security measure, the financial costs, the non-financial costs, the processing costs, the expediency in terms of the speed of the movement of goods and so on and so forth. Versus the costs of not applying the measures and having the situation that would . . . create direct first, second, third . . . rate impacts.[15]

Economic impact appears to feature strongly because it is tangible and, especially as regards direct impacts, quantifiable. Other impacts, such as social impacts, psychological impacts or political impacts, are no less important but much more difficult to measure.

Alongside the economic impact of measures, is the practical or operational impact of counter-terrorism measures, influenced in large part by a state's preparedness and response capacity. Using a before/after framework, policy-makers emphasized that the introduction of the European Arrest Warrant (EAW) had succeeded in speeding up extradition between Member States. Prior to the introduction of the EAW, delays experienced in securing extradition between Member States were a cause for concern. P6 noted that '[b]efore there was the European Arrest Warrant it could sometimes take decades to have somebody extradited between countries of the European Union and now with the European Arrest Warrant it can be two weeks so there you see . . . a real change'.[16] In contrast to the policy-makers, the civil society group was less positive in its assessment of the operational impact of the EAW.[17] It was only after the moderator specifically asked about potential positive impacts that the participants explored this idea. There seemed to be a general agreement that, indeed, the EAW might have positive impacts; one

12 European Commission *Impact Assessment Guidelines*, 15 January 2009, Sec (2009) 92.

13 Ibid., pp. 33–38.

14 SECILE/IV/1.

15 Ibid.

16 SECILE/IV/6.

17 The initial reaction of the civil society participants reflects the observations in the short overview of the civil society discourse on the EAW in JUSTICE *European Arrests Warrants, Ensuring an Effective Defence*, JUSTICE report, 2012, ISBN 9780907247548, p.8.

participant used the example where the EAW had enabled the arrest of an international child abductor. 'I mean, one isn't saying that the whole thing is wrong'.[18] Another participant added: 'I mean when a country continues to try to get somebody that committed a crime across state borders . . . you can't argue with that'.[19] But immediately after recognizing these possible positive impacts, the participants qualified their comments by mentioning 'the trouble is that there has been a number of cases where it was patently wrong. And the system has broken down'.[20] The operational impact of a measure depends in large part on the extent to which it is actually used in practice, a factor that arose in discussions on the Schengen information system (SIS). The decision to use the SIS is a matter of national discretion and it *supplements*, rather than replaces, national systems. In this respect, P6 explained that 'As a police officer you don't have to put your suspects in the SIS but if you do maybe if they travel around you get hits in other countries so it's more an additional tool' for national authorities.[21]

Besides impact on those targeted by the measure, participants recognized that 'everybody . . . who has some kind of obligations [*sic*] [under a measure] is impacted in a way'.[22] Thus, as well as facilitating faster extradition between Member States, the EAW has contributed to the development of a European judicial space. Related to this, is the impact of the EAW in the coordination of arrests across a number of states, which can be facilitated through joint investigation teams working through and with European institutions, such as EUROPOL and EUROJUST. These agencies create channels for formal and informal cooperation, training and coordination.[23] Impact then goes beyond the *who* and *what* a particular counter-terrorism measure impacts upon to include a beneficial impact for those operationalizing actors responsible for its implementation through the construction of a cooperative space (in this case of a judicial/prosecutorial nature).

The fourth impact identified by participants was unsurprisingly on security and levels of security. In this respect, they considered impact as including an analysis of whether the measure has created a legal framework in which the goal of a more secure Europe can be achieved. The civil society group focused on the methods used in achieving the important goal of security. They focused specifically on the impact of border surveillance, comparing the relative importance of the different aims of border surveillance, i.e. protecting the border and protecting the lives of migrants at sea. 'One of the many boats with 70 people that died last year had gone in and out of borders and people were aware! But they didn't share the information. So

---

18 SECILE/CS/2.
19 SECILE/CS/7.
20 SECILE/CS/2.
21 SECILE/IV/6.
22 SECILE/IV/2.
23 SECILE/IV/6.

the countries were not taking advantage of technologies, or utilizing data sharing technologies that they could utilize in a way that would save life'.[24] Of course, border surveillance technology was not intended for this use, thus raising concerns of function creep. However, there were differences of opinion in whether such function creep could potentially have a positive outcome, e.g., the ability to increase search and rescue at sea, or should primarily be seen as something negative and a potential slippery slope. The civil society focus group considered the impact of border surveillance as it is more broadly understood from a rights-based perspective. When asked to reflect on the impact of border surveillance and how to measure this, the first reaction was 'If it turns the Mediterranean into a cemetery, it's not good. That is my indicator'.[25]

Measuring impact

In order to measure the impact of a counter-terrorism measure, we need to understand first how that counter-terrorism measure is made and how it is assessed. In other words, analysis of impact includes an analysis of *ex ante* impact assessments in the process of law- and policy-making. A number of interviewees raised concerns in this respect. One interviewee particularly raised the issue of poor communication within the policy-making process, a feature exacerbated by the fact that people can find themselves in positions of making and assessing policy for which they do not necessarily have the requisite expertise.[26] Secondly, the 'one size fits all' approach to EU-wide measures and responses makes policy-making very difficult. Every country has a different legal and historical experience of terrorism, as well as different legal and political systems at the domestic level, but at an EU level one policy solution must be developed that fits all. This approach means that the detail required to address the original problem can become diluted in the final measure as this ultimate policy and/or legal instrument needs to work across all twenty-eight Member States. Reflecting somewhat similar concerns, the civil society group agreed that there can sometimes be a disconnect between problem definition and the proposed solution.[27]

The second stage in measuring impact is assessment. *Ex ante* and *ex post facto* impact assessments are the main tools used to measure impact. The European Commission impact-assessment process was heavily criticized by participants due to the absence of review periods in a number of measures.[28] *Ex ante* and *ex post facto* impact assessments usually examine the same

---

24 SECILE/CS/4.

25 SECILE/CS/3.

26 SECILE/IV/5.

27 SECILE/CS/3.

28 SECILE/CS/2. See further B. Hayes and C. Jones *Report on the Transposition of EU Counter-Terrorism Measures* (SECILE Consortium, 2014).

thing and engage with the same stakeholders, although there are scenarios in which people not consulted *ex ante* are then consulted in a later review.

A starting point in measuring the impact of any counter-terrorism measure is a statistical review of its operation and usage; however, statistics can tell only part of the story. For example, one civil society participant notes that the statistics on use of the EAW per country do not include information on whether the arrested individual is subsequently convicted of a terrorist offence; information she considered fundamental to assessing the measure's impact.[29] Another participant warned against over-reliance on quantitative data to assess impact, explaining that 'when you reduce the analysis of the impact [to] the quantitative and not the qualitative and . . . don't take into account the ethical and social perspective then you have a problem'.[30] This participant claimed that what is required is a more critically reflective approach to counter-terrorism measures, approaching impact assessment in a manner that acknowledges the strategic interests of 'who benefits, because there is a whole industry behind it'.[31] Second, she claimed that an increased openness and increased questioning around the cost of counter-terrorism was required in order to properly assess impact:[32] from her perspective there is a reluctance to question the cost of counter-terrorism, reflecting a distortion of political discourse.

To summarize, impact is best understood in relation to particular referents, depending on who we are measuring impact on and what we are measuring. It can be investigated at multiple levels and can be direct, indirect, national, transnational, uneven, positive and negative. The current tools for investigating impact are *ex ante* and *ex post facto* assessments. Similar to the other concept areas, participants felt that impact required policy-makers to be more critically reflective of the strategic interests at stake and the potential for differentiated impact.

4. Legitimacy

The second concept explored during the research was legitimacy and more specifically what constitutes legitimacy in the context of counter-terrorism. A number of definitions were proposed during the interviews, the most comprehensive of which was

> . . . compatibility with the Charter for Fundamental Rights, with primary law, compatibility with the secondary law including in terms of

29 SECILE/CS/2. See, for example, statistical information on the EAW in JUSTICE *European Arrests Warrants, Ensuring an Effective Defence*, JUSTICE report, 2012, ISBN 9780907247548, Annex 2, p.166. This report does not mention the number of convictions resulting from the use of the EAW.

30 SECILE/CS/3.

31 SECILE/IV/7.

32 SECILE/IV/7.

> due process and then there is a realm which goes beyond that; which goes into the moral, into the ethical realms. As regards terrorism this often involves the ratio between transparency and secrecy in society.[33]

This definition comprises three specific components: legality, due process and something which goes beyond the law into the area of morals and ethics. These factors were common across the interviews and the civil society focus group. Thus, this definition will be elaborated upon here and will be supplemented by two further components that arose: the question of the importance of output and the core values associated with legitimacy.

Defining legitimacy

For the policy-makers and civil society representatives who engaged with the authors, legality is a key factor in whether a particular measure is legitimate or not. This comprises analysis of both compliance with law *and* whether a particular measure is grounded in law. P1 pointed out that 'at the very least, the *sine qua non* condition for a policy to be considered (legitimate) is its compatibility with primary and secondary law'.[34] P5 agreed, stating clearly 'my personal opinion is that it must be normally always, with no exception, lawful'.[35] It must be in compliance with the European Convention on Human Rights (ECHR) and other international obligations.[36] P6 agreed that counter-terrorist measures must be legal, highlighting the EU choice of a criminal justice approach to fighting terrorism: 'we have not said "oh terrorism is so special that normal rules cannot apply"'.[37]

While participants considered legality to be a *sine qua non* of legitimacy, they also noted that legitimacy goes beyond mere lawfulness. The second aspect identified by participants in defining legitimacy is the process involved in the development and implementation of a counter-terrorism measure, i.e., 'how the law was adopted, by whom, under which processes'.[38] The process according to the civil society group should involve a democratic, transparent, accountable and legitimate authority.[39] P8 went a step further back to argue that the purpose of the measures itself feeds into a legitimacy analysis. The process of making law and policy can be divided into two phases: the development phase and the implementation phase.

In the development phase, legitimacy is linked to the procedures applied in developing the measure, including consideration of who is involved

33 SECILE/IV/1.
34 SECILE/IV/1.
35 SECILE/IV/5.
36 SECILE/IV/3.
37 SECILE/IV/6.
38 SECILE/IV/3.
39 SECILE/CS/4 and SECILE/CS/3.

in the development of the measure, and whether they are democratically elected. There was disagreement among participants in relation to time and the development phase. Some policy-makers noted that the process is time consuming – sometimes running to several years – but stated that the process involved in preparing proposals, white papers, communications and impact assessments was a real strength from a legitimacy perspective.[40] The civil society group, in contrast, argued that counter-terrorism measures were introduced too quickly.[41] The example of border surveillance was given, where it was suggested that technical amendments were being used to facilitate political amendments:

> [I]t really is technical amendments that are deciding or directing the fundamental changes they're making to the Schengen treaty, for instance. So they are not legitimate because we're not discussing the political issues at stake, but . . . technical amendments which are not technical at all; they are political amendments . . . So it's not legitimate because they are not following the procedure.[42]

The concern with the speed at which measures are introduced was fuelled by the exceptionalism argument, with several participants concerned that the events of September 2001 were framed as exceptional in order to justify the introduction of certain measures that would curtail civil liberties.[43]

The second part of the policy making process, following the development of a measure, is the implementation and the acceptance phase. Participants suggested that the level of implementation might tell us something about legitimacy because it might suggest a degree of acceptance at domestic level. A key component here is which actor should implement the measure. P6 explained that 'sometimes we don't have the legitimacy to pass certain measures but other people do and so it's also important to see clearly where can you be active and where is it [*sic*] better that you let others be active that are probably a lot more effective and a lot more credible'.[44] It may be more effective to support a civil society group than for a government to engage in direct implementation themselves. Who actually does the implementing raises questions about the relationship between legitimacy and good governance.

Participants raised some questions around whether implementation is exposed to the same public debate or rigour as the broader political policy and, if not, whether that has implications for legitimacy. A number of participants noted that while the top-line policy decision is made at European level, and attended by public debate, a large part of the systemic implementation

---

40 SECILE/IV/4.

41 SECILE/CS/3.

42 SECILE/CS/3.

43 SECILE/CS/7, SECILE/CS/2, SECILE/CS/3. See further Burgess and Martin-Mazé, this volume.

44 SECILE/IV/6.

of that policy is national and/or technocratic and may not attract the same level of debate and public scrutiny. This raises questions as to whether the legitimacy that attends the European policy-making phase is watered down in the implementation phase in such circumstances. A number of interviewees noted that review and evaluation might help to ameliorate such concerns,[45] particularly since legitimacy can vary over time depending on changes in the prevailing circumstances.[46] As P10 argued, 'every measure has it price . . . and at a certain moment you are willing to pay that price and give up certain privacy or rights and so forth, and then at a certain moment that may not look necessary anymore'.[47] Essentially, what is legitimate now may not necessarily be legitimate in the future.

There was criticism of the lack of review and evaluation within the EU with one policy-maker calling for increased evaluations 'both at national level and at European level'.[48] Hayes and Jones discovered in their research that of the eighty-eight legally binding counter-terrorism measures adopted within the EU since 2001, only twenty-two (25 per cent) have been the subject of an *ex ante* impact assessment. One third of these eighty-eight measures contain no provision for an *ex post facto* assessment.[49] P8 suggested that what is needed is an evaluation of outcomes rather than outputs and proposed a cyclical process of consideration, action, reaction, evaluation:

> If time is of the essence, you cannot do all the verification before, but then you should do [it] after. And it should be crystal clear that [if] the answer is negative, [the measures are] not acceptable. And, so . . . the question would be, please look back, how did it work out? Was there any effect at all? And how measures are working in practice is also a way of looking back. If the effectiveness was assumed [*ex ante*], but in practice [the measures] are not effective, I think then we should look back, go back, and reconsider the measure. So, I see legitimacy as . . . a circular process.[50]

Drawing on the example of the Data Retention Directive[51] to highlight the importance of evaluation, P8 noted 'we cannot wait seven to ten years until the legitimacy is finally decided. In the meantime it has already done

---

45 SECILE/IV/3 and SECILE/IV/10.

46 SECILE/IV/3.

47 SECILE/IV/10.

48 SECILE/IV/7.

49 B. Hayes and C. Jones *Report on How the EU Assesses the Impact, Legitimacy and Effectiveness of its Counter-terrorism Laws* (SECILE Consortium, 2013).

50 SECILE/IV/8.

51 Directive 2006/24/EC of the European Parliament and of the Council of 15 March 2006 on the retention of data generated or processed in connection with the provision of publicly available electronic communications services or of public communications networks and amending Directive 2002/58/EC, OJ L 105, 13.4.2006, pp. 54–63.

its damage'.[52] His final point was a critical one and was echoed by P7, who talked about the case of classification of documents and the difficulty of accessing such documents: 'the only way I can challenge that as an individual citizen is if I go to Court and that means . . . litigating five or six years, my costs, I mean that is prohibitive'.[53] Both policy-makers focused on the slow nature of court processes and highlighted their concern at the negative impacts a measure can have during this time.

There was disagreement among participants as to the importance of a measurable output in a legitimacy analysis, raising questions as to the relationship between effectiveness and legitimacy. According to P5, it is the most important part of the entire process. He explained that as a police officer 'you live for your investigation to bring it to prosecution to a court case. And if you don't reach that level you have worked for nothing'.[54] For this participant, input described in terms of person-hours applied to an investigation is largely irrelevant as measurement is on the basis of output or results. This was in contrast to P4 who argued that the prosecution is not in fact the most important feature:

> If it is not legitimate it will not lead to a solid trial case and you will not be very effective in bringing a presumed suspect terrorist to judgment. It might have saved lives, and this is then a good and noble cause, and if that is the case . . . then OK, there is no trial case, no conviction and this is not, at least for me as a person, and as a prosecutor has never been a big deal. It's about saving lives . . . that is a primary concern.[55]

These quoted policy-makers reflect different perspectives: judicial and operational. The civil society response to the question of the importance of output was different to that of the policy-makers. When asked about the importance of output of a measure and its link to legitimacy, the response was laughter by the whole group followed by an explanation that 'Legitimate is not the same as justified in the circumstances'.[56] CS7 explained why 'effectiveness' should not be a factor in measuring legitimacy. He warned of the situation where a measure might be implemented 'beyond the limits of the law', but which might retrospectively be justified just because the results were so good. Such an approach might lead to the slow erosion of human rights standards. Despite the lack of significance they placed on effective output, the civil society focus group nevertheless called for more information about the use of the EAW to assess its legitimacy.[57] So, as with measuring impact,

52 SECILE/IV/8.
53 SECILE/IV/7.
54 SECILE/IV/5.
55 SECILE/IV/4.
56 SECILE/CS/4.
57 SECILE/CS/2.

the actual use of the EAW and transparency about its use might influence the participants' perception of the legitimacy of the measure.

Going beyond legality and due process, there is a question of legitimacy in terms of moral and ethical considerations. The example given by P1 related to the dispersal of counter-radicalizing narratives through the financing of non-state organization's activities. Such an approach is legal and fulfils the criterion of legality from a legitimacy perspective. Furthermore, it is transparent as financial investment in such activities is transparent and subject to normal fiscal accountability processes. However, the activity remains necessarily covert: the counter-radicalizing message may originate with, or reflect the views of, a public authority but is communicated through a civil society group. For P1, this may raise moral or ethical questions relating to the tension between transparency and secrecy. Although these tensions are complex, ultimately policy-makers who addressed this were satisfied that resolving them is, and should remain, a political decision.[58]

Finally, participants identified certain core values that were said to relate to the concept of legitimacy: democracy, accountability, transparency, and participation. For participants, democracy was identified as a core and fundamental value of the European Union and thus as indispensable to legitimacy.[59] In terms of accountability, participants noted that legitimacy requires that 'if certain laws are adopted then those who have adopted them are accountable . . . to the [European] Parliament and to the public in general to say how [they] worked and whether [they] achieved the objectives'.[60] The civil society group was critical of the lack of accountability, with critiques ranging from the academic to the practical. For one participant, for example, 'you cannot have legitimacy without democratic accountability, and you can't have democratic accountability if you don't have a demos, and we don't have a demos in the European Union'.[61] The challenge of accountability was reiterated by CS3, who concluded, 'You need the legitimate authority but also the process that is open and accountable'.[62] Accountability depends, according to several of the participants,[63] on access to information and transparency, both highlighted as problematic in relation to legitimacy.

Transparency is the third core value that participants associated with legitimacy. It can be difficult to achieve transparency in the context of security as there is an inevitable tension between legitimacy and effectiveness. One response to the challenge of transparency could be the acceptance of different levels of transparency, which can be explained as follows.[64] While

58 SECILE/IV/1.
59 SECILE/IV/3 SECILE/IV/5 and SECILE/CS/6.
60 SECILE/IV/2.
61 SECILE/CS/2.
62 SECILE/CS/3.
63 SECILE/IV/2, SECILE/IV/3, SECILE/IV/6 and SECILE/IV/7.
64 SECILE/IV/3.

it may be difficult to have full transparency in the process of making counter-terrorism law and policy, policy-makers argued that it is important to have transparency of the final outcome. P2 explained that although 'you wouldn't be able to ask security services to be extremely transparent about their threat assessment and what they plan to do . . . I would think it's important to have transparency at least of the final outcome'.[65] The SIS is a good example of this in practice. The measure itself is public but the details of policy discussions and operational discussions around it are not. In certain cases, it might not be possible to be in any way transparent. There could potentially be scenarios where transparency would lead to assisting terrorists. In such cases, P3 argued that the appropriate response is to build in transparency through the use of safeguards, such as supervision by an independent authority.[66]

Achieving an acceptable level of transparency is complicated by the practice of classification of documents within the EU[67] and this was raised by a number of policy-makers. P7 complained of the routine classification of documents, which can undermine accountability as those testifying before a committee of the European Parliament may not be able to answer questions posed to them, for example, because the answers relate to classified documents. This has potentially serious consequences from a legitimacy perspective: when the evidence underpinning claims is not presented, this can lead to the fear that classification is used to hide a lack of convincing information and evidence.[68] Aside from the concern that the system would be used in such a manner, one participant claimed that there is a need to be able to brief the European Parliament in secret in order to bring balance to debates; at present, this participant considers that debates do not adequately include the perspectives of security services.[69]

Participation is the fourth value associated with legitimacy and identified by the participants; it is closely tied to transparency in the data. Who gets to participate in the decision-making process is a relevant factor in legitimacy. A potential gap arises here between strategic policy-makers and operational end users, which can affect the perception of end users of the legitimacy of a particular tool or measure.[70] However, who actually participates will vary from case to case and can range from high-level technical experts to radicalized terrorists' family members. Participation should not be confused with consultation or simply informing people.

65 SECILE/IV/2.
66 SECILE/IV/3.
67 Regulation (EC) No. 1049/2001.
68 SECILE/IV/8.
69 SECILE/IV/6.
70 SECILE/IV/8.

Measuring legitimacy

Having defined legitimacy, this section will focus on how we can begin to measure legitimacy and, indeed, who is involved in the process of measuring it. P2 suggested that for a measure to be legitimate, it must be 'appropriate, if it is appropriate it must be necessary so you don't have other means to achieve the same results, and then the broader proportionality' of a measure must be taken into account,[71] thus outlining three core legal terms of measurement that are relevant to a legitimacy analysis: appropriateness, necessity and proportionality. While a court may make the ultimate decision as to these benchmarks, in fact, decisions as to appropriateness, necessity and proportionality are made throughout the process of developing EU counter-terrorism measures. There are a number of stages involved in developing a legislative measure.[72] The Commission proposes the measure. There is an obligation to conduct a public consultation that allows for discussion with stakeholders. The impact assessment guidelines explain how, for each item, there needs to be an explanation, in light of the stakeholder discussion, of why a particular action is necessary. This then goes to an impact assessment board. The Parliament will look at it if it is a legislative measure. Other bodies will also be involved, such as the Committee of the Regions. This is important, as different bodies will have different priorities and values; in this way, the system acts as a check and balance. This is the process involved, but what ultimately determines the outcome is political will.[73]

Different types of legitimacy come under consideration here. On the one hand, the decision-makers have legitimacy by virtue of being elected, but on the other hand, we must consider the extent to which decisions on policy might be motivated by politics rather than being evidence-based. This politicization may be legitimized and justified in an *ex post facto* evaluation, but one participant questioned whether that would result in it having merely 'a light legitimacy',[74] reflecting the fact that the extent to which a decision is based on evidence is perceived as contributing to its legitimacy. This general principle can be complicated by panic or the need for speed in responding to a particular set of circumstances. Where time is of the essence, it may not be possible to obtain as full an evidence base as might be considered ideal, but difficult decisions still have to be taken. For one participant, this reality pointed to the ultimately political nature of the decision:

> In legal terms you would always ask for absolute proof and evidence but in a political arena you sometimes have to live with less and take

71 SECILE/IV/2.
72 See further Doody, this volume.
73 SECILE/IV/2.
74 SECILE/IV/2.

> a decision . . . just saying 'I will only take decision if it is based on all the evidence I have and otherwise I won't take a decision', if then something goes wrong I think they would be justifiably . . . accused of not taking their political responsibilities [seriously].[75]

To summarize, legitimacy can be measured through the lens of appropriateness, necessity and proportionality. The Court makes the ultimate decision on the legality of a measure. Various actors are involved in the process but what is clearly evident from the policy-makers' data is the prominent role of politics in legitimizing measures.

5. Effectiveness

It is critical that counter-terrorism measures are effective. But what does effectiveness actually mean? How can we define, understand and measure effectiveness?

Defining effectiveness

There was broad agreement among the policy-makers interviewed for the project that something is effective if it helps to achieve its objective; thus, objectives and purpose play a central role in defining effectiveness. A measure is deemed to be effective 'if it has achieved the purpose for which you adopt' it.[76] However there was a recognition that objectives may shift; e.g., 'that for the original idea you had in mind [the measure] turned out to be not so effective but actually it showed its effectiveness in another area and you think that for that purpose alone we could perhaps still maintain it'.[77] This has implications for the legitimacy of the measure, although what it may lack in process legitimacy, it might be perceived as gaining in output legitimacy due to its effectiveness.[78] The solution in such a situation, according to one interviewee, would be 'to re-think . . . to balance again and do the impact assessment as regards fundamental rights'.[79]

Linking effectiveness with objective and purpose is quite a simplified way of approaching the concept and it can be easily complicated with the introduction of other issues such as weaknesses in the policy-making process, a deeper excavation of the actual purpose, and the possibility of unanticipated consequences. Beginning with the idea of weaknesses within the policy-making process that make defining or measuring effectiveness difficult, P8 raised the issue of a possible disconnect through the example

75 SECILE/IV/2.
76 SECILE/IV/3.
77 SECILE/IV/2.
78 SECILE/IV/2.
79 SECILE/IV/3.

of the development of an EU-wide computer system to manage the issue of overstayers. The starting point was 'we need this big system'.[80] The issue, however, was that there was no European policy or harmonization in the area. He explained how, 'the measure was developed with a specific purpose in mind, but it was more that the tool was important and the policy had not been developed yet'.[81] The purpose evolved from something very specific to 'we need to modernize the way we manage borders . . . So you see there that the purpose moved from something specific, and I take this as an example, to something very general and therefore it makes it more difficult to measure whether the measures are effective or not. And whether they are legitimate'.[82] This echoes the earlier claim about the possibility of a disconnect between the original problem, which needed a particular solution to address it, and then what happens in terms of political narrative and discourse. Where this happens, one participant notes that a serious disconnect emerges and the ultimate solution might bear little or no connection to the original problem, although the repetition of the solution may help to legitimize the action taken.[83]

If effectiveness is linked to purpose, it is important to problematize the concept of 'purpose' itself. The perceived purpose of a measure may vary depending on the actor and perspective.[84] Participants in the project claimed that we should not assume that the purpose of a particular counter-terrorism measure is to increase security. The purpose may not, in fact, be to increase security but rather to increase people's *perception* of security. In other words, the purpose may be 'security theatre'. This claim was taken further by the civil society group, some members of which argued that 'effectiveness is not important. [CS3 looks sceptical] It's about . . . show. [Several Ps express agreement] . . . It's not about these technologies working, it's about them being there, showing that they are doing something [so] that the politicians can say "look, we tried to protect you"'.[85]

The final complication in terms of effectiveness relates to the unintended consequences of measures that are introduced under a counter-terrorism rubric.[86] What happens when actual output varies from projected output? P9 explored the conundrum that arises when a system is used for a completely unforeseen purpose. This scenario raises questions for both effectiveness and legitimacy. Do the operational end users go back to the political decision-makers and explain that the system is being used for a different purpose and not for the one for which it was originally established? How

80 SECILE/IV/8.
81 SECILE/IV/8.
82 SECILE/IV/8.
83 SECILE/CS/3.
84 SECILE/IV/9.
85 SECILE/CS/1.
86 SECILE/IV/10.

can this be monitored? There is no check that a system only does what it was established to do.

Ultimately, there was some disagreement among participants about the importance of the effectiveness of a measure. Within the policy-maker group, P8 stated that 'if the effectiveness was assumed, but in practice [the measure is] not effective . . . we should . . . go back and reconsider the measure'.[87] Several participants within the focus group, however, believed that even if a measure proved to be ineffective, this would not have severe consequences. One participant argued that 'once you introduce them, you can't get rid of them. So even if the evidence said it's a crock, it is a pile of rubbish, once it is deployed everyone thinks it's really valuable'.[88] Similar sentiments were expressed by CS3 and CS2. This led participants in the focus group to wonder how relevant the effectiveness of a measure actually is. To this end, in discussing whether border surveillance and CTF measures were effective, CS7 stated 'It doesn't matter whether it works or not'.[89] This demonstrates a sharp divergence between policy-makers and the members of the civil society focus group on this matter.

Measuring effectiveness

In the counter-terrorist context, some participants considered effectiveness to be a particularly challenging concept to measure 'because obviously when you prevent attacks then you might not know that there would otherwise have been an attack'.[90] Or, as a participant in the civil society group remarked, 'No result is a good result'. The absence of an attack is in itself a measure of effectiveness, but as it cannot always be proven that the attack would have occurred were it not for the particular measure in question, participants considered that we need to consider other components of effectiveness. The research highlighted the importance of three different factors: perspective, statistics and output.

The first factor to be considered here is that of perspective. From a legal perspective, 'you can say the definition of the crimes is effective when it covers everything'.[91] From an operational perspective, in contrast, effectiveness might be considered by reference to rate, ease and speed of usage. A societal perspective might consider the effectiveness of a measure in terms of the wider impact that it has on society and on particular communities within society. The complex nature of perspective was touched upon in the focus group, where CS7 noted 'not everything is effective for everyone at the same time. So it might be effective from a state perspective, but really

87 SECILE/IV/8.
88 SECILE/CS/7.
89 SECILE/CS/7 and SECILE/CS/4.
90 SECILE/IV/6.
91 SECILE/IV/6.

challenging from a human security perspective [CS3 nods]'.[92] It follows that counter-terrorist measures that are effective from one perspective may be ineffective from another: it might improve security but curtail the civil liberties of a particular group, for example. Thus, it may be useful to consider the possibility of accepting different levels of effectiveness. These can then be transferred to a matrix where we can begin to prioritize costs and benefits according to predetermined criteria. Added to this complexity of perspective is the fact that effectiveness changes over time. As one measure is effective, terrorists innovate and identify new routes, opportunities and means, so that the effectiveness of counter-terrorist measures ought to be continually re-evaluated.[93]

A second factor to consider in measuring effectiveness is the role of statistics. From a law enforcement perspective, it may be possible to use statistics to measure the effectiveness of certain kinds of measures, such as the EAW; in such circumstances, as P6 pointed out, 'you have the statistics, you have x amount of arrests, you have x amount of prosecutions'.[94] P3 agreed, noting that a quantitative analysis of the effectiveness of a measure such as the EAW ought to be relatively straightforward,

> . . . the fact that you can say . . . we have arrested so many people because they were under a European Arrest Warrant it's easier . . . because every time someone is check[ed] and there is a measure to be taken against this person there is a specific report or this is reported somewhere and then you have, you can have in this case, you can have figures about the use of the system.[95]

However, for many participants in the research, using statistics was seen as a somewhat simplistic means of measuring effectiveness. Statistics reflect the extent of the use of a measure, which as P10 noted is discretionary in respect of things such as SIS, and where usage is discretionary statistics may not be especially meaningful as to effectiveness per se, not least because there can be a lack of uniformity in the extent to which states use it.[96] Whether or not to use a measure will depend on a number of factors across the Member States, not least the fact that 'the phenomenon of terrorism is different in each and every country and the people there based on social historical involvement in different countries'.[97]

Using statistics to measure effectiveness is also extremely complicated in the case of counter-terrorist finance where financing pathways, strategies and

---

92 SECILE/CS/7.
93 SECILE/IV/6.
94 SECILE/IV/6.
95 See *supra* note 30.
96 SECILE/IV/10.
97 SECILE/IV/5.

processes can be complex. There is immense difficulty involved in proving the intent or purpose of monetary transactions, where the money in question may have been collected in a legal manner. CSP6 pointed out that 'large amounts of money will pop-up as an alert, but when you look at terrorist financing that's often small amounts of money from small institutions or from people transferred to other accounts. So it's very difficult for financial institutions to trace these kinds of amount because it is not out of the ordinary, they can be about ten euros that are transferred on a weekly basis. So it's much more difficult to apply algorithms or systems to these kinds of finance traces'.[98] A further complicating factor is that the financing of terrorism comes in many non-monetary forms, such as drugs and weapons, implying that the tracking of financial transactions might have little effect in terms of countering terrorism overall. Using statistics to measure effectiveness in this field arguably ignores the complexity and often-invisible nature of the world of terrorist financing.

Furthermore, statistics can be manipulated or presented in a particular light for a variety of political or economic reasons, and should therefore be approached with caution. Statistics are also limited inasmuch as not everything is quantifiable. There are certain measures, such as training and best practice sharing, for example, which are not susceptible to statistical quantification for the purposes of understanding or assessing their effectiveness.[99] Rather than focusing on statistics alone, P9 suggested that the most appropriate way to understand effectiveness is through a broader process of evaluation going beyond statistical enquiry.[100]

Evaluation relates to the third aspect of effectiveness: output. Does a measure achieve what it set out to achieve? This is identified through evaluation. Cost-benefit analyses are already conducted as part of the European Commission's guidelines. The value of these analyses was questioned, however, '[The Commission says] they will perform a cost-benefit analysis (. . .) but what they actually do is they do a cost effectiveness study (. . .) they leave the effectiveness part as being self-evident. (. . .) it's the analysis on benefit which needs to be done (. . .). I have never seen an example of that being done'.[101] Evaluation needs to go beyond a financial or economic calculation and must include an evaluation of the effect the measure has on citizens.[102] P9 pointed out that there is, however, sometimes an unwillingness to evaluate the effectiveness of security measures for political reasons. Using the example of border surveillance, he explained the unwillingness to conduct an experiment into the effectiveness 'because they are scared of what they will find. If they find that none of those people are detected can

98 SECILE/CS/6. See further Murphy *et al.*, this volume.
99 SECILE/IV/5.
100 SECILE/IV/9.
101 SECILE/IV/9.
102 SECILE/IV/9.

you imagine what the repercussions would be for their jobs, for the whole edifice, for the whole . . . theatre of security the curtain would come crashing down'.[103] Furthermore, evaluations must be done against the backdrop of knowledge of the strategic value of the industry to our economy, an issue mentioned by other interviewees. Counter-terrorism employs hundreds of thousands of people as border guards, airport checks, etc. and has a huge impact on our economy.[104]

6. Conclusion

This chapter set out to improve our understanding of the impact, legitimacy and effectiveness of counter-terrorism measures, drawing on research conducted with members of civil society and key policy-makers. It questioned the common assumption that policy-makers merely develop measures while civil society merely criticizes them. It demonstrated that both groups in fact are critically self-reflexive. The conclusion will summarize the key findings for each concept before considering the relationship between the three concepts and between civil society and policy-makers.

First, the participants indicated that there can be several different types of impact: economic impact, legal impact and practical impact. Furthermore, impact can be direct or indirect. Impact can vary according to the measure in question, depending on whether it is a legislative tool, a Council Conclusion, a statement, a strategy, etc. The variety of possible impacts identified in the research begs the question of whether it is possible to balance different types of impact or whether we should consider prioritizing them. Economic impacts are tangible and quantifiable unlike other impacts such as social impacts, psychological impacts or political impacts, which are much more difficult to measure, particularly at the *ex ante* stage. According to civil society, concerns about the impact of measures relate primarily to the risk of discrimination through profiling and the targeting of NGOs, which were both considered negative impacts. In terms of 'who' we are looking at when we consider impact, we can approach this on two levels: the individual and the societal. Understanding the impact of a counter-terrorist measure on an individual necessitates an appreciation of the extent to which a human right has been infringed. There was a recognition that individuals do not exist in a vacuum but rather come together to form communities and societies and therefore impact can be approached from this broader level. Considering impact at the societal level entails exploring how counter-terrorist measures affect democratic values, practices and principles.

Legitimacy can be viewed through two different lenses. First, from a legal perspective, does it comply with primary and secondary legislation and

103 SECILE/IV/9.
104 SECILE/IV/9.

fulfil the lawfulness criterion? This is seen as the starting point. Second, was the process of development legitimate? Is it necessary, proportionate and fair? Is it being implemented? Implementation moves us from the legal perspective to the political perspective as implementation and uptake can be a reflection of political and social acceptance. As we move from legal acceptance to technical implementation, how does this impact legitimacy? Core values of democracy, accountability, transparency and participation all raise separate challenges, particularly around the policy-making process and the secrecy involved in the classification procedure within the EU. These challenges underline the importance of review mechanisms and the need for evaluation.

Effectiveness relates to the degree to which the measure is able to reach its stated aims. However, the stated aims might differ depending on perspective. In addition, it was felt that measuring effectiveness in the case of counter-terrorism was particularly difficult and in some cases not particularly relevant. The main issue relating to effectiveness is that participants felt that its measurement heavily depends on political agendas and aims. A key issue when measuring effectiveness is the fact that participants have conflated the concepts of effectiveness and impact and do not distinguish between them. This raises particular issues for our definition and measurement of the concepts.

Based on the discussion with civil society, there seemed to be little correlation between the effectiveness of a measure and its impact or legitimacy. This lack of correlation was particularly apparent in the discussion of CTF where participants perceived the measure to be ineffective in countering terrorism, while in fact having a large negative impact on the ability of NGOs to do their work. The disconnect between effectiveness and legitimacy seemed even stronger. According to the participants, the effectiveness of a measure *should* have little influence on the legitimacy. This was primarily related to the fear that the effectiveness of a measure might be used to justify retroactively an otherwise illegitimate measure. This lack of correlation between the concepts was not shared by the policy-makers, however, who did see a link between them. In one particular example given by P4, two different measures of effectiveness are identified: (1) a solid trial, which could lead to a prosecution and (2) no trial but lives were saved. The latter measure may be prioritized sometimes in a hierarchy of effectiveness. Viewing the legitimacy-effectiveness relationship in this way suggests that a temporal factor is at play. Saving lives is an immediate type of effectiveness, whereas prosecution followed by a trial is a more long-term type of effectiveness. We also need to consider the wider societal impacts of short-term effective but illegitimate measures. Finally, we can see from this example that effectiveness is prioritized over legitimacy. P1 agrees that there is a relationship between all three:

> So no CT policy can ever be effective if it's illegitimate . . . it can't because . . . it can be effective for the narrow purpose for which it was

> built but it will be potentially ineffective for the whole CT strategy at the grand level because it will destroy confidence.[105]

What emerges most strongly is the similarity in responses from both groups, with both groups demonstrating a healthy critical awareness. In addition, the role of purpose and statistics, and an understanding of wider policy-making and perspective is critical, as is the willingness to appreciate the nuances of layers of impact, effectiveness or legitimacy in order to understand their inter-relationship.

---

105 SECILE/IV/1.

10 Governance gaps in EU counter-terrorism: implications for democracy and constitutionalism

*Fiona de Londras**

Introduction

The EU is constitutionally committed to a number of fundamental values. Article 2 of the Treaty of the European Union names 'human dignity, freedom, democracy, equality, the rule of law and respect for human rights' as values upon which the Union is founded. Furthermore, Article 3 commits the Union to the promotion of peace and well-being within and beyond the Member States. These values and principles, together with the fundamental rights protected in Article 6 and the Charter of Fundamental Rights of the European Union, help to constitute both the institution of the EU as a social and legal phenomenon *and* act as regulatory and constitutionalist limits on the EU in its activities. By their endorsement of the Treaty, the Member States have consented and committed to these values and principles. Thus, in the context of counter-terrorism (as well as the rest of the Union's work), these constitutional foundations 'perform the fundamental function of granting legitimacy to EU counter-terrorism law and policy and ensuring its recognition as socially acceptable'.[1]

However, the making and implementation of EU counter-terrorism law and policy raise serious questions as to the extent to which this limb of the Union's activities is undertaken in accordance with the constitutionalist spirit of the Union and, if not, what implications this may have for constitutionalism and legitimacy within the EU. Although some of these concerns have been doctrinally (if not yet practically) resolved through the dissolution of the three pillars and further empowerment of the European Parliament in the Lisbon Treaty, a number of fundamental concerns persist. Building on engagement with stakeholders over the course of the past eighteen months,[2]

---

* Professor of Law, Durham University. This chapter builds on research undertaken as part of the Securing Europe through Counter-terrorism: Impact, Legitimacy and Effectiveness (SECILE) project that has received funding from the European Union Seventh Framework Programme (FP7/2007–2013) under grant agreement No. 313195.

This chapter reflects the views of the author only, and not of the entire consortium.

1 Bruno Oliveira Martins, this volume, p.136.

2 See Doody and Van der Hilst, this volume; Murphy, Zammit Borda and Hoyte, this volume.

this chapter first outlines the scope and scale of formal EU counter-terrorism and then considers key constitutionalist and legitimacy concerns relating to provenance, process, democratic oversight and effectiveness.

The stakeholder perspectives that are presented at points in this chapter, and which inform its structure, were gleaned as part of a European Commission funded project entitled SECILE (Securing Europe through Counter-Terrorism: Impact, Legitimacy and Effectiveness), which engaged with (1) operational end users through focus groups,[3] (2) civil society through a focus group,[4] (3) policy-makers in EU counter-terrorism through semi-structured interviews[5] and (4) a mixture of categories (1) to (3) through a one-day workshop run on a 'Chatham House rules' basis. While the views of these stakeholders are not represented here as being generalizable beyond the research subjects who participated, they are nevertheless important perspectives through which some on-the-ground concerns about the nature of EU counter-terrorism and the governance thereof can be identified.

This chapter starts by outlining the scope of the EU's counter-terrorism activities since 2001, before going on to consider the paper's framing concepts of constitutionalism and legitimacy. Building on this, the chapter then assesses EU counter-terrorism by reference to provenance, process, democratic oversight and effectiveness in order to consider the extent to which EU constitutionalism may be compromised or called into question in the field of counter-terrorism as so far engaged with by the Union. The chapter argues that the EU experiences constitutionalist tensions in its making and implementation of counter-terrorism law and policy, some of which are resolved by the courts of the EU, but the nature of which point to the need to build further constitutionalist structures into EU counter-terrorism.

Part I EU counter-terrorism: scope and nature

While the EU has long been involved in security to some extent – not least in finding ways (such as the Schengen systems and its associated databases and protocols) to spread and manage the risks to security that come from fundamental freedoms, such as freedom of movement – counter-terrorism was not part of the EU's working agenda at the time of the attacks of 11 September 2001. Rather, counter-terrorism was predominantly managed

---

3 See C. C. Murphy, A. Zammit Borda and L. Hoyte, *Law Enforcement Officers Perspectives on Impact, Legitimacy and Effectiveness of EU Border Control Databases* (SECILE Consortium, 2014); C.C. Murphy, A. Zammit Borda and L. Hoyte, *Counter-Terrorist Finance Operatives Perspectives on Impact, Legitimacy and Effectiveness of EU Counter-Terrorist Finance Law and Policy* (SECILE Consortium, 2014); C. C. Murphy, A. Zammit Borda and L. Hoyte, *Prosecutor and Government Officials Perspectives on Impact, Legitimacy and Effectiveness of the European Arrest Warrant* (SECILE Consortium, 2014).

4 See R. van der Hilst, *Civil Society Perspectives on the Impact, Legitimacy and Effectiveness of European Counter-Terrorist Measures* (SECILE Consortium, 2014).

5 F. de Londras and J. Doody, *Policy-Maker Perspectives on Impact, Legitimacy and Effectiveness in EU Counter-Terrorism* (SECILE Consortium, 2014).

by the Member States themselves, sometimes with formal or informal cooperation existing between them where appropriate, and largely without EU involvement. Certainly, informal networks existed in the EU that assisted in addressing early security challenges and the establishment of the Terrorism, Radicalism, Extremism and Violence International (TREVI) group in 1975 (in response to the Munich Olympics attack) arguably marked the beginning of European cooperation in the area of counter-terrorism. This was an intergovernmental forum composed of interior and justice ministers working outside formal treaty structures. They used the informal grouping to exchange information and best practices.[6]

A formal institutional role for the EU was not developed until the Conclusions of the extraordinary EU Justice and Home Affairs Council convened on 20 September 2001. The European Council met the following day in an extraordinary session 'in order to analyse the international situation following the terrorist attacks in the United States and to impart the necessary impetus to the actions of the European Union' and adopted Conclusions and a plan of action.[7] This was supplemented by an EU anti-terrorism roadmap listing forty-six measures, adopted on 26 September 2001 and which has subsequently been revised. Some new institutional structures have been developed at EU level, such as the position of EU Counter-Terrorism Coordinator (CTC) established in 2004 in the aftermath of the Madrid bombings. The role of the CTC is to coordinate counter-terrorism activities within the Council, monitor the implementation of measures, communicate and ensure cooperation. The importance of this position was reaffirmed in the Stockholm Programme, which provides 'The European Council reaffirms the importance of the role of the EU Counter-terrorism Coordinator in ensuring implementation and evaluation of the Counter Terrorist strategy, coordinating Counter Terrorist work within the Union, and fostering better communication between the Union and third countries'.[8]

As well as building some institutional infrastructure to address terrorism, the European Union has been an active (if not, in Kent Roach's term, hyperactive[9]) law- and policy-maker in this field over the past decade. Between September 2001 and July 2013, the EU introduced 238 counter-terrorist

---

6 See Doody, this volume.

7 European Commission, Conclusions and Plan of Action of the Extraordinary European Council Meeting of 21 September 2001, SI (2001) 990; Available online at http://europa.eu/rapid/press-release_DOC-01-13_en.htm (accessed 17 January 2015).

8 On the development of formal EU institutions on counter-terrorism, see Doody, this volume; on the development of horizontal networks in EU counter-terrorism see M. den Boer, C. Hillebrand and A, Nölke, 'Legitimacy under pressure: the European web of counter-terrorism networks' (2008) 46(1) *Journal of Common Market Studies* 101.

9 K. Roach, *The 9/11 Effect: Comparative Counter-Terrorism* (Cambridge: Cambridge University Press, 2011).

measures, including eighty-eight 'hard law' measures, adopting a criminal justice approach to EU counter-terrorism.[10] The breakdown of these measures by instrument type illustrates the range of political, legal and operational approaches taken to counter-terrorism at EU level. In that time period, the EU introduced twenty-six action plans and strategy documents, twenty-five Regulations, fifteen Directives, eleven Framework Decisions, twenty-five Decisions, one Joint Action, three Common Positions, nine Recommendations, four Resolutions, 111 Council Conclusions, and eight International Agreements in the counter-terrorism field. Among these is the EU's Action Plan on Countering Terrorism in which broad objectives and the approach to countering terrorism are outlined. Its Action Plan on Countering Terrorism, and the revision thereto, outlines seven strategic objectives for countering terrorism broadly categorized as protect, prevent, pursue and respond.

The development of a comprehensive strategy and range of measures of this nature in such a short period of time is remarkable; not only did it display a kind of hyperactive legislative and policy activity that has been observed elsewhere in counter-terrorism, but it was also a rare example of speedy and concerted cooperation across the Member States of the European Union. In the European Union, however, as elsewhere, the emergence of a concerted phase of counter-terrorism had the potential to raise serious questions of constitutionalism and legitimacy: concepts to which this chapter now turns.

Part II Constitutionalism and legitimacy

Countering terrorism always poses challenges for constitutionalist states committed to the maintenance of core values and principles such as democracy, accountability, transparency, human rights and the rule of law. This is because those states are caught between two seemingly (although not necessarily) competing activities: providing the social good of security against violent attacks, on the one hand, and maintaining constitutionalist characteristics on the other. Times of perceived terrorist violence test the bounds of constitutionalism, understood here as 'the extent to which [a legal system] satisfies desirable precepts of good governance which go beyond those normally expressed within the constitution itself',[11] namely accountability, good administration and the maintenance of human rights.[12] The constitutionalist challenge experienced in countering terrorism across different polities can generally be characterized as follows: repressive, security-oriented measures (at least some of which have been desired security or executive policy prior

10 For the full catalogue see B. Hayes and C. Jones, *Catalogue of EU Counter-Terrorism Measures* (SECILE Consortium, 2013); see also Hayes and Jones, this volume.

11 P. Craig, 'Constitutions, constitutionalism and the European Union' (2001) 7(2) *European Law Journal* 125, p.128.

12 Ibid.

to the emergence of the crisis) are proposed by a strong executive supported by moral and/or norm entrepreneurs steeped in a security community and mindset,[13] the political oversight role of the legislature is weakened and policies that would 'normally' be considered disproportionate are introduced, purportedly to address the crisis as framed by the executive and security professionals. Civil society and human rights voices are marginalized and ineffective and the security community adopts a prominent role in shaping policy and legislative change, and a significant portion of the work of maintaining constitutionalism is borne by courts, to varying degrees of 'success'.[14]

Adherence to law is an essential part of constitutionalism, conceived here as the mindset that government and governance are limited by a commitment to constitutional values, principles and laws so that the making of law and policy is undertaken with a constant constitutionalist awareness and a determination not to exceed constitutional limits. This does not mean, of course, that institutions at domestic or transnational levels would *never* make unconstitutional decisions: the collaborative nature of constitutionalism whereby constitutional meaning is derived from a dynamic and often dialogic relationship between different institutions (e.g. executive and judiciary) makes this almost inevitable.[15]

The challenge to constitutionalism in a counter-terrorist context is significant in established, mature democracies where constitutionalism is deeply entrenched. Thus, it seems reasonable to hypothesize that such a challenge would arise to at least the same extent in relatively less mature constitutionalist polities such as the EU.[16] Indeed, looking at the EU's approach to counter-terrorism through a legitimacy lens, one can discern a number of challenges from a constitutionalist perspective within the activities of even a relatively constrained security actor such as the European Union.[17]

---

13 This draws clearly on Stan Cohen's concept of moral panic as outlined in S. Cohen, *Folk Devils and Moral Panics: The Creation of the Mods and Rockers* (London: MacGibbon & Kee, 1972). For an application of this theory in the context of domestic law-making in counter-terrorism see F. de Londras, *Detention in the 'War on Terror': Can Human Rights Fight Back?* (Cambridge: Cambridge University Press, 2011), Chapter 1.

14 On the role and success of courts in acting as an oversight mechanism in counter-terrorism see generally F.F. Davis and F. de Londras (eds), *Critical Debates on Counter-Terrorism Judicial Review* (Cambridge: Cambridge University Press, 2014).

15 On collaborative constitutionalism see E. Carolan, 'Between supremacy and submission: a model of collaborative constitutionalism?' (1 July, 2013). Available online at SSRN: http://ssrn.com/abstract=2309875 (last accessed 17 January 2015).

16 On EU constitutionalism see, for example, R. Schütze, 'Constitutionalism and the European Union' in Catherine Barnard and Steve Peers, *European Union Law* (Oxford: Oxford University Press, 2014).

17 The constraints of the EU here are related to the fact that security remains a largely domestic, sovereign matter for the Member States.

Legitimacy is a contested concept across numerous different disciplinary frameworks.[18] However, there are a number of insights that can be drawn from across disciplines in order to develop an understanding of legitimacy in this context.[19] In addition, the concept of legitimacy was explored with research participants in SECILE in order to enrich disciplinary perspectives on legitimacy with those of key stakeholders who were asked to expound on their conception of legitimacy.[20] Reading these cross-disciplinary perspectives together with the views of stakeholders through a constitutionalist lens, a number of elements or indicia of legitimacy are identified here.

Within a constitutionalist polity, legality is generally considered to be closely associated with legitimacy. In this respect, legality might be said to be a *sine qua non* of legitimacy inasmuch as illegal or unconstitutional actions are automatically relegated to the category of illegitimacy. However, simple legality is not sufficient. In this respect, adherence to law can be seen as conferring normative legitimacy on a measure or action, whereas matters beyond law can be said to relate to descriptive legitimacy.[21] Descriptive legitimacy then appears to relate to processes rather than to lawfulness per se; in other words, descriptive legitimacy relates to 'people's beliefs about political authority and, sometimes political obligations', whereas normative legitimacy relates to 'some benchmark of acceptability or justification of political power or authority and – possibly – obligation'.[22] The benchmark of acceptability or justification that might be applied in a legitimacy analysis is not necessarily limited to law; rather, the effectiveness of a measure or

18 For a range of views on the concept of legitimacy in the context of counter-terrorism see M. Martin-Mazé, *Report on Societal Understandings of Impact, Legitimacy and Effectiveness in the Counter-Terrorism Context* (SECILE Consortium, 2013); Y. Chistyakova, *Report on Democratic Understandings of Impact, Legitimacy and Effectiveness in the Counter-Terrorism Context* (SECILE Consortium, 2013); F. de Londras, J. Doody and E. Downing, *Report on Operational Perspectives on Impact, Legitimacy and Effectiveness in Counter-Terrorism* (SECILE Consortium, 2013); M. Vermeulen, D. Deering and S. McCarthy (with research assistance from C. Möller), *Report on Legal Understandings of Impact, Legitimacy and Effectiveness in Counter-Terrorism* (SECILE Consortium, 2013).

19 See F. de Londras, J. Doody, J. Supe and S. Zalkalne, *Cross-Disciplinary Perspectives on Impact, Legitimacy and Effectiveness in the Context of EU Counter-Terrorism* (SECILE Consortium, 2013).

20 See C. C. Murphy, A. Zammit Borda and L. Hoyte, *Law Enforcement Officers Perspectives on Impact, Legitimacy and Effectiveness of EU Border Control Databases* (SECILE Consortium, 2014); C. C. Murphy, A. Zammit Borda and L. Hoyte, *Counter-Terrorist Finance Operatives Perspectives on Impact, Legitimacy and Effectiveness of EU Counter-Terrorist Finance Law and Policy* (SECILE Consortium, 2014); C. C. Murphy, A. Zammit Borda and L. Hoyte, *Prosecutor and Government Officials Perspectives on Impact, Legitimacy and Effectiveness of the European Arrest Warrant* (SECILE Consortium, 2014); R. van der Hilst, *Civil Society Perspectives on the Impact, Legitimacy and Effectiveness of European Counter-Terrorist Measures* (SECILE Consortium, 2014); F. de Londras and J. Doody *Policy-maker Perspectives on Impact, Legitimacy and Effectiveness in EU Counter-Terrorism* (SECILE Consortium, 2014).

21 M. Vermeulen, D. Deering and S. McCarthy (with research assistance from C. Möller) *Report on Legal Understandings of Impact, Legitimacy and Effectiveness in Counter-Terrorism* (SECILE Consortium, 2013).

22 S. Fabienne, 'Political Legitimacy', in E. N. Zalta, *The Stanford Encyclopedia of Philosophy*. Available online at http://plato.stanford.edu/entries/legitimacy/ (accessed 28 October 2014).

policy is closely associated with societal and democratic perceptions of legitimacy, as well as with perceptions of legitimacy on the part of those actors seized with the responsibility of implementing measures (i.e. 'operational end users' in security parlance). In terms of descriptive legitimacy adherence to expected protocols in terms of process, deliberation, sound and evidence-based law- and policy-making, participation, transparency and accountability (reflecting autonomy) is key.

In short, legitimacy is a nebulous term but when broken down to measurable elements we might say that a legitimacy analysis of EU counter-terrorism can be conducted by reference to five *indicia*: (1) legality, (2) provenance, (3) process, (4) democratic oversight and (5) effectiveness. While these indicia admittedly overlap, they are also capable of being considered individually. These elements reflect core values of constitutionalism and are, thus, an appropriate framework through which to consider the EU's activity in counter-terrorism from a constitutionalist perspective.

Part III Legality

Legality is a non-negotiable element of EU counter-terrorism from a legitimacy perspective. Unlike in some other legal systems, there has been no debate about the acceptability or otherwise of countering terrorism in a zone beyond law[23] or, indeed, of adjusting fundamental legal norms in order to accommodate counter-terrorist measures or policies that are justified purely on the basis of 'necessity'.[24] This, of course, is related to more than the constitutional commitment to values and principles outlined above within the EU. As a polity, the EU simply has not had to consider many of the areas in which illegality, extra-legality, and excessive legalism have arisen in many domestic counter-terrorist contexts: it has no power to detain, thus internment and treatment in custody by EU agents simply did not arise for consideration. However, questions of legality have nevertheless arisen in the context of EU counter-terrorism, not least in relation to measures introduced to disrupt terrorist financing, highlighted in the famous *Kadi* litigation,[25] and the Data Retention Directive,[26] which was struck down by the Court of Justice of the European Union in the spring of 2014.[27]

Building on the conception of constitutionalism outlined above, critical examination of the legitimacy of counter-terrorism by reference to legality

---

23 See, for example, O. Gross, 'Chaos and rules: should responses to violent crises always be constitutional?' (2003) 112 *Yale Law Journal* 1011; O. Gross, 'Extra-legality and the ethic of political responsibility' in Victor Ramraj (Ed), *Emergencies and the Limits of Legality* (Cambridge: Cambridge University Press, 2008).

24 For a meditation on necessity reasoning see, for example, O. Gross, 'Are torture warrants warranted? Pragmatic absolutism and official disobedience', (2004) 88 *Minnesota Law Review* 1481.

25 Joined Cases C-402/05P & C-415/05P *Kadi and Al Barakaat v Council* [2008] ECR I-6351.

26 Directive 2006/24/EC.

27 Joined Cases C-293/12 and C-594/12, Judgment of the Grand Chamber, 8 April 2014.

should consider not only where measures are ultimately found to have breached constitutional or other legal limitations, but also the extent to which the original decision-makers consciously opted to push or test the boundaries of the constitutional meta-structure within which they operate.

The domestic history of countering terrorism through legal measures is resplendent with examples of governments, and in some cases legislatures in defiance of the executive branch,[28] taking a counter-constitutionalist stance by introducing legislation that seems to defy constitutionalist limits.[29] In the domestic sphere, such actions are at least partially explicable by the political effects of both top-down and bottom-up panic; as I have written before, '[p]anic, fear and populist impulses can conspire to create an atmosphere in which the imperative turns towards combating a risk, and where that risk is presented or conceived of as being particularly grave or dangerous'[30] thus greasing the wheels for especially repressive laws and policies to be introduced in haste. At the transnational level, however, a number of insulating factors tend to make it more difficult to take such swift and, arguably, instrumental advantage of a state of terroristic violence.[31] Notwithstanding that, the EU did engage in swift law-making and, indeed, law-making that has been characterized by some as incoherent, ineffective and disproportionate by reference to the situational risk.[32] This was at least partially, connected to the then-extant three pillar structure of the EU, which is considered further under democratic oversight below, but it also constituted an instance of opportunity-maximization by the Member States, which introduced a raft of measures in the wake of terrorist attacks that they had failed to introduce in 'normal' times.

The Data Retention Directive serves as an excellent example of this. Data retention was on the political agenda in the European Union for an appreciable period of time before the Directive was finally introduced. As Hayes and Jones have noted, attempts to introduce Europe-wide systems of data retention can be traced back to the early 1990s,[33] with a concerted effort

28 On this, see F. de Londras, 'Guantánamo Bay, the rise of courts and the revenge of politics' in David Jenkins, Anders Henriksen and Amanda Jacobsen (Eds). *The Long Decade: How 9/11 Has Changed the Law* (Oxford: Oxford University Press, 2014).

29 K. Roach, 2012.

30 F. de Londras, *Detention in the 'War on Terror': Can Human Rights Fight Back?* (Cambridge: Cambridge University Press, 2011), p.8.

31 Ibid., pp. 203–212. I name these as structure (international institutions are not normally designed to allow for quick decision-making of a legally binding nature), situation (relating to the cognitive distance between the international institution and the panicked domestic polity), constitutive (the 'democratic deficit' of international institutions), and constitutionalist (international values and global goods).

32 G. Edwards and C. Meyer, 'Introduction: Charting a Contested Transformation' (2008) 46(1) *Journal of Common Market Studies* 1.

33 B. Hayes and C. Jones, *The EU Data Retention Directive: a Case Study in the Legitimacy and Effectiveness of EU Counter-terrorism Policy* (SECILE Consortium, 2013), pp. 6–7.

to introduce such a system having taken place in the context of the e-Privacy Directive[34] in the early 2000s. Although that Directive included a provision requiring some data retention by telecommunications providers, attempts to introduce a more comprehensive regime were rejected, largely on privacy grounds,[35] until representations were made in the aftermath of the London and Madrid bombings that this was insufficient, leading to the introduction of the Data Retention Directive. In spite of clear advice from key rights-related office holders and the NGO sector that a turn towards mass blanket surveillance would constitute a disproportionate interference with fundamental rights and thus be unlawful, the Directive was passed; indeed, serious infringement proceedings were brought against states that failed to implement it out of concern about its incompatibility with their domestic rights protections.[36] This clear counter-constitutionalist turn ultimately led to the Court of Justice of the European Union (CJEU) striking the Directive down[37] for precisely the reasons of disproportionality that had been highlighted at the time of its design and promulgation (considered further below), as well as by the expression of serious concerns by numerous apex courts across the Member States of the European Union.[38] Illegitimacy here stems not only from the ultimate unconstitutionality of the promulgated measure, but also from the determined political turn away from constitutionalism when introducing it in the first place.

This highlights an important constitutionalist concern in the form of a cognitive governance gap. Although governance is a multi-actor activity, ultimate responsibility for decision-making in the EU (as in domestic systems) rests on the political actors with the institutional, constitutional and political responsibility to make policy and legislative decisions. These actors are, thus, key in maintaining constitutionalism and legitimacy as they carry

---

34 Directive 2002/58/EC.

35 B. Hayes and C. Jones, *The EU Data Retention Directive: A Case Study in the Legitimacy and Effectiveness of EU Counter-Terrorism policy* (SECILE Consortium, 2013), pp. 8–9.

36 On infringement proceedings in relation to the Directive, see Hayes and Jones, Ibid., pp. 15–21.

37 Joined Cases C-293/12 and C-594/12, Judgment of the Grand Chamber, 8 April 2014.

38 European Digital Rights (2008) 'Bulgarian court annuls a vague article of the data retention law', *EDRi-gram*, 17 December 2008. Available online at http://www.edri.org/edri-gram/number6.24/bulgarian-administrative-case-data-retention (accessed 17 January 2015); Constitutional Court of Romania, Decision no.1258, 9 October 2009. Available online at http://www.legi-internet.ro/fileadmin/editor_folder/pdf/decision-constitutional-court-romania-data-retention.pdf (accessed 17 January 2015); Cyprus Supreme Court (Civil applications 65/2009, 78/2009, 82/2009 and 15/2010–22/2010). Available online at http://www.supremecourt.gov.cy/Judicial/SC.nsf/All/5B67A764B86AA78EC225782F004F6D28/$file/65–09.pdf (accessed 17 January 2015); Leitsätze zum Urteil des Ersten Seants vom 2. März 2010–1 BvR 256/08–1 BvR 263/08–1 BvR 586/08', *Bundesverfassungsgericht*, 2 March 2010. Available online at https://www.bundesverfassungsgericht.de/entscheidungen/rs20100302_1bvr025608.html (accessed 17 January 2015); 'English translation of the Czech Constitutional Court decision on Data Retention', 22 March 2011. Available online at http://www.slidilove.cz/sites/default/files/dataretention_judgment_constitutionalcourt_czechrepublic.pdf (accessed 17 January 2015).

out self-governing and self-regulatory functions that are fundamental to the functioning of constitutionalism through institutional design, processes and participation.

Part IV Provenance

Numerous stakeholders in EU counter-terrorism who engaged with the SECILE project expressed concern as to the provenance of a number of EU counter-terrorism measures.[39] This relates to legitimacy and constitutionalism in two ways. First, it reflects a suspicion that some measures introduced under the rubric of counter-terrorism might be unnecessary and in fact a reaction to an exogenous pressure to legislate, rather than to a rigorously analysed situational risk. Second, there is a concern that at least some of these measures might not relate to terrorism at all, but might in fact be previously desired measures promulgated in the environment of legislative permissiveness that tends to emerge in a situation of terrorism-related crisis.

(i) Unnecessary measures

Due in part to the internationalization of counter-terrorism in the wake of the 11 September 2001 attacks,[40] and the decision of EU Member States to implement some international obligations flowing from Security Council Resolution 1373 in a unified manner through EU law, the Union has introduced a number of measures that appear justified by exogenous factors, rather than having a clear basis in evidence-based assessments of necessity and threat within the European Union itself. Thus, for example, the operational end users involved in the implementation of counter-terrorist financing laws and systems within the EU who participated in the SECILE project raised some concerns about the extent to which these measures had been introduced as a response to international and US-based pressure to address financing in Europe without the need for such measures having been clearly established.[41] Similar concerns might be legitimately raised in relation to the measures that will be introduced to deal with foreign terrorist fighters pursuant to Security Council Resolution 2178, as well as to the EU's agreement

39 Interview transcript 7; C. C. Murphy, A. Zammit Borda and L. Hoyte, *Counter-terrorist Finance Operatives Perspectives on Impact, Legitimacy and Effectiveness of EU Counter-terrorist Finance Law and Policy* (SECILE Consortium, 2014).

40 On internationalization, regionalization and hybridization of counter-terrorism see F. de Londras, '(Counter)Terrorism and Hybridity' in N. L. Herbert and R. Freedman (Eds), *Hybridity* (forthcoming, 2015).

41 C. C. Murphy, A. Zammit Borda and L. Hoyte, *Counter-terrorist Finance Operatives Perspectives on Impact, Legitimacy and Effectiveness of EU Counter-terrorist Finance Law and Policy* (SECILE Consortium, 2014), pp. 12–14.

to measures such as the SWIFT Agreement, which were clearly motivated by requests from the United States, rather than having any particular provenance within an evidence-based assessment of situational risk within the European Union per se.[42]

(ii) Opportunism and 'creep'

A further concern as to provenance arises in relation to opportunism and 'creep' in EU counter-terrorism. Opportunism in the context of counter-terrorism, which is by no means unique to the European Union, comprises the use of a counter-terrorism framework to introduce measures that 'norm entrepreneurs' might otherwise not succeed in having introduced, often because of concerns about their non-compliance with human rights standards. Measures of this kind have a tendency to capitalize on the moment of opportunity created by crisis, which was considered above, and extend the extraordinary grammar of counter-terrorism across a range of fields that are only tangentially associated with countering terrorism. The Data Retention Directive, the introduction of which was considered above, is arguably an example of such opportunism. However, as well as opportunism, concerns as to provenance also arise in relation to 'creep'.

In the EU, as elsewhere, counter-terrorism measures are rarely single-use; rather, they tend to have scope to apply to a range of criminal justice and other issues. This is reflected in the fact that I categorize such measures as falling into three types: capitalizing measures, terrorism-related measures, and terrorism-specific measures.

I define capitalizing measures as measures that reflect policy choices pre-dating major terrorist attacks but in relation to which the political impetus for implementing these policy choices first became available in a post-attack atmosphere. These measures might not strictly be considered counter-terrorist in ordinary circumstances; in fact, they are more likely to be described as general criminal justice measures, and those practitioners who use them on a relatively frequent basis may not conceive of them as having much, if anything, to do with countering terrorism. However, as they were introduced under the heading of counter-terrorism they are rightly considered to be part of the EU's broader counter-terrorism law and policy. Two prime examples of capitalizing measures, although introduced at different times, are the European Arrest Warrant and the European Data Retention Directive (now struck down).

Terrorism-related measures are here defined as measures that are introduced in order to respond to general security concerns, including terrorism. As with capitalizing measures, these are unlikely to be perceived as primarily

42 On the SWIFT Agreement and its implications for EU governance, see M. de Goede, 'The SWIFT affair and the global politics of European Security' (2012) 50(2) *Journal of Common Market Studies* 214.

or even largely 'counter-terrorist', although they have a clear counter-terrorist application and in some cases the justificatory rhetoric surrounding their introduction referred expressly to the threat from terrorism. An example of terrorism-related measures is the introduction and implementation of major border control databases across the Member States of the European Union such as the Schengen Information System (and soon SIS II), the European Border Surveillance System (EUROSUR) and others. These databases are, in essence, necessary corollaries of the opening up of borders within the European Union; with freedom of movement comes a certain risk that states perceive needs to be managed through a coordinated system of border control and/or surveillance. Operational actors both at borders and in Frontex do not tend to characterize these databases or measures as being counter-terrorist. Indeed, a representative of Frontex interviewed for SECILE expressly rejected any such characterization,[43] although this is entirely at odds with the views expressed by civil society in a focus group on the matter.[44] However, the political discourse surrounding border control does have an increasingly strong counter-terrorist tone, and terrorism related security concerns are increasingly part of the rhetoric around border control, a situation that seems only exacerbated by the introduction of Security Council Resolution 2178.

In contrast, terrorism-specific measures are ones that were introduced in order to respond to a perceived risk from terrorism, rather than being general criminal justice measures. As the Member States of the European Union retain the vast majority of counter-terrorist and security competence, these measures are, in truth, relatively sparse at the EU level and relate to matters in which a transnational approach is required. The primary example of this is the EU's system for the disruption of terrorist financing, in relation to which other concerns as to provenance, considered above, might be said to arise.

From a constitutionalist perspective, anxieties as to provenance raise serious concerns. Establishing the necessity of introducing a measure is a key element of its legitimation;[45] the imposition of the coercive force of law, governance and bureaucracy is premised on the implicit pact of self-restraint by government. Where coercion is based on something other than necessity,

---

43 According to the interviewee: 'I think that in general when it comes to EU border security or counter-terrorism it hasn't really been established as a field of work. If you look at Frontex mandate, our tasking, there is no specific reference to counter-terrorism at all. And if there is anything it is disputed by member states . . . I don't think [Schengen Information System] was designed . . . as a tool to counter terrorism. It is there to . . . help with border management and movement of people and then [to] enable that there is such a thing as the Schengen Information System but . . . I don't think that those responsible for countering those activities really consider Schengen Information System as their tool or some resource that they [have].'

44 R. van der Hilst, *Civil Society Perspectives on the Impact, Legitimacy and Effectiveness of European Counter-terrorist Measures* (SECILE Consortium, 2014), pp. 13–16.

45 On legitimization and counter-terrorism see Burgess and Mazé, this volume.

serious questions as to legitimacy arise. This is even more so in situations where the measure(s) introduced have serious implications for the limited power of the state and supra-state apparatus and the protection of human rights. As considered above, counter-terrorism as a field of legal, political and operational practice poses specific challenges to constitutionalism and rights, not least because of the commitment to a grammar of 'balancing' that both represents rights and security as being in tension *and* tends to overweight security concerns.[46] A similar legitimacy concern arises in relation to creep by means of capitalizing and terrorism-related measures: not only do such measures emerge from political and deliberative processes that tend to be distorted by the counter-terrorist environment and framing, but they also extend the products of these distorted processes – with their associated troubling in-built assessments of balance – to fields of operation beyond terrorism. As remarked by Edwards and Meyer, 'the very fact that the fight against crime and illegal migration is framed as part of the fight against terrorism underlines the point that the politics of counter-terrorism have set the EU off on a widely contested course that could affect its role, functioning and claim to legitimacy'.[47]

Part V Process

Over recent years, the EU has been committing significant resources to improving the quality of its law and regulation, stemming from the criticisms of the quality of existing EU legislation levied by the Working Group on Regulation.[48] Since 2002, *ex ante* impact assessment has been a core element of this initiative towards better regulation, which is intended to 'enhance the rationality of the EU emerging regulatory state while at the same time democratizing its decision-making process'.[49] Although the use of *ex ante* impact assessment in EU counter-terrorism is by no means yet systematic, twenty-two of the eight-eight legally binding measures identified by Hayes and Jones were the subject of such assessments.[50]

In essence, *ex ante* impact assessment is designed to verify the existence of a problem or challenge, explore potential solutions to it and present evidence-based options to the political institutions of the EU, which then decide what, if any, option to pursue in order to address the identified

---

46 On the problematic nature of balance in counter-terrorism and security see, for example, J. Waldron, 'Security and liberty: the image of balance' (2003) 11(2) *Journal of Political Philosophy* 191.

47 G. Edwards and C. O. Meyers, 'Introduction: Charting a Contested Transformation' (2006) 46(1) *JCMS* 1, p.3.

48 Report of the Working Group on Better Regulation (Group 2c), May 2001, White Paper on European Governance, Work Area no 2, p.21.

49 A. Alemanno, 'A meeting of minds on impact assessment: when *ex ante* evaluation meets *ex post* judicial control' (2011) 17(3) *European Public Law* 5.

50 Hayes and Jones, this volume.

challenge. While impact assessments are intended to provide an evidence base for, rather than to replace, political decision-making, it is clear that the European Commission places a very heavy premium on these assessments, describing the *ex ante* process as 'an essential tool for producing high quality and credible policy proposals . . . increas[ing] the legitimacy of EU action from the point of view of stakeholders and citizens'.[51] However, within this process, concerns arise in the counter-terrorist context about the extent to which 'societal impacts' including rights and values are adequately factored in.

In making an *ex ante* impact assessment, the Commission takes into account the environmental, economic and 'social/societal' impacts of proposed changes. Social impacts here include impacts on rights, democratic principles, senses of security and societal values. While economic impacts might be susceptible to relatively scientific forecasting, it is not clear that societal impacts can truly be assessed in a quantitative way and, as a result, there is a real possibility that they might not get an appropriate weighting in what is, essentially, a pre-legal proportionality analysis in the form of an impact assessment. While we might be able to predict that implementing Measure X will cost €4 million per annum spread across twenty stakeholders, for example, we cannot predict that it will lead to an 11 per cent reduction in the effective enjoyment of privacy, or a 5 per cent reduction in social cohesion. In such circumstances, the qualitative analysis of impact on rights is not easily assessed alongside the quantitative analysis of impact on economics, with more 'concrete' data often appearing to receive more analytical weight. This does not mean that those conducting these assessments are not concerned with rights, but rather that such assessments are evidence-based and other forms of impact can usually, although not always, be assessed by reference to more, and more verifiable, 'evidence' than can potential impacts on rights.

This is not to suggest that *ex ante* impact assessments are undertaken without care, attention, or the commitment of resources. In fact, in the general course of events these *ex ante* impact assessments are usually done over a period of a year or so, and involve thirteen key steps.[52] The formal impact-assessment process aims to be both participatory and predictive. However, in reality it is participatory only inasmuch as those identified by the Commission as relevant stakeholders are engaged, and predictive only in relation to what are deemed economic, social and environmental impacts, and even then only inasmuch as these impacts can be accurately forecast and effectively factored into the analysis which, as mentioned above, can be especially challenging in respect of rights. It is also important to note that in formal *ex ante* impact assessments, participation seems to serve three

51 European Commission, Impact Assessment Guidelines, SEC (2009) 92, p.18.

52 Ibid., p.7.

functions (identification and shaping of the problem, generation of options to address said problem and assessment of the potential impacts of such options), raising some questions about the extent to which participation is designed to confirm, rather than inform, decision-making. This is all the more worrisome when one recognizes the long-term significance of these *ex ante* impact assessments throughout the life cycle of a measure.

The shape, nature and findings of *ex ante* impact assessments can be relevant in designing *ex post facto* reviews of EU counter-terrorism measures. Although, as outlined further below, there are serious concerns about the extent to which EU counter-terrorist measures are exposed to effective and regular review, where such reviews do take place the measures tend to be reviewed against the objectives that were outlined in the *ex ante* impact assessment. In other words, this assessment not only defines the problem to be addressed and shapes the discourse around potential options for doing so, but also substantively shapes subsequent discourses around the effectiveness and success of the measure on the occasions that we ask these kinds of question about counter-terrorism. This is not to suggest that *ex post facto* reviews will entirely or necessarily mirror the questions asked in the *ex ante* assessment, but rather to note that this speculative and prospective assessment can shape the discourse around a measure in a way that is influential in respect of this later assessment of the operation of the measure, whether by indicating potential review questions for the Commission to ask or by influencing the terms of reference of an externally conducted review.

A further important function of these *ex ante* impact assessments is suggested by an emerging pattern in other parts of EU law whereby the Court of Justice refers to *ex ante* impact assessments in the course of deciding upon the constitutionality of EU laws. By institutional design and substantive competence, the Court is not well placed to determine the practical operational effects of EU measures, especially in technical and technocratic areas such as telecommunications, climate change or pharmaceutical regulation. When considering the impacts of a measure for the purposes of assessing its proportionality, the Court is assessing legal impact: what changes to the pre-existing laws did the measure in question result in? Do those changes constitute a *prima facie* interference with fundamental rights? If so, is that interference proportionate? These are the questions that courts ask when assessing all measures, including counter-terrorism measures. To the extent that the court might take into account burdens that the measure places on industry, for example, or other implementing actors, it is reliant on information about something that is not law and thus on information from another source. In this respect, *ex ante* impact assessments and *ex post facto* review may coincide in what Alberto Alemanno describes as an 'indirect encounter'.[53]

53 A. Alemanno, 'A meeting of minds on impact assessment: when *ex ante* evaluation meets *ex post* judicial control' (2011) 17(3) *European Public Law* 5.

In spite of their lack of formal legal status, these impact assessments can then be used as aids to the parties and to the court, not least when the court pursues a line of reasoning that suggests that 'the institutions must at the very least be able to produce and set out clearly and unequivocally the basic facts which had to be taken into account as the basis of the contested measures of the act and on which the exercise of their discretion depended'.[54] This suggests, at the very least, that in assessing the proportionality of highly technical measures, the Court may find it useful to have a resource, such as an impact assessment, which has made something similar to a preliminary proportionality assessment, at its disposal.

Thus, having in place an effective and rigorous system whereby all impacts, including those that are classed as societal, are properly accounted for in the policy-making process that precedes the introduction of an EU counter-terrorist measure is significant not only for the content and quality of the measure itself but also, in at least some cases, for how it is subsequently assessed in and beyond courts. The process of forming policy, thus, has serious implications for constitutionalism and the system's capacity to maintain and safeguard it.

Part VI Democratic oversight

Not all EU counter-terrorism measures are subjected to *ex ante* impact assessment; it is required only for major initiatives and, furthermore, a substantial amount of core policy decisions in the counter-terrorist field are already made at a political level before such an assessment, and then operationalized through legal or logistical measures. However, there are other opportunities for impact, and especially societal impact in the form of impact on rights, to be taken into account in advance of the formal adoption of measures through mechanisms of democratic oversight; for example, democratic debate on proposed measures and consideration of measures by parliamentary committees that receive evidence from specialist stakeholders. As well as offering further opportunities for assessment of potential impact, mechanisms of democratic oversight can also shed light on the operation, effectiveness and actual impact of EU counter-terrorism measures once they have been implemented. Impact and effectiveness assessment through democratic oversight improves governance and democratic legitimacy and thus aligns with constitutionalist values. Concomitantly, a lack of democratic oversight can undermine the legitimacy of such measures and raise questions of constitutionalist tension in the counter-terrorist field. However, the history of EU counter-terrorism to date suggests that democratic oversight emanating from the European Parliament has been somewhat lacking. Thus, the democratic processes that we rely on to provide effective oversight in

54 Case C-310/04 *Spain v. Council* [2006] ECR I-7285 [123].

law-making activities is challenged, if not compromised, in a counter-terrorist context. This has been the case in the EU since 2001,[55] as well across a number of domestic politico-legal systems.[56]

The record shows that neither public consultation nor pre-legislative scrutiny occurs frequently in the security context nor, indeed, achieves much purchase in the process to understand and ameliorate the societal impacts of counter-terrorism measures.[57] Hayes and Jones claim that only 3.4 per cent of the counter-terrorism measures introduced by the European Union between 2001 and 2013 were subject to public consultation before their introduction, and even within these consultations they are critical of the extent to which human rights concerns were actively folded into the analysis.[58] Furthermore, while co-decision now applies to counter-terrorism, this was not the case prior to the introduction of the Lisbon Treaty, which dismantled the three pillars of the European Union and further empowered the European Parliament. Indeed, largely relating to the then-extant institutional and constitutional structure of the European Union, co-decision took place in respect of only twenty-three of the eighty-eight legally binding counter-terrorism measures introduced between 2001 and 2013.[59]

When considering the apparent marginalization of the European Parliament in the context of counter-terrorism since 2001, two important factors must be borne in mind. First, at least part of the reason for the apparent marginalization of the European Parliament in the initial phase of EU counter-terrorism must be the then-constitutional and institutional structure of the Union. The three-pillar structure meant that the European Parliament's marginalization was, to some extent, a simple function of the categorization of some elements of counter-terrorism (while not denying that categorization may, at times, have been instrumental in order to reduce parliamentary scrutiny and debate). In this way, it ought to be seen as a further manifestation of the general, and generally problematic, marginalization of the Parliament prior to the changes introduced by the Lisbon Treaty. To at least a doctrinal or formal extent, then, the dissolution of the pillar structure and empowerment of the European Parliament in the Lisbon Treaty may address some of this marginalization in the future.

Second, marginalization of the European Parliament has at least something to do with the mindset of MEPs, including those who sit on pertinent committees within the Parliament. While there are certainly real challenges

55 B. Hayes and C. Jones, *Report on How the EU Assesses the Impact, Legitimacy and Effectiveness of its Counter-terrorism Laws* (SECILE Consortium, 2013).

56 For a comparative overview, see F. de Londras and F. F. Davis, 'Controlling the executive in times of terrorism: competing perspectives on effective oversight mechanisms' (2011) 30(1) *Oxford Journal of Legal Studies* 19.

57 See Hayes & Jones, this volume.

58 Ibid.

59 Ibid.

that flow from secrecy protocols from the perspective of effective democratic oversight, and while the document classification system within the EU is deeply problematic, it is also the case that MEPs have been reluctant to sit in closed sessions or negotiate those challenges through procedural innovation. Furthermore, Wills *et al.* found considerable concern among some MEPs about the potential implications of security clearance for their capacity to speak out.[60] However, although there is of course a risk that security clearance might undermine a politician's capacity to 'make noise' about security concerns as well as genuine concerns about capture, the lack of such clearance makes democratic oversight extremely challenging: information flow is stymied and building trust between the overseer and overseen is deeply challenged. To the extent to which the European Parliament might be said to have been marginalized as a matter of mindset, this presents an interesting variation on the domestically observed patterns of legislative compliance with executive policy in counter-terrorism and/or hyper-politicization of terrorism.[61]

Part VII Effectiveness

Counter-terrorism law and policy can push the boundaries of acceptable (supra-)state behavior, empowering the authorities to engage in repressive activities that would otherwise be considered clearly disproportionate and are unlikely to be successfully steered through a parliamentary process. Thus, there is a clear constitutionalist importance to ensuring that the effectiveness of these measures is assessed in order to discern the extent to which they actually achieve their stated specific- and meta-objectives. While we might accept that a measure to address a particular terrorist phenomenon is necessary, thus lending its introduction some *prima facie* constitutionalist legitimacy, this cannot be the end of the enquiry, for necessity is just one element of establishing legitimacy within a constitutional polity. Ineffectiveness of a measure negates the claim to necessity; that which does not work to counter terrorism cannot be necessary in order to do so. Thus, examining the effectiveness of counter-terrorist measures is elemental.

As well as testing the necessity basis for the measure (i.e. its justifiability by reference to situational risk and practical impacts), review of a measure's effectiveness contributes to constitutionalism in a number of ways. First, it provides an opportunity to reassess the original evidence base for the introduction of the measure: Does the problem still exist? Has it changed in its form or nature? Are the responses, as implemented, still appropriate? Reassessing the evidence base for a measure enhances its claim to legitimacy.

60 A. Wills, M. Vermeulen, H. Born, M. Scheinin, M. Wiebusch and A. Thprnton, *Parliamentary Oversight of Security and Intelligence Agencies in the European Union* (LIBE Committee, 2011).

61 F. de Londras, *Detention in the 'War on Terror': Can Human Rights Fight Back?* (Cambridge: Cambridge University Press, 2011), Chapter 4.

This is not least because such a review also offers the opportunity to assess proportionality based on practice rather than speculation, taking into account both the quantitative and qualitative experiences of communities, operational end users, and other relevant stakeholders of the actual operation of these measures. This in turn injects a level of transparency into the operation of the measures through, ideally, the public reporting of (for example) the frequency with which they are applied, the kinds of results that have been achieved through their application, their reception in target and other communities, and the range of burdens and benefits they are perceived to have brought to relevant stakeholders.

When properly implemented, a public policy feedback loop that includes effective, evaluative review of the operation of measures thus contributes to the maintenance of constitutionalism through transparency, participation and quality assessment through which legitimacy is enhanced. In spite of the benefits of *ex post facto* review from a constitutionalist perspective, such review is rare in the context of counter-terrorism. The (generally put) trend in counter-terrorism tends to be to implement measures, and then to implement more measures, and then more with little or no assessment of the effectiveness and impacts of these policies, laws, instruments and approaches or, sometimes, of their necessity. This is not universally true: in both the UK and Australia, for example, there is a trend of independent review,[62] albeit one where the institutional structure of the review in question is in some flux, and researchers are sometimes engaged by government or other funding bodies to study the impacts and effects of such measures. But as a general matter, security appears to be treated as an exception to our commitment to good governance of this kind, and this is also the case in the European Union.

This is evident from both a statistical and a substantive analysis of the review of EU counter-terrorism over the past twelve years.[63] Of the eighty-eight legally binding measures that were introduced under the rubric of counter-terrorism between 2001 and 2013, fifty-nine contained Commission review clauses and a further nine contained clauses providing for review by the Council. Thus, approximately one-third of the legally binding measures introduced in this period of time contained no formal review clause. Of those that did, sixty-two in total, only thirty-three have taken place on time,

62 On independent review in the UK and Australia, see J. Blackbourne, 'Independent reviewers as alternative: an empirical study from Australia and the United Kingdom', in F. F. Davis and F. de Londras (Eds), *Critical Debates on Counter-terrorism Judicial Review* (Cambridge: Cambridge University Press, 2014).

63 In this respect, I discount European Commission supervision or review of the formal transposition of measures where such transposition is legally required. These reviews are formalistic rather than evaluative or qualitative and, while transposition and implementation are sometimes considered as indicators of the 'effectiveness' of EU counter-terrorism measures, they do not take operational and rights-related analyses into account. For an account of transposition of EU counter-terrorist measures see B. Hayes and C. Jones, *Report on How the EU Assesses the Impact, Legitimacy and Effectiveness of its Counter-Terrorism Laws* (SECILE Consortium, 2013).

a further ten had not reached their time limit, and sixteen had not taken place or could not be located.[64] The picture is hardly more positive when one considers the non-legally binding measures. Of eight Agreements, three require review, and only one (on the EU-Canada PNR/API Agreement) has taken place, although it cannot be publicly accessed. One of the Common Positions has been reviewed,[65] eleven Decisions have been reviewed, thirteen Directives have been reviewed (reflecting the well-established systems for reviewing Directives), nine Framework Decisions have been reviewed, the Joint Action has not been reviewed and five Regulations have been reviewed.[66] A further five externally contracted reviews have been carried out.[67]

It is important, however, to bear in mind that formal review is only part of the picture: additional, *de facto* review takes place in a variety of other institutional, informal and ancillary ways, including through formal peer review.[68] Institutionally, the reports of office holders such as the Counter-Terrorism Coordinator can operate as a kind of quasi review of the measures under consideration, although such reports do not have the benefits of participation and transparency in terms of their preparation that formal reviews benefit from. In addition, there are formal and informal peer reviews, working group meetings and side meetings in which the practical operation of measures is often discussed; these discussions can feed into political decision-making with consequences for the continuation, repeal or adjustment of existing measures. Again, however, these processes are very operationally-oriented, placing the experiences and perspectives of state actors, likely to have security biases, in a position of privilege. Furthermore, many of these processes are closed, so that they do not have the characteristics of participation and transparency, undermining their contribution to legitimacy and constitutionalism in EU counter-terrorism.

Thus, while the matter of formal review does not tell the whole story about the review of EU counter-terrorism, it is clear that reviewing does not happen in a consistent, systematic and regular manner. Thus, many individual EU counter-terrorist measures effectively remain operational

64 Ibid., p.17.

65 2005/69/JHA of 24 January 2005 on exchanging certain data with Interpol, reviewed in 2006. European Commission 'Report from the Commission on the operation of Council Common Position 2005/69/JHA', COM (2006) 167 final, 21 April 2006. Available online at http://eur-lex.europa.eu/LexUriServ/LexUriServ.do?uri=COM:2006:0167:FIN:EN:PDF

66 B. Hayes and C. Jones, *Report on How the EU Assesses the Impact, Legitimacy and Effectiveness of its Counter-terrorism Laws* (SECILE Consortium, 2013), 18–19.

67 Ibid., p.20.

68 The peer review mechanism was introduced in 1997 by means of Joint Action 1997/827/JHA of 5 December 1997, adopted by the Council on the basis of Article K.3 of the Treaty on European Union, establishing a mechanism for evaluating the application and implementation at national level of international undertakings in the fight against organized crime. Available online at http://eur-lex.europa.eu/LexUriServ/LexUriServ.do?uri=CELEX:31997F0827:EN:HTML

The relevant reviews were General Secretariat, 'Second round of peer evaluation: preparedness and consequence management in the event of a terrorist attack – final report', 8568/10, 16 April 2010. Available online at http://register.consilium.europa.eu/pdf/en/10/st08/st08568.en10.pdf

without formal review and, as a result, without a clear indication of their implications on a systemic level for the effective enjoyment of rights across the European Union.

Even when formal reviews mandated by the terms of EU counter-terrorist measures do take place, there can be substantial challenges in ensuring that they actually achieve participation, transparency and a meaningful effectiveness assessment. This can be illustrated, once again, by reference to the Data Retention Directive. This Directive was subjected to an *ex post facto* review carried out by the Commission.[69] The review comprised a conference in 2009 at which stakeholders from data protection authorities, industry, civil society and academia contributed to an evaluation of the Directive.[70] The conference was supplemented by a questionnaire sent by the Commission to these stakeholder groups and to which approximately seventy responses were garnered.[71] There was then a second conference in December 2010 at which preliminary assessment and future challenges were discussed.[72] In spite of the well documented and widespread concerns about the rights implications of the Directive[73] and, especially, about its instigation of blanket surveillance with vastly different processes across the Member States of the EU, the continuous difficulties in securing statistics as to the use of the Directive from the Member States themselves,[74] and the disquiet that had been expressed by domestic courts in Romania,[75] Germany[76] and the Czech Republic,[77] not to mention substantial concerns about the economic and operational burden imposed by the Directive from industry,[78] the Commission concluded that data retention is a necessary tool and plays an important role in criminal investigations (including in securing acquittals) and should, thus, be continued. While the Commission acknowledged that transposition was uneven, the operational burden was costly, and there were concerns about proportionality, it nevertheless concluded that data retention was necessary, albeit it would recommend a revision of the framework that was then in operation.[79]

For many, this review simply confirmed what was perceived as the essentially political nature of such exercises and seemed to draw conclusions that

69 European Commission, *Evaluation Report on the Data Retention Directive (Directive 2006/24/EC)* (2011).

70 Ibid.

71 Ibid.

72 Ibid., pp.1–2.

73 Ibid., pp.28–30.

74 Ibid., p.19.

75 Decision no 1258 from 8 October 2009 of the Romanian Constitutional Court.

76 Bundesverfassungsgericht, 1 BvR 256/08, para 1–345.

77 Judgment of the Czech Constitutional Court of 22 March on Act No. 127/2005 and Decree No 485/2005.

78 European Commission, *Evaluation Report on the Data Retention Directive (Directive 2006/24/EC)*, COM(2011) 225 final, pp.26–27.

79 Ibid., pp.30–33.

were not supported by industry perspectives, rights-based concerns or indeed the statistics (such as they were) that were provided by Member States. Indeed, so substantial was the reaction that a shadow review was prepared by the NGO, European Digital Rights (EDR).[80] In contrast to the Commission, this shadow review argued that '[o]ver the past five years, the Data Retention Directive has proved to be an unnecessary and unprecedented violation of the fundamental rights of 500 million Europeans'.[81] This simply added to a chorus of concern about the Directive, including from the European Data Protection Supervisor, who had described it as 'the most privacy invasive instrument ever adopted by the EU'.[82] Indeed, the experience of this review process was so negative from the perspective of stakeholders that it appears to have undermined Commission-led review, described in the EDR shadow report as having been 'fundamentally flawed' as '[r]ather than procuring an independent assessment that satisfies scientific standards, the Commission [had] produced a political document'.[83]

Part VIII Constitutionalism and the courts

It is important to acknowledge that at least some EU counter-terrorist measures are, and have been, subjected to what we might describe as 'indirect review' by national and European courts. This form of review is termed 'indirect' here because it is not a formal, participatory, rounded review of the operation and impact of a measure; rather, it is a judicial review of the *lawfulness* of the measure that is being challenged. While judicial review of these counter-terrorist measures has important legal and regulatory roles to play,[84] it is, thus, a limited exercise in some important ways. Judicial review asks questions relating solely to legal matters and is often contingent on a particular factual scenario; it does not always achieve the levels of participation, transparency and broader quality assessment that a policy-oriented review might do. This is not least because, in the context of security, we must always grapple with the problematic but unavoidable fact that those who are to be reviewed effectively monopolize the information we need in order to be able to undertake meaningful review.[85] That said, the Court of Justice of the European Union has engaged in constitutionalist 'heavy lifting'

80 EDR, *Shadow Evaluation Report on the Data Retention Directive* (2006/24/EC) (2011).

81 Ibid., p.2.

82 P. Hustinx, 'The Moment of truth for the Data Retention Directive', Paper presented at 'Taking on the Data Retention Directive', Brussels, 3 December 2010. Available online at https://secure.edps.europa.eu/EDPSWEB/webdav/site/mySite/shared/Documents/EDPS/Publications/Speeches/2010/10–12–03_Data_retention_speech_PH_EN.pdf (accessed, 3 June 2014).

83 EDR, *Shadow Evaluation Report on the Data Retention Directive* (2006/24/EC) (2011), 2.

84 See F. de Londras, 'Counter-terrorism judicial review as regulatory constitutionalism' in F. F. Davis and F. de Londras, *Critical Debates on Counter-terrorism Judicial Review* (Cambridge: Cambridge University Press, 2014).

85 Burgess and Martin-Mazé, this volume.

in at least some cases relating to EU counter-terrorism since 2001, although the overall picture of its record in this field is somewhat mixed.[86]

Returning, once more, to the Data Retention Directive, we can see the operation of such indirect review in the context of EU counter-terrorism. Not only was the Directive subjected to review – and the subject of expressions of serious judicial concern – in domestic courts (as discussed above), but it was ultimately reviewed by the Court of Justice of the European Union, which struck it down. In joined challenges taken by Digital Rights Ireland and Kärntner Landesregierung,[87] the Court accepted that data retention constitutes a *prima facie* interference with fundamental rights, not least because so-called metadata 'may allow very precise conclusions to be drawn concerning . . . private lives'.[88] However, the Court also accepted that the retention of data for the purposes of counter-terrorism and the disruption of serious crime is done in pursuance of a genuine goal. This does not mean that security has some kind of hyper-weighted status within the Court's analysis; rather:

> [I]t must be held that the fight against serious crime, in particular against organised crime and terrorism, is indeed of the utmost importance in order to ensure public security and its effectiveness may depend to a great extent on the use of modern investigation techniques. However, such an objective of general interest, however fundamental it may be, does not, in itself, justify a retention measure such as that established by Directive 2006/24 being considered to be necessary for the purpose of that fight.[89]

In spite of this legitimate aim, the Court found that the system of data retention introduced by the Directive was disproportionate. This hung on reasons such as the blanket nature of the surveillance,[90] the failure to discriminate between different forms of data,[91] the retention period,[92] the lack of clear limits on, or processes relating to, access and use of the data by state authorities,[93] and the failure to specify 'objective criterion' for and judicial control over access to data.[94] The Court also expressed significant

86 See C. C. Murphy, 'Counter-terrorism law and judicial review: the challenge for the Court of Justice of the European Union' in F. F. Davis and F. de Londras, *Critical Debates on Counter-terrorism Judicial Review* (Cambridge: Cambridge University Press, 2014).

87 Joined Cases C-293/12 and C-594/12, Judgment of the Grand Chamber, 8 April 2014.

88 Ibid., para 27.

89 Ibid., para 51.

90 Ibid., paras 57–58.

91 Ibid., para 59.

92 Ibid., paras 64–65.

93 Ibid., para 60.

94 Ibid., para 62.

concerns about the security of retained data and found that the Directive 'does not provide sufficient safeguards . . . to ensure effective protection of the data retained against the risk of abuse and against any unlawful access and use of that data', not least because it does not guarantee that it will remain within the European Union.[95]

The decision of the Court of Justice on the Data Retention Directive was significant, not only because it struck the Directive down, but because of how it related to the *ex ante* impact assessment and the *ex post facto* review. In both cases, these same concerns that ultimately led to the striking down of the Directive had been raised, and in both cases the Commission had argued – seemingly in defiance of common experience and, perhaps, common sense – that the Directive was sufficiently clear, limited and harmonizing to mitigate these concerns and make it proportionate. In this case, then, judicial review by the Court of Justice was, in the end, the only effective review of the Directive. While the example of the Data Retention Directive may suggest that such indirect (judicial) review is sufficient because, ultimately, a result was rendered that forced a more appropriate accounting for rights in the context of data retention, this came after many years of blanket surveillance, the bearing of significant costs by industry, costly breaking down of relationships of trust and effective governance between civil society and the institutions of the EU, effective sidelining of important and critical analyses of the Directive from Member State courts and European offices and institutions such as the European Data Protection Supervisor, and – of course – immense privacy infringements. Remedying the situation now requires significant activity at both national legislative and European levels and is costly in terms of economic and human resources. One cannot but conclude that more robust *ex ante* and *ex post facto* impact assessment would have been preferable from a constitutionalist perspective to this judicialized outcome.

Conclusions

The analysis presented in this chapter illustrates that a number of constitutionalist concerns arise when one considers EU counter-terrorism as system and process. While some of those constitutionalist concerns may be addressed through judicial review, this is merely a partial solution. The constitutionalist concerns and anxieties identified above are likely to be best addressed through the instigation of a means for closing the loop in EU counter-terrorism by introducing a system of evaluative, participatory and rights-oriented effectiveness review.

Such review would allow for the impact of a measure on rights, as well as more broadly, to be properly identified and understood (if the relevant

95 Ibid., para 66.

information were given to the reviewing party or parties), which in turn would aid legitimacy by testing the rationale for the measure's introduction in the first place against the reality of its operation. In order to be meaningful, such reviews ought to be regular, participatory, public (to the extent possible and bearing in mind the challenges of transparency in the security context considered in relation to legitimacy) and capable of bringing about policy, legal, practical and political reorientation by providing a rigorous evidence base for policy (re)evaluation.

Undoubtedly, instigating such a system of review at EU level is challenging, not least because of potential reluctance on the part of Member States to share relevant information with a European-level reviewing entity *and* the challenges of institutional design. However, if the EU is truly committed to the principles and values outlined in the Treaty and to its continuing constitutionalist evolution, this would seem to be a challenge that must be addressed.

Index

For Product Safety Concerns and Information please contact our EU
representative GPSR@taylorandfrancis.com
Taylor & Francis Verlag GmbH, Kaufingerstraße 24, 80331 München, Germany

www.ingramcontent.com/pod-product-compliance
Ingram Content Group UK Ltd.
Pitfield, Milton Keynes, MK11 3LW, UK
UKHW022131190926
475702UK00013B/1754

* 9 7 8 1 1 3 8 0 9 7 9 5 7 *